FROZEN VOICES

A SPEECH THERAPIST'S ALASKAN MEMOIR

Kit Roberts Johnson

 The names of the people in this book have been changed to protect their identity with the exception of a few who have asked to use their real names.
Published by Dynamic Communication Press
www.kitrobertsjohnson.com
Cover Art: Kit Roberts Johnson
Covers: Eric Johnson and Kit Roberts Johnson
Map: Melinda Bessett
Author Photo: Eric Johnson
Interior Design: Kit Roberts Johnson
979-8-9887949-0-5 e Book
979-8-9887949-4-3 Kindle
979-8-9887949-1-2 paperback
979-8-9887949-2-9 hardback
979-8-9887949-3-6 audio
Printed in the United States.

To Alaska— Its Beauty, Its People.

To those who struggle to communicate.

To sentience, which holds all of us with love.

CONTENTS

PLACES I WORKED IN ALASKA

Anaktuvuk Pass, Aniak, Barrow, Bethel, Brevig Mission, Chevak, Cordova, Elim, Fairbanks, Fort Wainwright, Fort Yukon, Gambell, Glenallen, Golovin, Healy, Homer, Juneau, Kenai, Ketchikan, Klawock, Kodiak, Kotzebue, Nenana, Nome, Nikolaevsk, Nuiqsut, Point Hope, Point Lay, Saint Mary's, Savoonga, Shaktoolik, Shishmaref, Skagway, Soldotna, Soloman, Stebbins, Tuntutuliak, Unalakleet, Umiat, Wainwright, and Wasilla.

CHAPTER1

Seven-Year Itch

A spouse is not a destination but a fellow traveler.
—Sadhguru

"I'm thinking of taking a job in Alaska," Bill had said.

We had been together for seven years—had reached that seven-year itch period, when couples either made it or they didn't—and now Bill had left for Alaska without me. He had done the same thing when we had moved to Seattle. He left for a job two months before I could follow, before I had finished my master's degree in Los Angeles and my speech-language pathology job in the school district. I always followed. I always stayed behind and arranged the emptying, the shuttering, and the evacuating. And this time would be no different.

We were living on Vashon Island, a small island just a fifteen-minute ferry ride to Seattle. It is located at the southern end of the Puget Sound between Seattle and Tacoma and is an idyllic suburb of Seattle. I would miss Seattle and the fresh fish, produce, and handcrafted creations I bought at Pike Place Market. I would treasure the pine-coned trees that remained evergreen even on a winter's day. I would remember sailing through the iridescent waters of the Puget Sound to go island hopping with friends in the summer.

When we were together, Bill and I made the best of it. On weekends, Bill donned his wetsuit, threw his speargun and boat bag into our small aluminum craft, and hunted for octopus, red snapper, and anything else that might be edible. Whatever he brought home, I cooked, and we enjoyed eating it together. We loved exploring—seeing the Pacific Northwest, breathing the sea air, feeling a damp breeze on our faces, tasting the blackberries we had just picked off a wild bush, skipping that polished beach rock across a calm sea, picking up curious pieces of driftwood for the yard, and gazing at the stars at night, undimmed by thousands of city lights, as in Los Angeles. But this part of our life was over now.

We had chosen Vashon Island because it was halfway between both our jobs—his with the Bremerton Shipyards on the Olympic Peninsula and mine with the Seattle Public Schools. We both caught different north-end car ferries in the morning. His ferry went west, and then he drove north to Bremerton for forty minutes. Mine went east, and then I drove an equal amount of time on the Seattle freeways to get to my two schools.

After commuting for one year, after the uniqueness of ferry travel had worn off, the fates presented me with a gift. The only speech-language pathology (SLP) job with the Vashon public schools opened, and I was thrilled to be hired. My schools were now a mere seven miles away. It was heaven to leave for work at seven-thirty in the morning instead of five-forty, to catch the six o'clock morning ferry. For three glorious months, my Seattle commuting was ancient history. Getting to work was finally easy. My elation did not last long.

Bill's declaration, announced just before Christmas, that he wanted to take a job in Alaska surprised me. He had been working in the shipyards for a year and a half, and I was settling into my convenient job on Vashon. We had just bought a house, and we both loved the island and being so close to the city. Now he was thinking of going to Alaska, of all places.

"Alaska? Really? What kind of a job is it?" I calmly asked. I tried not to upset Bill. It wasn't his temper that I feared; he wasn't abusive. He did have a mean streak, but I had been raised to believe a woman supports her husband, that the man makes the important decisions. Now he was telling me he might take a job in Alaska. I didn't know what to say. Alaska. My feelings ranged from dread, to sadness, to defeat. Alaska. It seemed like we were going backward, but I decided there was no point in arguing about it. Alaska. It wouldn't matter how I felt. I would go along with whatever he wanted to do in the end. I loved him.

"Well, Darrel saw a job posted in the breakroom," Bill said, as casually as if he was talking about buying a used car, not uprooting our lives. "It's with the Federal Aviation Administration, and he got hired. He and Holly already moved, but he says they need more ETs. He thinks I'd like it." Both Bill and his friend Darrel had become electronic technicians during the Vietnam War, Bill in the Navy and Darrel in the Air Force. Thankfully, the war had recently been declared over.

I had met Darrel and his wife, Holly, at a lake one afternoon. Bill and I took a ride in their boat, and we had a picnic. Holly, a nurse, seemed friendly and intelligent. They were about our age and childless, like us. Unfortunately, they didn't live on Vashon Island, so we never knew each other very well as couples. But now Bill was telling me we might be following them to Alaska.

Unbeknownst to me, Bill had applied for the job and even interviewed with the Federal Aviation Administration, or FAA, over the phone.

"If an offer comes through, it's for two years, which isn't that long, and the FAA will pay for our move there and back again. What do we have to lose?" he asked.

I could hear the excitement and determination in his voice. If the offer was made, then it was a done deal. At least the FAA would foot the moving costs.

"When would it start?" I asked, thinking it would be next summer.

"I'd report the beginning of January," he answered.

"But that's only a few weeks away. I can't leave my school job in the middle of the semester. I've signed a contract," I replied, dismayed. As the lone SLP on Vashon Island, I didn't want to abandon my students mid-year.

Bill was a military brat. He was used to moving. I wasn't. In the seven years since we'd met in 1968, we had already moved nine times. I wanted to stop moving.

My thoughts flurried here and there like a squall at sea. I calculated what moving entailed—all the packing and unpacking would be my responsibility. I'd have to leave my job and new friends and sell the house I loved—which meant fixing that up as well. And what about our three cats? We couldn't leave them.

But I didn't have any real power when it came to Bill. He was in charge, just like all the men in my life had been. If I wanted to get my way, then I would have to do it alone, without their support. I was a wife now, and that meant surrender. Whatever frustrated inner voice I had, I would freeze it. Whatever fear, confusion, or disappointment I felt, I would stuff it. I didn't have the guts to express my thoughts, feelings, or other possibilities. There was no point in sharing them. My concerns and desires would be disregarded. So I did what I always did—I disregarded my own concerns and desires as well. How many other women did the same thing? That's how we were raised and conditioned. I never saw my mother argue with my father, so why would I argue with my husband?

The more I thought about it in the days that followed, the more I rationalized what I didn't like about Vashon. Its rural countryside filled with massive lawns, thrilling fir trees, and large, expensive homes was too perfect. It seemed that half the population had retired, and the other half had young families. Those were the people I met at school—the parents of my students. Being young and childless, Bill and I didn't have much in common with either group. And the truth was, we didn't explore much together anymore. He increasingly wanted to go out on the water alone or with his buddies. While Bill went spearfishing, I stayed home with the cats and made macramé plant hangers.

Once, I attended a consciousness-raising meeting for women at a local Victorian home. The woman running the group had a chubby husband with a Freudian beard and a PhD in psychology. She ran the meeting, but he was there and supportive. Other than what I had heard about women's liberation in the media and read in magazines, which I totally supported, this was the first in-person gathering I had ever attended.

I started to think about feminism in a more nuanced way.

I learned that I was not responsible for my husband's behavior, how he spoke to people, or how he dressed—all things that had made me cringe at one time or another. But at the same time, I didn't learn that I was responsible for my own choices in life. Once married, I gave that responsibility over to my husband.

I didn't see myself getting too involved with the women's group. I overloaded myself getting an education, working in a profession, and contributing to our finances. I thought I was already liberated. I saw no contradiction in subordinating my life to my husband's while feeling liberated through my work.

These women didn't get it, I reasoned as I contemplated leaving Vashon. It was a small town of seven thousand people. Everybody seemed to know everything about everyone. I could picture myself dead, in a casket, in the graveyard, having never done anything exciting—each typical day just like the last. I was only twenty-six years old, yet living in such a laid-back place, I already felt like I was retired. Going to Alaska, especially if it was just for two years, started to sound exciting. In no time, I began to picture myself living like a modern pioneer.

By the time the job offer was made to Bill, I was convinced. I talked with my principal. He agreed to let me out of my contract after the semester ended in February. I could deal with that. When Bill returned home from work, I told him I could join him in a couple of months. Since it followed our pattern—him leaving ahead of me, me catching up a couple of months later—it was all good, I told myself. I was responsible, diligent, and compliant. I could handle it on my own. No complaints, just planning. No whining, just packing. No looking back, just moving forward. We were going on an adventure, just for two years.

To get ready for the cold, we drove to REI, the store that sells camping and hiking gear, and bought everything we could possibly foresee needing. Down parkas, thermal underwear, rugged boots, and thick gloves and socks. We bought camp stoves and flares and emergency kits, warm hats, and anything described as "insulated." We were determined to buy our way out of the cold. And of course, we threw in a *Rand McNally Laminated Easy to Fold Map: Alaska* and the *Rand McNally Guide to Alaska*, then bought three cat carriers. It wasn't cheap. Our two, matching down parkas alone cost two weeks' salary. Thankfully, we were as ready as we could be. We had just enough time to enjoy the holidays before Bill left.

Had I given deep thought to all I had to do before I moved, I would have collapsed. Instead, I did as I always did: I worked on autopilot and finished the work. While I prepared our house for sale, Bill packed his bags. Finally, on January 2, 1976, just a few weeks after Bill had sprung the idea on me, I drove him to the airport in the used, gas-guzzler sedan we'd brought up from Los Angeles, kissed him good-bye, and returned home—to sell the house and car, finish packing, and wrap up my semester. He gave me a big bear hug, like when we first met, and headed north to Alaska.

I knew little to nothing about Alaska except that it was cold. Alone in my home and surrounded by my boxed-up life, I unfolded the map and studied it carefully. The size and scope of Alaska surprised me—it was huge. The bulk of Alaska stood on two arched legs: the Aleutian Chain—scooping to the west toward Japan, and the Southeast—bordering Canada on the southeastern coastline. When I superimposed the Alaskan map over a map of the contiguous United States, those legs stretched from California to Florida. Water surrounded Alaska on three sides. Only the border with Canada joined it land-to-land, from top to bottom along the east.

The *Rand McNally Guide* told me a different story: there are only a few highways in Alaska. The main road goes around in a circle. Looking at a map and seeing a place with your own eyes, however, are two completely different experiences. Just weeks before, I was in love with Vashon and never wanted to leave. Now I couldn't wait to see Alaska, to be there beneath the northern lights, feeling the arctic chill on my face, walking across the blue-white snow as it crunched beneath my feet, walking alongside my husband, bundled in our down coats, warm and happy. Finally, that day came.

Now I boarded the plane, eight years after meeting Bill and three years after marrying him, flying to Alaska to be by his side. I drifted off to sleep thinking how wonderful it would be to see him again and get another bear hug.

CHAPTER 2
Down on the Farm

Niceness stays quiet. Kindness speaks up. Niceness is toxic. Kindness is healing. Niceness lies to keep the peace. Kindness moves forward with humility, gentleness and grace.
—Decolonize Myself, Facebook

Sitting back in my seat after eating a full, hot airline meal, I closed my eyes to rest on the three-and-a-half-hour flight to Alaska. I thought about my life and how I had become a speech-language pathologist.

"Mommy, Donny is hitting me," I yelled from the hallway by our bedrooms at the age of six.

"Donny, don't hit your sister," our mother yelled back from the kitchen.

If I got mad enough, I would fight back, like a wild cat. It wasn't right that my older brother could hit me.

My three brothers and I had grown up on a farm in eastern Washington. I was the second oldest. They wanted to wrestle, fight, and kill. They wanted to be in control and yell. They didn't like girls, so I had to be like them if I wanted to be with them, and I did. I was lonely.

After exhausting myself playing soldiers and cops-and-robbers and digging forts for our shootouts, I calmly withdrew into quiet activities by myself. I drew house plans in the driveway gravel with a stick or played in my room with dolls. If I needed to disappear, our yard had a great tall tree in the corner. I climbed as high as I could, hid in the leaves, and scanned the big, wide world below. There I saw other small farms and rows of Concord grapes. I inspected cactus country, a frightening field full of sagebrush and cactus across the street. Here we explored for anything interesting, like old bones, and avoided rattlesnakes in the summer. I also gazed at the wide-open, quiet sky.

Exalted, my imagination soared over vast distances while I observed the world from my lofty vantage point. I believed that someday, somehow, I would travel over there, or down that way, or up in that direction. Reality eventually returned as my senses reminded me that I was perched on a limb. I climbed down the tree like a cat who had been stuck long enough. Contemplating the future had momentarily soothed my soul.

Of course, I would never tell my brothers about any of this. They would not understand. My imaginings were not to be shared with others. There was no time for that in our house. It was too busy.

When we had moved to Pasco, I was three months old. My father had taken a job as an accountant at Hanford, where atomic bomb research transpired in secret. He started that job right after graduating with a degree in accounting from the University of Washington in Seattle in 1950. In 1953, he contracted polio after a fishing trip to a lake near Pasco. He had three children at the time, one of them my newborn brother. It devastated my mother.

All the doctors in town were at a symposium in Seattle that weekend on how to treat polio. From his hospital room, Daddy phoned my mother constantly, shrieking in pain, begging her to help him, to do something. Of course, she could not do a thing. As his wife and a registered nurse, filled with fear and grief, she felt helpless. She tried to hide it, but it seeped into me.

At the time, the medical community thought he might be able to give her polio, so she wasn't allowed to see him. I didn't know how much time had passed without my daddy. To help me fall asleep, he used to lay on my bed at night and read the newspaper under my headboard lamp. I'd roll to my side and put my arm across his warm chest, hear the paper crackling, and smell the newsprint. Soon I'd be fast asleep. If he wasn't there, I feared the wolves that were surely under my bed, and I couldn't fall asleep. Suddenly, he had stopped reading the paper with me. He was gone. When the day came that we were allowed to see him in the hospital, I was ecstatic.

"Mommy, can I take some chocolate chip cookies to see Daddy?" I asked before we left.

"Yes, that's fine," she said, "Get in the car."

I gathered up two cookies and thrust them in my pocket, eager to give them to Daddy.

After we arrived at the hospital, I stood on the blistering asphalt and watched as they wheeled him out. The nurse put my daddy at the top of the cement stairs that led to the back door of the hospital. We weren't allowed to go near him for fear that we might catch the polio. This isn't what I thought would happen. I wanted to sit on his lap and have him put his arms around me and tell me, "Everything will be all right."

I felt the two chocolate chip cookies in my pocket—his favorite kind. I wanted to give them to him so he would know how much I loved him, but I couldn't even tell him I had them; he sat too far away to hear me. The chocolate chips were melting in the heat, and I felt awful. The scorching sun blinded my eyes and made it hard to see him. I tried to understand. He was my daddy, but I couldn't get to him. He wouldn't hold me. *He must not love me anymore*, I reasoned.

My heart was breaking. I needed my father. I needed his love, but I couldn't get it. Desperate, I had to do something. So at the age of three, I put my father in limbo. I created an invisible sound bubble around myself and separated from him. I had to detach from him or I would have died of sadness. From then on, my cries for him could not get out, and his calls to me could not get in. As they rolled him back into the hospital, I felt numb, and we left.

Even after he had recovered and returned home, I remained anxious around him, never knowing if he would disappear again. Whatever bond we had had together before, his love never came back. How could it? I didn't know I had created the bubble that prevented him from getting in or me from getting out. And I didn't know the bubble worked the same way for everyone in my life. I didn't know I had created my core wound, that moment in time that I separated from my own life force, my inner source of love. Self-abandoned, neglected, and unsupported, I was doomed to a sad, closed heart and a fearful soul. Even kindergarten scared me.

Dad had a long recovery. With lots of help from my mother rehabilitating him at home, giving him shots, and taking care of things he normally handled, he made a full recovery. As I grew, I internalized my sadness, fear, and anger. I never heard the words to express feelings. No one ever asked me how I felt. My feelings remained inside, like something long dead and buried. There they were safe, and there they were hidden, because the world was, after all, a man's world. Girls took care of the house; men took care of the world. Girls were quiet and unassuming. Boys were loud and rude. That was their nature, just as being quiet and invisible was ours.

# # #

When Alaska achieved statehood in 1959, I was nine years old. That's when I started to see soothing, colored lights as I fell asleep at night. Soft purple, green, and red swirled back and forth beneath my eyelids. As my eyes followed the drifting light, my body relaxed, and my mind filled with comfort and love. Any fear or tension I had melted away. Within a few minutes, I surrendered to sleep. I didn't know what the mysterious lights were. I had never seen or felt them before. I never asked my mother about them. I thought the lights were normal and everyone saw them. The swirling sweetness stopped after a few weeks, just as I started the fourth grade.

On the first day of school, I had wandered down the hall to find my classroom. "Hello," a voice said. "I'm Mrs. Baker. Who are you?"

My new fourth-grade teacher kindly asked me my name, but I couldn't see her face or answer. My eyes were fixed on the tiny baby hand hanging from the end of her elbow.

"What's your name?" she inquired again.

I looked up and saw her smiling face. "Kit Roberts," I replied quietly.

"It's nice to meet you, Kit. You'll be sitting right here."

She walked me to the end of row three and showed me my desk. I watched as other kids arrived and were directed to their places. I kept my eye on my teacher's hand. It was just like my little brother's hand when he was a baby, except her fingers didn't move, they just flopped. I wondered if it hurt or if she was sad about it. Somehow, I took my seat, but all I remember is staring, immobilized, at that baby hand.

Then, speaking to the entire class, Mrs. Baker told us she had a birth defect. Her left arm never grew all the way, and her baby-sized hand just hung there, not working. It worried me. I felt sorry for her. Most of the time, her sleeves covered it up, and then I forgot all about it.

I adored Mrs. Baker because she was so kind. She never ridiculed us or made us feel foolish or stupid, like my second-grade teacher who yelled at me after I raised my hand and answered a question without enough confidence. (Don't worry, I never raised my hand again.) Even with a birth defect, Mrs. Baker was the best teacher I ever had.

I liked being in the fourth grade but didn't understand why the other kids avoided Stanley. He sat across from me at the end of row four. A gentle and agreeable boy, unlike my brothers at home who beat me up and threw spiders at me, Stanley had a little scar on his lip and spoke softly. Some of his words sounded like there was air coming out of his nose. The boys ignored him. I treated him with kindness. I wished other people knew how kind he was, too. They should all be Stanley's friend, I thought, just like me.

Then, at recess one day, I heard a lot of commotion and saw a bunch of boys surrounding someone. Carefully, I inched closer. *What's going on*?

There, cornered against a brick wall of the school, stood Rose. She was in the third-grade handicapped class and had a hard time talking. My attention focused. *Why are the boys screeching such horrible names at her? Her face is all red. She just spit at them. She can't even talk. Why don't they leave her alone?*

Rose was a sweet girl. Why were the boys being so mean to her? Stunned and inept, I felt sorry for her and ashamed that I didn't help. Frozen in horror, I just stood there. The recess bell rang, and we all went running back to class.

As time went on, my compassion, empathy, and fondness for Mrs. Baker, Stanley, and Rose only grew. I liked them and hoped they liked me. I always tried my best to be polite around Stanley and Rose, and I never understood people who didn't. If they needed help and protection from those other kids who were so mean, I resolved to give it to them. After all, I could beat up my brothers. *I won't back down the next time*, I decided. *I'll stick up for them.*

As traumatized as I felt by these incidents, I could not imagine how Rose and Stanley dealt with them. It must have happened over and over. My heart pounded with compassion and care; I wanted to connect with them, help them, and protect them. They were suffering. Their lives were at stake. I wasn't having it. I made a vow. I wouldn't abandon or neglect them. Instead, I would support them. I stayed on the lookout, but I never saw anything bad happen again on my watch.

I did not know that most handicapped children, as they were called then, were all together in one room. The only time they spent with the other kids was at recess and lunch. I didn't have lunch at school because I walked home to eat. The lunchroom was overwhelming for me, with too many kids making too much noise. At home, I ate my bologna sandwich and a bowl of tomato soup with saltine crackers in peace and quiet in my frozen bubble.

Although I did not know what happened to the kids during school lunch, I did know that my bubble had cracked a bit. In my own mind, I started to come out of the frozen shell I had created, at least when it came to Rose and Stanley. Fighting for someone else gave me the courage to open my mouth, use my voice, and say something—something I wouldn't do for myself, like during one incident in sixth grade.

At the end of that school year, my teacher, Mr. Carlton,

walked from child to child and stopped at each desk to predict our futures—out loud. As he paused at my seat, he made an announcement to the whole class.

"You will start college, but you'll drop out after the first year," he declared.

At the age of twelve, I was demoralized. To me, Mr. Carlton appeared as a hulk of a man. When the boys misbehaved, he pinned them to the wall by their collarbones, their feet dangling off the floor, their voices shrieking in pain. I was afraid of him.

But that settled it. He had just confirmed what I already suspected: *I'm not smart enough to go to college.* He earned a promotion to principal and moved to Olympia. As a chronically overwhelmed child in a state of chronic defense, I did my best with the humiliating and discouraging sentence I had just received.

He never said why I would drop out. I didn't have the best grades in class, but I didn't have the worst either. It never occurred to me to refute his claim. I believed him. He was a man, my teacher, and my elder. I could not tell him how I felt because I did not know the words. Anyway, I knew better than to talk back to an adult. That would only get me into trouble.

I didn't really understand the concept of college anyway; I just understood that it was a good thing, a thing that both of my parents had done, and a thing that I would not get to do. Oh well, there were no colleges in Pasco. Just check that off the list of future possibilities.

Finally, school finished for the summer. The next year I would be in a different school. I had never seen the junior high school building. I could not walk to it, like my elementary school. Instead, I thought about summer vacation. We would pack the car and go to Coulee Dam to be with my grandparents —in the best place, with the best food, and the best swimming. I could think about junior high later. For now, I would take a break from my farm chores and relax in the glow of my grandmother's love, the best grandmother in the world.

CHAPTER 3

Growing Pains

Vocation does not come from a voice out there calling me to be something I am not. It comes from a voice in here calling me to be the person I was born to be.
—Thomas Merton

"Would you like a pillow or a blanket?" asked the stewardess.

Interrupting my memories, I accepted both. We were halfway to Fairbanks, the food had been cleared, and people were settling in for a nap or a smoke. I closed my eyes and heard my mother's voice.

"Everybody, come here and sit down. We have something to tell you," Mommy said. "We're not going to Coulee Dam this summer."

My brothers and I, now aged fourteen, twelve, ten, and eight, looked at her like she had two heads.

"Your father has taken a job in California, and we're leaving in ten days. The movers will be here in a few days to start packing, so we have to stay home and get ready to go."

"How long will it take to get to California?" I asked, completely clueless about it.

"It's going to take three days. We'll be staying at some motels with swimming pools," she added, to distract us from not swimming behind Coulee Dam.

The rest of the move is a blur to me now—although I do remember in the dark of evening, putting on my new swimming suit, pink with black polka dots, and swimming in warm motel pool water. Arriving in Reno late, my mother promised we could go swimming, and so we did.

That summer, instead of our usual visit to Coulee Dam to swim and picnic on the Columbia River with our beloved grandparents—our grandfather, who supervised everything painted in the dam from turbines to handrails, and our grandmother, so full of love, gentleness, and the best apple pie ever—our family moved from our farm in Pasco, a town of fourteen thousand people, to a suburb of Los Angeles, California, the San Fernando Valley (where the term Valley Girl came from), with its multiple towns of one million people.

On the first day of school, I arrived in the seventh grade, about to turn thirteen years old, in scuffed, brown-and-white, lace-up saddle shoes, dingy white anklets, and an old, little-girl dress. My hair did what it wanted. As soon as I arrived, I yearned to crawl into a hole for the rest of the day.

Hundreds of kids rushed between bells to get from one class to the next. Many of the classes were in a portable somewhere in the schoolyard. (What was a portable? I didn't know.) All the girls wore black flats with pointy toes, tight straight skirts, and long hair ratted up four inches high. I had never seen a pair of flats, but I understood immediately that I looked like a country bumpkin right off the farm, and that is how I felt: ashamed, embarrassed, and completely overwhelmed.

There had not been any "come to junior high school early day" to get acquainted with my unknown surroundings. The temporary two-classroom, rectangular buildings known as portables sat behind the school on the lawn or on asphalt to solve the over-crowding problem. I had been thrown into the deep end—and toting a violin no less. That completed my nerd-on-steroids look. I enrolled in orchestra and played violin because my grandfather played violin. Since my father was a child prodigy at piano, each kid in my family had to take lessons in piano and one other instrument. This was my third year of violin and it didn't sound much better than the first.

It took a while for me to adapt to my fast-paced surroundings. My mom finally bought me a pair of flats and a straight skirt, and I learned how to rat my hair. There wasn't much extra money for my clothes because Mom was having a baby. That "surprise" baby would be my youngest brother, and two years later, when I turned fifteen years old, she gave birth to my only sister.

My mother, who had been a full-time registered nurse specializing in surgery, labor, and delivery, until she delivered me, became a stay-at-home mom, and a busy one at that. When we lived on the farm, she did everything but milk the cow. She had taught Sunday school, attended Parent Teacher Association meetings, and made our lives as happy as possible. She had co-led a Blue Bird/Camp Fire Girl group so I could meet some girls, learn how to be a good citizen, and help the less fortunate. Now, she busied herself raising the two youngest children.

Mom cooked three delicious meals a day out of a small kitchen, shuffled us to various appointments and church (picking up doughnuts on the way home), and kept the house tidy. We four older children became responsible for ourselves. That meant no help with homework or checking on school projects. I learned to take care of myself, finish my homework without prodding from my parents, and get babysitting jobs for neighborhood children to make fifty cents an hour.

As I approached my senior year of high school, my mother made a pronouncement. "You are going to college. You have to get a degree in something. I don't care what it is. That's your insurance, in case you have to take care of yourself."

Of course, I wanted to go to college. I did not expect a man to take care of me. Unsure if he would ever come back, my boyfriend at the time lived in Vietnam as an Army medic. Unfortunately, no particular professions appealed to me, but by now, I realized the importance of a college education.

My horizons had broadened with the women's movement, which had evolved at just the right time in the 1960s. My mother had been a nurse and my paternal grandmother a teacher in the one-room schools of Canada. The other acceptable vocations for a woman in the past were mother and secretary. But with the advent of the 1970s, women believed they could be anything.

Men liked the idea of women bringing in some money, but they found it difficult to let go of female stereotypes and didn't make it easy for us to enter traditional male careers, which covered pretty much everything except the four I just mentioned. My thoughts turned gloomy. *I don't want to be a nurse, a teacher, or a secretary. What am I going to do? I don't know what I want. I only know what I don't want.*

During my second year of junior college, my family moved to Chicago for my father's work. I didn't want to see him go, but I had detached from him emotionally as a little girl. In California, he had become caught in the corporate model of working long hours to provide for his family. I rarely saw him, except for birthdays and holiday celebrations, which my mother always arranged and prepared with great joy and abundance. She did everything to keep the family happy. Now, as a comptroller for a large corporation in Los Angeles, with facilities across the country, a promotion required that he move to Chicago to oversee the finances on an airport project. We agreed that I could stay in California and finish college. I didn't have to leave home; my family left me.

I kept the fear and overwhelm I had picked up from my mother as a little girl during Daddy's illness. But I never expressed it because those feelings, and all my feelings, good or bad, were frozen inside my bubble and unable to get out. Feelings were still tucked deep inside and not to be expressed, like the loss I felt when my little brother and sister moved away. I loved watching them grow up, playing with them, and taking them for rides in a stroller after school. I could focus my love on them. Now, focusing on my housing problem, I started looking for a place to live, just like my mother would have done.

The college had a message board that posted odd jobs and rooms for rent. I phoned a woman whose house was within walking distance to the college. From her, I rented a room with a bath for seventy dollars a month. I had kitchen and pool privileges, and she and her teenage daughter and I became friends.

I enrolled in Psychology 101 that semester. The course required ten hours of community service. I arranged to volunteer at Crippled Children's Services, where my landlady worked as an administrative assistant. As I walked through the facility on the first day, I noticed my first speech-language pathologist (SLP). Although I didn't have to, I decided to pass by her office every day and observe her work. Something about her intrigued me.

This well-groomed woman looked to be in her mid-thirties. Petite, with dark-brown, shoulder-length hair, she calmly busied herself with her work, which I only saw through a window.

On the first day, she sat with a little girl wearing bilateral hearing aids. I watched through a one-way mirror window while both of them looked into the mirror and the girl imitated the speech therapist. The SLP held a picture under her mouth while the girl focused on it. Then the girl, gazing into the mirror, said the word a few times by herself. The SLP presented the next picture, and the girl imitated the therapist once again. Sometimes the speech therapist directed the girl's attention to a specific part of her mouth—her lips or tongue, for example. They practiced over and over.

On the second day, I saw the SLP meeting with a well-dressed, silver-haired woman in a wheelchair. They sat side by side in the middle of the room, away from the mirrored-window, so I couldn't hear what they were saying. The SLP showed the woman a picture, and I noticed that they repeated the name of it together.

By the third day, I summoned the courage to introduce myself and ask the SLP about her profession.

"What do you do?" I asked her.

"I'm a speech-language pathologist."

"How do you help people?"

"I work with people who have communication disorders, like the little girl with bilateral hearing loss. I'm helping her improve her oral speech and language. I see her three times a week for an hour. The woman in the wheelchair had a stroke, which affected her ability to speak. I'm working to stimulate her understanding and expression of speech and language. I'm with her for an hour, twice a week."

Talking with this SLP, I remembered the anguished look on Rose's face and Stanley's loneliness. More importantly, I felt the compassion and respect I had for both of them. That had been the first time my self-imposed bubble started to crack, and out I came, ready to fight for a cause. My heart quickened with an unfolding recognition of my future.

Wanting to know more, I asked, "What kind of a degree do you have?"

"I have a master's degree in communication disorders. The company I work for contracts with different facilities, and to work with them, I have to have a master's."

Okay. A master's degree. Those take at least two more years of college after the bachelor's degree. That's going to be expensive. I have to find a university that will accept me. I have to find out where these programs are being offered. There's a lot to do, but I'm ready for the challenge.

"Can you support yourself on your salary?" I asked.

"Yes. No problem."

This is good. I might be single for a long time, and I'll need to make a living wage.

"Do you get paid vacation?"

"Yes. I started with two weeks a year, and I now receive three weeks a year. My husband and I are traveling to Europe this summer. I also get sick leave and have an employer health insurance plan."

Even at the age of nineteen, I understood that insurance and paid vacation were valuable benefits. I started to realize that a *profession* enhanced one's prosperity, as opposed to a *job* such as the one I had at the local dry cleaners. There, the Old Greek, as he nicknamed himself, chewed on a pipe as he spotted the stained clothes with toxic chemicals on an old ironing board in the back room.

While I cleaned pockets and stapled numbered tags on the clothes, he told me, "My son works with his brawn. It's hard work, and he doesn't make much money. Stay in college. Get a job where you can work with your brain, not your brawn."

I made minimum wage, $1.67 an hour. That was barely more than babysitting. I had never heard anyone say it as plainly as the Greek, and I took his advice seriously.

As the SLP answered each of my questions, my resolve strengthened. I could help people and earn enough income to support myself. It felt right, and it had happened so naturally. *This is what I'm supposed to do.*

Transferring to California State University, Northridge (CSUN) in 1970, I went to the Communications Disorders Department and examined the coursework for a degree in Communication Disorders: Phonetics, Voice Science, Language Development and Disorders, Hearing Science, Marriage and Family Relations, Fluency Disorders, Linguistics, and more. *Wow, I'm not smart enough to get through all of that,* I thought.

As I judged the difficulty of the curriculum, I chickened out. Remembering Mr. Carlton's prediction, I didn't think I could hack it. I switched my major to communications.

Instead of helping people with communication disorders, I now pictured myself as a news anchor, reading the six o'clock news on television each night. All my classes emphasized radio and television production: History of Broadcasting, TV-Film Aesthetics, Mass Communication Arts, and Broadcast Workshop. Having lived in Tinseltown for eight years, I imagined myself in the land of movies and television. Dumb blonds and tough guys, cowboys and honest lawyers—all these stereotypes saturated the handful of TV stations in Los Angeles during the 1960s and '70s. ABC, NBC, and CBS had the most viewership. Local independent stations—channels 5, 9 and 11—filled the airwaves with old movies and some locally produced shows.

I watched the evening news for signs of how the anchors performed their jobs, as well as the actual information they were broadcasting. One thing that stood out. Most of the female broadcasters were blond—check! I was blond!

After reading news copy in class one day for a mock radio

show, my professor critiqued it as being "too authoritative; no one wants to hear a woman with authority in her voice on the radio."

I heard that comment as an insult to women in general and myself specifically. I realized I did not have to stomach this humiliation nor perpetuate it. This was a whole system that dictated how women were supposed to be to please the men in power who ran everything. It made me angry, and I felt it. I wanted to correct it, but what could I do? *Read the news with a nice voice, not an authoritative voice.* It never entered my mind to challenge the system. Instead, I challenged myself. At the end of the semester, I reevaluated my options.

Communications hadn't inspired or interested me at all. It seemed like a lot of busy work with nothing important to show in the end. It had been a cheap substitute, something familiar to do because I didn't think I was smart enough to do what I really wanted to do. When a classmate selected me to demonstrate mouth-to-mouth resuscitation on a good-looking guy for a mock talk-show, the jig was up. I understood: *These guys are trying to make me into a blond bimbo.* I wasn't having it.

In the 1970s, holes were being punched through the walls of patriarchy. Television shows like *Leave It to Beaver,* with the knowledgeable and calm father who came home to a wife wearing a dress and a pearl necklace, were replaced with the *Mary Tyler Moore Show,* about a young woman living alone, working full-time, without a husband or a boyfriend. Shocking, yes. But real? Absolutely yes.

Holes were also being punched through the walls of racism and sexism. Women had marched to dismantle both, and their voices were raised for the first time in a long time. The memory of having my mouth washed out with soap, discouraging me from speaking out, faded like a bad dream. "Say it proud, say it loud" was the new battle cry.

I watched these women on the evening news coverage, apprehensive but hopeful. I knew how it felt to have that champagne-bottle cork stuck in my neck, with the bubbles of my speech attempting to arise. Stuck in my throat, the pressure in my gut wanted to release, but some primitive and fearful force inside me stopped it. These women gave me hope. They gave me courage. They gave me will.

With that hope, I ran to the Communication Disorders department and registered as quickly as possible. What a relief. A profession where a woman could speak with authority had opened its doors to me. To walk through those doors required intelligence, compassion, and courage. I accepted the challenge of all three. I entered a career that demanded problem-solving skills and changed peoples' lives for the better.

All that I had frozen in my emotional bubble became useful. The sadness in my bubble craved connection. The fear drove my desire to protect others. And my anger inspired me to correct the wrongs in the world. How can I live in a world so filled with wrongs, with people who needed help neglected and unprotected? Who was going to help them if I didn't? I had to make it right. These pent-up feelings veritably burst open, and I threw myself into the work. This I had to do.

On this path, whatever I faced, I analyzed it in my own, no-nonsense way. I wasn't into having fun; I was into getting results. Problem-solving gave me joy. Information and efficiency soothed my soul. I had found my home. There had been no need for me to worry. My calling had mysteriously presented itself. I saw it through a window and didn't need to fear my future after all.

At about the same time, Bill enlisted in the Navy when his draft number was getting close to being called. If he didn't enlist in a branch of the military he wanted to be in, he would be randomly placed in the Army or Marines. Since he had grown up as an Army brat, he knew all about that. He had attended twelve different schools before graduating from high school. As the new kid in school, he learned to protect himself from the bullies by making friends with them. In return, he did their math homework and became a tough guy himself. He became angry and needed everything to be his way.

Having learned his own dysfunctional communication skills, he needed to boss everyone around, including me. It was his way or the highway. Therefore, I was perfect for him. I had honed that communication style with my brothers and craved connection from inside my frozen bubble. I would do whatever he wanted, within my power. We were perfect for each other. He could dish it out. I could take it.

For a year, he trained at the naval base in Long Beach and came home on weekends. Then he deployed to sea for eighteen months. Based in the Philippines, he never landed in Vietnam. Because he had completed college credits to become an electronic technician, he parlayed that into attending the Navy school for electronics. He became certified and took care of the equipment on his ship. This required that he work in an air-conditioned room, which was highly beneficial in the south seas. Eventually, he moved his mattress into the cooled-off room and lived in it. His popularity increased, and he had many visitors during his shifts. He made the Navy work for him.

In his absence, I worked hard finishing my bachelor's degree and starting my master's. We wrote many letters back and forth, and one time, he called me from Japan on his R&R —his rest and recreation holiday. Luckily, he wasn't in combat, so I didn't have to worry about him getting killed. But one day, I received a letter in the mail with unfamiliar handwriting on it and a hospital return address from the Philippines. I immediately thought the worst—that he'd been wounded in some kind of a battle. I ripped open the envelope and quickly read it. It had been written by a nurse. She explained that Bill's appendix had ruptured, and he had an emergency appendectomy. He was doing fine and would join his ship as soon as he recovered. What a relief.

We had met, after graduating from high school, on the way to cruise Van Nuys Boulevard, the local Friday and Saturday night hangout for kids with cars. When he pulled up next to my friend Melissa and me in his gold, fadeaway GTO, he motioned for me to roll down my window.

"Where you going?" he yelled.

"To Bob's," I shouted back.

He looked at the two other guys with him and replied, "We're going to bed!" Then he threw his head back and cackled like he had just said something hysterical. I rolled up my window.

They followed us into the hamburger joint known as Bob's. When he got out of his car, I saw a tall, blond, handsome guy. As we got ready to leave, he took my phone number and then inexplicably put his arms around me in a big bear hug, lifted me off the ground, and put me down. My heart started beating with love, and that was that. We got married after he returned from Vietnam. Instead of becoming Mrs. Tate, I kept my maiden name, Roberts, which was a new, feminist custom. Plus, Kit Tate just didn't sound right.

As soon as I finished my master's degree, we left the desert heat of Los Angeles for the cool green of the Pacific Northwest. Rather, he left about a month ahead of me, and I followed, sharing the journey with a friend of his on a non-stop drive to Vashon Island in our gas-guzzling sedan. Luckily, gas was only fifty cents a gallon.

CHAPTER 4

Genie

I shall never forget the surprise and delight I felt when I uttered my first connected sentence, "It is warm." True they were broken and stammering syllables, but they were human speech. My soul, conscious of new strength, came out of bondage, and was reaching through those broken symbols of speech to all knowledge and faith.
—Helen Keller

Out of all my classmates, why was I chosen by my professors to work with Genie through a summer internship? What were they thinking when they assigned this girl to me? Genie had been criminally neglected with no social interaction for the first thirteen years of her life. And my task? Help this traumatized child learn to communicate.

Genie had been born with hip dysplasia, a fairly common and correctable condition. Her parents made no effort to get her the corrective surgery she needed, however, and instead just toted her home and waited for her to die. Reportedly, they believed she was hopelessly deformed and would be dead within a few months. Thus, they condemned her to her crib. They fed her but had minimal interaction with her. Unloved and unwanted, baby Genie was abandoned in her room and ignored.

Genie lived. As she grew and developed physically, her parents wrapped her crib in chicken wire, which prevented her from climbing out. They left her in diapers and fed her mostly milk and cornflakes. When she matured beyond the crib, they tied her to a potty chair during the day, her legs and arms securely bound, and confined her in a sleeping bag on the floor at night. Her room had one window in it, the only natural light she ever saw. If she made any sound, her father beat her, and instead of speaking to her, only grunted or growled, baring his teeth and barking like a wild dog. For the next thirteen years, she rarely left her room. Finally, when Genie's mother applied for disability benefits in 1970 and took Genie with her, a social worker saw the malnourished, uncommunicative child and became suspicious.

Child Protective Services rescued Genie and removed her from her home. Her parents were charged with her abuse and neglect. On the morning of the trial, however, her father shot and killed himself. Her mother, who had also been abused by the father and was deemed to be cognitively impaired, lived out her life in a group home.

Genie was placed with a couple who were both psychologists. They became her guardians and did their best to undo the damage that such extreme neglect had done. Like Helen Keller's teacher, they taught her how to eat, how to dress herself, and how to talk. Genie lived in this new world for four years before she entered my world—the world of speech-language pathology.

I mustered all my logic, knowledge, and courage to help Genie. None of my classes had addressed how we could help a client like her. With Genie's history, not only was she profoundly different from any other child with a speech disorder, but I would have to be different, too. It had been three years since Genie's rescue, and in that time, she'd become known the world over as a "feral child," drawing the attention of some the world's most skilled and renowned psychologists and linguists.

Still in graduate school, I had been chosen to participate in a five-week summer practicum focusing on helping Genie gain speech. To be selected to join such an illustrious team of speech experts was an honor, and soon, like these others, I became obsessed with figuring out how to create and execute a unique plan for her, a plan that would help her to speak and understand human speech.

Pleased and anxious to have the internship, I prepared for the challenge. Mass-produced speech therapy materials were scarce and expensive in 1973, so I created my own. After walking to a local bookstore, I scoured the children's section and purchased picture-vocabulary books. Returning home, I cut out the colored pictures, pasted them to colored construction paper, and covered them with a roll of clear plastic shelf liner for durability. I couldn't afford to have them laminated. Each picture showed a child using an object, so the photos were filled with possibilities: using pronouns, *he/she*; naming nouns, *milk/girl*; saying colors, *green/red*; using is + verbing, *is pouring*; and articles, *a/the—a girl is pouring the milk*.

But then came the day I met Genie. Now sixteen, she stood a head taller than I, and I was five feet, seven inches. Her thick brown hair fell indifferently to her shoulders, and her porcelain skin affirmed that she hadn't been exposed to sunlight for most of her life. One of her hips tilted higher than the other. With her slim build, she appeared gangly and wended her way as gently as a soft breeze as she walked. Her eyes turned to the right as far as possible when she wanted to study something. Genie's personality radiated pure curiosity, without destructiveness or guile.

CSUN, where I studied, hosted a summer day camp for children with special needs. The camp included swimming in the campus pool, arts and crafts, dancing, games, social skills, and other activities. I functioned as Genie's speech therapist and camp assistant. If she played basketball, I played basketball; if she danced, I danced; if she painted, I painted, all the while emphasizing speech and language to accompany our activities.

Bringing Genie's senses to life kept me busy. As we walked across the lush, green campus lawn, I took a deep breath and commented, "They cut the grass. The grass smells sweet." I pointed to the royal blue sky on a bright sunny morning, "Look at that blue sky." The door leading to the pool had bushes on both sides. I stopped her and had her look at them and touch a leaf. It was soft. "Say soft."

She replied in a high, whispered voice, "Soft?"

"Look how small it is, only about two inches long. Say small."

"Small?"

"What color is it? It's green! Say green."

"Green?"

"Feel all these leaves on the plant. Say leaf."

"Leaf?"

"What is it? Tell me now? What color? Green. Say the whole thing. The leaf is green."

"Leaf is green?"

"Good talking!"

She pricked her finger on the tip of a leaf and pulled it back, like Sleeping Beauty at the spinning wheel.

"Ouch. It's pointy," I said.

"Pointy?"

"That's right. Be careful."

Genie wanted to interact with the other kids, but she wasn't sure how to approach them. She frequently drifted off into her own inner world and I had to attract and strengthen her attention to get her back outside. I'd yell, "Genie, catch the ball!" Throwing the ball to her brought her back to the present.

She had limited control over phonation (voice) and spoke in a whisper most of the time. The rest of her speech manifested in a high, singsong pitch. She communicated mainly with gestures or single words. Genie had been taught to use sign language, of which I knew very little at the time. But I bought a beginner's sign-language book and learned to use it simultaneously with simple speech. Although she wasn't literally deaf, her poor pitch control may have indicated cortical deafness.

Cortical deafness happens when the brain lacks stimulation for sound after birth. There are different causes of cortical deafness, such as hearing loss or, in Genie's case, an absence of sound stimulation. Over time, the failure of synaptic stimulation causes neurons to die, and the part of the cortex (temporal lobes/gray matter) that analyzes sounds atrophies. Genie may have lacked the neurons to hear the way a person who has heard sounds from birth normally hears. Inadequate neural development would make it difficult for her to get feedback from her brain to alert her that she was doing something different with her speech than other people were doing.

Watch it. You're doing too much for her. Just guide her to something or someone. Tell her what to say; let her imitate you. Encourage her to have verbal interactions. Help her. These thoughts ran through my head as I tried to help too much. I had to constrain myself. Genie needed to communicate independently. I aimed to encourage verbal interaction. I believed in being friendly—but I didn't want to be her "buddy." That role should be for one of the camp kids.

Each day, I filled out a form describing her Activities, Attitudes, Peer Relationships, Language, Signs, and Tantrums. One of her behaviors that needed to be extinguished was spitting. From the time Genie had been found by social workers, she'd had difficulty swallowing because she had been denied solid food. Instead, she spat. Now, three years later, although she had been taught to swallow, the spitting had persisted. If she drank from a water fountain, she quickly spat in it. Sometimes, she took hold of her shirt collar, turned her head away, and pretended to wipe her mouth on it. But she wasn't wiping her mouth. She was spitting into her shirt. This was a self-stimulatory behavior, done for her self-preservation.

Whatever is paid attention to is reinforced and increases—good or bad. If I pointed out her spitting, she became more aware of it. The more aware she was, the more likely she would be compelled to do it again. To avoid this from happening, I narrated to her everything she and I did, and I steered her behavior in the right direction. Instead of saying, "Don't spit in the water," I said, "Time for a drink of water. Drinking, drinking, drinking. All done."

But five days later I blew it. I saw her spitting on her collar—and made the mistake of telling her. For the rest of the day, that's all she thought about. We danced—but she left the group and spent her time staring at the wall. When I invited her to get involved with the campers again, she decreed, "Don't spit," or "Genie no spit," in a self-deprecating tone. I couldn't get her to change the subject or calm her down. I had failed her and sent her back inside to her traumatized self. I had learned my lesson.

If she ever spat again, I'd keep my mouth shut.

At the close of summer camp, I wrote a report on her status. She now spoke at a two-and-a-half to three-year age level, even after being out of solitary confinement for over three years. At her best, she uttered simple two- and three-word sentences, such as "I like swim," "my book," and "thank you, Kit."

Communication, however, meant more than talking. Communication includes intonation (how we stress words), prosody (the emotion or melody we give to our speech), pitch, volume, facial expressions, and gestures. Genie exhibited severe weaknesses in all these areas. She rarely showed any facial expression. I worked with her to increase vocal inflection by having her voice go up at the end of a question. She had improved in this area but didn't use a question word, such as "who," "when," "where," or "why." So instead of "When is lunch?" she might say, "Lunch?" I wasn't able to lower her pitch either, partly because I didn't have that training yet. Her pitch remained high, in falsetto, and weak.

Was Genie's speech spontaneous, or did it have to be prompted? Most of her speech answered a question that I asked her, and we practiced the answer ahead of time. Therefore, it was prompted. She could label something for me—for example, "ball"—but I first had to ask her, "What is that?" She seldom spoke spontaneously, and she required cueing. While Genie made good progress over the summer, she needed perseverance to complete the journey to communication. But I was patient. I knew the day would come that the light would suddenly turn on and she would use language as a tool.

Genie was indeed closer to being a feral child than anyone had witnessed in modern times. Because she lived in such isolation (her father forbade his wife or son from speaking above a whisper, and no television or radio was permitted in the home), Genie's speech and language hadn't developed. I strived to stimulate the regrowth of her lost neurons by giving her as many new experiences as possible in the short amount of time I had with her.

I was bewildered by this young woman and her fly-paper life. If only I had had more experience or modeling from my professors, I knew I could have done better. I researched everything available, I made materials, and I spent every waking moment thinking about her. I had expected to teach her better communication and more quickly, but no matter what I tried, I didn't succeed. Five weeks wasn't enough for those neurons to regrow.

Though I had been unable to teach Genie all I'd hoped to in our short time together, she had taught me so much. Neglecting a baby, withholding food, movement, and sound are deadly. Terrorizing a child makes her retreat inside her body to preserve herself, where she must self-stimulate that body, which needs to move and feel sensation to know it is alive. Just because she has been freed from the fly paper, that doesn't mean the toxic damage can be reversed, yet it is worth all the effort in the world to try.

Years later, I met a speech-language pathologist who knew about Genie. She informed me that Genie eventually transitioned into a group home. She hadn't overcome her childhood isolation enough to live at an independent level. Additionally, she had visitations with her mother during that whole time. This information had been concealed from me when I worked with her. I had mixed feelings about that, but given that her mother had some cognitive disabilities and had been manipulated and severely abused by her husband, she didn't have the wherewithal to get help. Even highly intelligent, well-educated women don't leave abusive relationships. Yet Genie's mother never did exhibit much concern for the suffering Genie had endured. Still, I knew that it was probably her mother who kept Genie alive.

Genie never gained the ability to use grammar, as those parts of her brain had never developed. After a series of foster homes and institutions, and even returning to live with her mother for a few years, Genie became withdrawn and rarely spoke. Fortunately, she was eventually made a ward of the state and placed in a supportive group home where she did learn to verbalize and to communicate through sign language.

Genie, one of my first clients, had lived through a traumatic childhood and had a severe disability. I saw her as a rare human being, deserving of everything I had to offer—empathy, compassion, and the best treatment I could deliver—yet that treatment had not been enough. And though I knew I was unlikely to encounter another client quite like Genie in my career, I knew I'd encounter many more abused, neglected, and wounded children—children I could help with communication but not with the psychic wounds that haunted them.

Could my heart remain big enough for them all? After all, I had suffered my own wounds in life, wounds that had silenced me in different ways. I had learned to remain silent when I wanted to speak up. To accept abuse when it was undeserved. To bury my own emotions as I focused on the emotions of my clients. If I could not speak up myself, could I truly help my clients to be heard? Was speech therapy a calling for me or just a job? It would take moving to Alaska, where my skills and talents were put to the test daily and often in harsh and brutal conditions, for me to learn the answer.

CHAPTER 5
The Greatland

To the lover of wilderness, Alaska is one of the most wonderful countries in the world.
—John Muir

Beyond the deserts of California, beyond the drizzle of the Pacific Northwest, beyond the forests of British Columbia lies a distant land known only to a few who have dared to seek her fierce grace, known to most only by stories and imagination. But to the privileged few, it is a real place, a sacred place, a good place.

This land, like a hidden gem discovered in a lost cavern that leads to another world, was a secret hideaway for some ancient Snow People. The sentient land knew at all times who was walking on her, living in her field of consciousness, and worthy of her abundance.

Those who did not belong in this land were swallowed by the cave and excreted back to where they came from within six months. The rest stayed until they were sick or dead. For once a human was enveloped by her aura, there was no escape. That person was there as a witness to the beauty and greatness of the Greatland and a lover of the harsh and wild life that became Alaska.

After a long Pan American flight over spectacular snowcapped mountains, the plane landed in Fairbanks, a city in the cold interior of Alaska. As I descended the stairs that had been rolled up to the plane, my eyes shifted from wide-open curiosity to squinting at the ground. Cautiously, I stepped onto two feet of snow as hard as concrete. Even though I paid guarded attention to each specific action I took, some lofty, protective awareness encircled me. I felt completely comfortable.

Bill was waiting for me and the cats at the little terminal. I was already dressed in the blue down parka with the big hood that we had bought at REI, and I felt like an Eskimo as Bill gave me that big bear hug and a kiss. It was so good to see him again.

We drove to the place he had rented near the University of Alaska. It was a far cry from the cozy little house we'd had on Vashon, but at least it wasn't a Quonset hut. It was one unit in a triplex in a modern housing tract and had been built on permafrost, which freezes in the winter and thaws to about five feet below ground in the summer. All the homes were sinking and would have to be abandoned someday. Ever since the Alaskan oil boom that had started in the late 1950s, housing had been scarce and rents high. Consequently, even though we only planned to be there for two years, we wanted to buy a home as soon as we could afford it. But for the meantime, this quirky little house would have to do.

We leased the largest unit with three bedrooms, but each bedroom had been rented to a different person. While Bill and I had the corner bedroom with an attached bathroom, a guy who worked with Bill at the FAA and another man looking for work rented the other two. We all shared the living room, main bathroom, and the kitchen and dining area. A communal laundry downstairs was inconvenient, but at least we had one. The place was clean, and knowing it was temporary, I was happy to be there. It was all part of our arctic adventure.

"I want to warn you about the water," Bill said after we'd settled in. "We're not supposed to drink it."

"Not drink the water?" I asked, bewildered. I hadn't been there even an hour and already the adventure was a lot less fun.

"It's full of sulfur. It makes the water orange, stains everything, and smells like rotten eggs. It's all over this area of town. Don't brush your teeth in it either, and don't wash your hair in it or it'll turn orange," he warned.

"So what are we supposed to do for drinking water, buy it?" We had such pristine water on Vashon. It never entered my mind that Alaska would have undrinkable water.

"Don't worry. I bought three five-gallon jugs," Bill said, proud of his own resourcefulness. "On Sunday, we'll go to Fox;

it's about fifteen miles north of town and fill the jugs with river water. That's where everybody goes. It's clean enough for drinking and cooking—once we boil it. And we can brush our teeth with it, and you can use it to wash your pretty blond hair. In the meantime, I bought a couple of gallons of water at the store."

Okay, I told myself. That's okay. I can deal with that. No biggie. River water it is.

That night, I tried to take a bath. I had spent four hours in a plane full of smokers and reeked of cigarette smoke. Cautiously, I put my foot into the murky water. It disappeared under the smelly solution. Disgusted, I removed my foot, drained the tub, and took a quick shower after hiding my hair in a shower cap. My hair still smelled like cigarettes.

I slept very well that night. It was good to be back with Bill. Once the cats were snuggled in, all was right with the world.

I woke up starving. After bundling myself in a warm robe and slippers, I went to the kitchen. Nothing in the fridge but beer and soft drinks. I opened the cupboards. No food, just junk, like chips and crackers. It had to be somewhere.

I trudged back to the bedroom, the air frigid in the early morning hour. Shaking Bill awake, I asked, "Where's the food?"

"Well, I was waiting for you to get here to stock up," he said as he rose from his pillow. "Do you want to go to the store now?" He waited *two months* to stock up? He was a grown man. I thought he would have food waiting for his life partner so she wouldn't have to go to the grocery store on her first day in town. So that was how it was going to be. My adventure grew more dismal by the minute.

We drove to the grocery store. As if on a quest, I snagged a rusty metal grocery cart with my gloved hands, and we looked over the fresh food. I balked at the singular pathetic head of iceberg lettuce in the bin—small, dried out, and brown. It looked tasteless and cost six dollars. I decided not to get it. A loaf of bread, which just the week before on Vashon had cost a dollar and fifty cents, sold for four dollars. I didn't buy that either.

There wasn't anything in this store I could afford! I left with five things in my cart: a can of tomatoes, a package of dried beans, a pound of hamburger, chili powder, and saltine crackers. We would have chili for breakfast. And lunch. And dinner.

When I returned home, I had a dismal appreciation of why Bill didn't have any groceries in the house. I changed the way I shopped. I couldn't look for the best price anymore. In fact, I ignored the price completely. If I needed it, I bought it. End of story. I fancied myself a modern pioneer. Apparently, I could be rattled by the shocking prices for a moment, an hour, or even a day, but adaptation comes quickly to a human being who wants to survive. I chose survival. Hence, food would be a big expense.

Sunday afternoon, after warming the truck engine, we hustled into the front seat to explore Alaska and get some water. Within a few blocks, we were out of the city and into the wild. The ground was flat and covered with snow. Clustered here and there were frozen deciduous trees with no leaves. Desolate hills strayed in the distance. No activity—no sign or sound of man, not even birdsong—to distract my mind could be found. I sat quietly in the warm truck, completely relaxed and feeling only happiness and joy to finally be in the Alaskan wilderness beside my husband.

Soon we reached a river, frozen in ice. Earlier in the day someone had chopped a hole through the ice, so by the time we arrived in the afternoon, fresh water was available. We weren't the only ones; it was a water convention. Bill grabbed the three empty five-gallon jugs and climbed down the bank of the river. I followed close behind. After Bill filled each jug with the river water, he handed them to me. Five gallons is heavy. Hoisting the first one with all my strength, I staggered to the truck, deposited it, and came back for the second five gallons. After Bill returned to the truck with the third jug, we started back home. There was no complaining; it was just an Alaskan pioneer thing that needed to be done.

It had only been a weekend, but I could see how Alaska was testing me. She perceived I was breathing her crisp air.

She understood I had grown up on a farm and was used to hard work, responsible, and dependable. She believed I had something to offer the people, so she had brought me here for them. With her aura, she had captured me. Lured and buoyed by her greatness, I put one foot in front of the other and became more present to the present. The rest of the world was somewhere far away, erased by the spell of Alaska.

On Monday, finding myself a job became priority number one. With the prices of rent and food, I realized we needed more money. Fortunately, a law had passed in 1975 that mandated all public schools provide speech therapy to children with communication disorders. It was a great boon for the children. It also meant there was a considerable demand for SLPs in the schools.

After phoning the local school district, I discovered their one and only speech therapist position was filled. I also learned that my $11,500-per-year salary from Vashon Island would double to $22,000 in Fairbanks. Of course, things were more expensive up here, but not *that* much more. Maybe I could afford to buy groceries after all. They asked me to send a résumé for their files, which I did. Then I wondered what I would do for employment in the meantime.

I checked the want ads in the local newspaper. I wasn't trained for any of them. I looked through the Fairbanks and Anchorage yellow pages for speech-language pathology. I was disappointed that Fairbanks had nothing. I collected information about a couple of organizations that provided speech therapy in Anchorage and sent them my résumé. Then there was nothing more to do but wait.

Our household goods and white pickup truck had already arrived in Fairbanks, but the little red sports car, shipped via Sea Land, hadn't appeared yet. I couldn't wait to get it. Bill drove the truck to work five days a week, leaving me stranded in the sinking house. I wasn't used to being stuck at home. It was boring. There was nothing to do, and I didn't know anyone. We had television part of the day, but this was long before cable, much less videos. Programs were mailed on a reel and broadcast two weeks later. Every show was delayed by two weeks, even the Super Bowl.

I listened to the local radio station for current news and information. I had never relied on the radio for anything but music. In Alaska, the radio took on a sense of importance. I felt as if I had gone back in time to my parents' generation before television, when people went about their lives unattached to the tube. It was quiet and calm.

Nonetheless, I was restless, and wanted to explore my unfamiliar city. One morning, several days after arriving, I dropped Bill off at work and took the truck. As I drove around Fairbanks, it looked as if the town itself had remained frozen in time. Buildings painted institutional green and gray resembled those from the 1940s and '50s. They were built during an economic and population boom during the New Deal and World War II.

The downtown area, which consisted of about four streets, concluded at the frozen Chena River, which bordered the city in ice-chunked silence. No blue ripples of water on the banks. No smell of the splashing fish that would fill the most popular river in interior Alaska during the summer. The river, like the city, was noiseless.

I drove across the Chena Bridge to the other side of the river. Randomly situated Victorian-style homes, small houses, and even log cabins resembling what one might imagine from a Jack London novel came into view. I didn't see any new homes. No tract housing like ours, either—each house was unique in this town of about twenty-two thousand people. There were some nice neighborhoods, and I figured we could find something to buy eventually. For now, we had to stay in our sinking rental; we only had one income. That wasn't enough to buy a house.

Turning back across the river, I parked downtown to check out the stores. Walking down First Street, I looked through a tourist shop on the corner and bought some paperbacks about Alaskan native history and culture. As I continued down the street, I noticed some grown men lying on the sidewalks in the middle of the day. Puzzled, I thought, *What the heck? Who are these guys?* They were all men, about seven of them. A few sat on the concrete with their backs slouched against the buildings. They drank from bottles in brown paper bags. When they spoke, their speech was slurred. Their eyelids hung heavy, and their heads drooped after taking a sip.

The rest of the men were supine on the sidewalk, dead to the world. Some were white men and some were dark-haired and dark-skinned men. As I stepped around several drunks, I discovered that most of the town's bars were located on that street. With an immediate twinge of sadness, I realized that I had seen my first Alaskan native, and he was passed out on the sidewalk. Alcohol doesn't care what race you are. Once it grabs hold of you, it ruins your life.

Even though all the inebriates wore jackets, I worried that they might be cold, even get frostbite—their breath was easily visible in the frigid air. Seeing a stricken person passed out in a warm-weather town was bad enough, but it seemed crueler and far more alarming in an ice-cold town.

Were they in jeopardy of freezing to death? Should I speak to a policeman or call an ambulance? Who took care of these unfortunate people? This was my first visit to downtown. I didn't know what systems were in place.

Where were the locals? Had they abandoned these men, who were presently dead to the world? Or did they know better than I, a cheechako, a greenhorn, what the human body could withstand? Did they grasp that these guys would live to drink another day? Disturbed and sorrowful, I tiptoed past, trying not to stare. This was the first time I had witnessed the intersection of alcohol and Alaskan natives, but it wouldn't be the last.

Driving around Fairbanks, it seemed like I had gone back in time. I had entered an episode of the *Twilight Zone*—the sort of show where a guy is driving and has to turn off the main highway to a small town. Everything appears normal, but something is waiting for him, something that will reveal his character, provoke a challenge, or defy his imagination. I seemed to be that person as I drove around town. I felt I was being watched over, as all that I had experienced washed over me, like the smelly water in our shower. Alaska was showing me what I needed to see: the harshness, the wreckage, and the ordinary. How would it affect me? Would I give up on it, or would it make me even more determined to survive there?

I thought about these questions all day as I drove around town, memorized the main streets and intersections, and stopped at the store. Eventually, I picked up Bill from work, and we went home to the sinking house.

For the next several days, I focused on my recent books. I shut the door to our bedroom, lay in our warm waterbed—which we'd had since college days—snuggled in with our Ragdoll cats, and read. I was fascinated by the Russian history of the region, including how they were the first to bring smallpox and other diseases that killed, in some cases, almost every person in an entire village. Some indigenous Alaskans were treated as slaves, used to harvest fur. But members of a few tribes fought back and killed their overlords. Unfortunately, Russia sent a regiment back to kill everyone in the village: men, women, and children. Without guns and manpower, the Alaskans were helpless, and countless were slaughtered.

Many First Peoples, as the indigenous Alaskans call themselves, used to be nomads. They followed the fish in the summer and the game in the winter. They didn't always stay in one place. They had established trading posts where a population remained year-round. The coastal people had permanent settlements, depending more on the sea for food than inland tribes, who followed the game: caribou and moose. Both "Eskimo" and "Indian" people, as the white people had named them, lived in coastal and inland Alaska, and they spoke at least twenty different languages.

When the white man came along, he made the indigenous Alaskans settle down in one place. The Americans, who had bought the state from Russia in 1867, banned the Alaskans from speaking their native languages or worshipping in their traditional ways.

Our government contracted with churches to provide their schooling and Christianization, because, after all, they were considered heathen. We Americans took away their clothing, their dancing, and their singing. They couldn't just subsist as they had for thousands of years; they needed to be like us—get a job and make money.

We gave them alcohol to negotiate contracts and keep them quiet. The leaders of the churches molested their children. The leaders of the schools made the children sit at desks all day and be still, something they had never done before. They were punished if they spoke their own language. We sent their children far away to boarding schools, severing ties with their families and their culture. Arrogant and ignorant, we tried to make them in our image: greedy, mean, sinful, hypocritical, and suspicious.

After we abolished their culture and the results became evident, we wondered, *Why didn't they flourish? Why didn't they do well in school? Why didn't they talk like us? Why didn't they work as we did?* Those actions had consequences that have lingered to the present.

It is evident now that indigenous Alaskans have lived in Alaska for thirteen thousand years. They walked here as intrepid explorers, looking for food, for a place to flourish at the end of the Ice Age. They mastered the environment, these People of the Snow, with their intelligence and God-given intuition, by honing their ways, their culture, and their stamina.

Indigenous Alaskans are a strong and beautiful people. They are intelligent. They live in unusually harsh conditions and are extraordinarily inventive and talented. They have mastered how to survive in a tough and sparse environment for thousands of years. I just hoped they could teach me how to survive in this environment for the next two years.

CHAPTER 6
There's No Place Like Home

Home is the nicest word there is.
—Laura Ingalls Wilder

When Alaska was young, people carved a home out of whatever they could find. Warmth was always at the forefront, and survival. The people dug out permafrost to make a floor, which they covered with furs and skins. A domed roof made from the permafrost chunks—dirt and grasses—kept out the snow and rain.

In 1976, when we had first moved to Fairbanks, native Alaskans could still remember living in those houses, everyone sleeping on the floor together to stay warm at night. Most of the sod houses had sunk back into the earth, and now the people lived in Western-style houses. But I hadn't seen any of their homes because I hadn't been to their towns or villages. Whatever homes they built had to withstand the fury of the winds, the frigidness of the air, and the frostiness of the ground. Whatever Alaska forced on them they had to accept and endure. And now that we were living there, we had to accept and endure the brutal climate as well.

As spring arrived, our attention turned to finding a home to buy. Even though Fairbanks was the second largest city in Alaska, and one of the coldest, hundreds of people lived in cabins without running water or electricity. They stoked the fire of their wood stove for heat in the morning and cooked on it. Coleman lanterns and candles provided light. And just like us, they acquired their water from the river in Fox. Dirty clothes were washed at one of the two laundromats in town. Many people showered at the university. That's not what I had in mind.

I didn't mind having a wood stove for extra heat—we had

one on Vashon—but I wasn't going to be cooking on it. I didn't want to haul my water from the river. And I didn't want to take a shower in sulfur-stinking water that turned my hair orange. I wanted a modern home in a modern neighborhood.

Living in a sinking house was acceptable for a few months, but in the long run I wanted electricity, city water, and a sewer. Mostly, I craved a garage and a fireplace. If I drove the truck first, I ran outside ten minutes early, sat on the rock-hard frozen bench seat, and started the engine. Next, I scraped the ice off the windshield. Then I dashed back inside the warm house and waited another ten minutes for the truck to warm. If I forgot to direct the heater fan toward the windshield on the inside, my body heat would fog up the glass when I drove it. Then I would have to open the window to let the steam out, to get the fog off the windows, which was the last thing I wanted to do. A garage would eliminate all this rigamarole.

Eventually, we found a small split-level home in a neighborhood west of downtown. It had two bedrooms, a nice bathroom, a bonus room, and a laundry closet. Most importantly, it had the attached garage I wanted, but no fireplace. That didn't matter now, as I had already learned that a room loses more heat from a wood-burning fireplace than it actually provides. And if it's one thing we didn't want to lose in the winter, it was heat.

Luckily, we had moved our uber-heavy cast iron, wood-burning stove from Vashon Island to Fairbanks. I watched as three men carried it, grueling step by grueling step. One guy's knees bent backward and I thought his legs were going to snap. Men were indispensable in Alaska for their physical strength, but I hoped I wouldn't cripple anyone with my urge to stay warm.

I didn't have any friends yet. We visited Holly and Darrell a couple of times at their home about twenty minutes out of town in a rural area. They were both working and busy, and they had a baby girl now, so I didn't have as much interaction with Holly as I would have liked. The only other people I knew were the guys we had lived with, and since we moved to our own home, I didn't even have them to talk with now. Our cats were my main companions.

By March, our planet had started its tilt toward the sun, giving the frozen town of Fairbanks twelve hours of daylight. But the sun did little to thaw the frozen earth. The temperatures were still below freezing and plunging close to zero at night. Spring didn't start in March, there were no April showers to bring May flowers. It even snowed in May. Spring, the kind of spring I thought about, where the awakened grass was tender and bright, the trees budded out into leaves, and the first daffodils showed their joyful petals, was completely different here. It unfolded within a short, few weeks in June. It was winter, winter, winter, then suddenly it was spring.

I delighted in seeing the surrounding vegetation come to life in Fairbanks. It seemed that overnight, deciduous trees, like the beautiful May Day tree, flowered with an intoxicating, sweet scent. White birch, with silver-sheened leaves that glistened in the breeze, for some reason were my favorite. But where were all the big Christmas trees I had imagined? I had envisioned enchanted fir forests, but there were none to behold.

The evergreen trees on Vashon Island were large, lacy, and beautiful. Now, as far north as I had ever been in my life, I expected to see the biggest conifers ever. Sadly, I was mistaken. The extreme cold this far north stunted evergreen growth, rendering them scrawny, scraggly, and almost black.

Within four months of arriving, I came to know Fairbanks in the summer. Basically, the circling, worshipped sun never set, stealing sleep from my brain and making it forget the lateness of the hour. I cultivated unique ways to trick my brain into sleeping. My watch became indispensable, and I looked at it often. *What? It's eleven o'clock already? I have to get to bed.* We installed black-out shades in the bedroom windows, ordered from a Sears catalogue. They protected my eyes from the relentless streams of radiant light. As I integrated the unaccustomed, light-sky world into my being and let my old paradigms drift away, I fell more in love with Alaska.

We spent the summer exploring our unfamiliar surroundings. We battled super mosquitoes, took long drives, went camping, and danced the night away in grungy taverns with floors covered in peanut shells. Little by little, I became accustomed to the never-setting sun, the dilapidated infrastructure, and the limited groceries. These were small prices to pay to be living among such natural abundance.

As summer turned to fall, the green leaves faded to yellow, but they never reached red. Temperatures veered too cold too fast. By Labor Day everything had frozen, and I was once again scraping the ice off the windshield.

September also was the time when the men went moose hunting. They motored boats upriver, into the wild—boats loaded with as many cases of beer as possible. Bill always came back with some moose meat, which was systematically divided among all the men on the trip. The first time I tried it, I wanted it to be my last. I didn't like it. After that, I refused to cook it. If Bill wanted to eat it, that was his choice, but he could cook it himself. The longer I endured the challenges of Alaska, the tougher I became. And the tougher I became, the more lines I started to draw in the sand. Maybe if people weren't tough before they came to Alaska, they toughened as they went along.

When Christmas arrived, we needed a Christmas tree. "Let's go get a Christmas tree today," Bill suggested, his face gleaming with excitement. We both loved Christmas.

"I've only seen a couple of tree lots, and the trees are all frozen," I replied. "They don't look that good. Maybe we should buy a fake one this year."

A fake tree was heresy. Bill wouldn't hear of it. "No. Let's go to that field of little trees. We can get three of them and tie them together to make one good tree." He had it all planned out.

"But it's forty below today! Are you serious? And they're frozen stiff, they won't look good at all."

In response, Bill threw an ax and a chainsaw—an expensive Alaskan toy—in the bed of the pickup and gave it several minutes to warm up. Not only was the temperature cold that day, but there was also a breeze, lowering the temperature even further with the wind chill. But I concluded this wouldn't be an issue I'd prevail on, so I dressed warmly for the adventure. After a fifteen-minute drive, there it was, the miniature fir forest of black spruce trees. We left the warm cab and stepped over a wire fence to get to them.

"Are we trespassing?" I asked, looking at a NO TRESPASSING sign.

"Don't worry about it," he replied. We started our search for the best tree, but none of them looked any good. We went deeper into the forest. Within a couple of minutes, my eyelashes were frozen. I hadn't brought my face mask with me, and my cheeks were stinging with cold.

"Bill, your mustache has icicles on it. I'm freezing. Hurry up. Just pick one. I don't care anymore," I begged. Ignoring my pleas but seemingly aware that there were limits to my patience, he cut down three small and stunted trees and threw them in the bed of the pickup. It was a six-minute logging expedition to find the best of the bunch. Ten minutes at forty below can cause frostbite, so I was glad it was over. On the way home I looked back and noticed one of the trees flying out of the truck bed.

"One of the trees just blew out," I yelled. "Didn't you cover them or tie them together?"

"That's okay, we still have two left," he reassured me.

"What about the tree on the road? We need to clear it off."

"The wind will take care of it."

As I looked back again, he was right. The wind had grown so strong that it had swept the tree to the shoulder of the road. Home at last, our struggle over, we realized what we had: the saddest Charlie Brown trees ever. One of them wasn't worth saving. We eagerly decorated the few branches of the last tree standing and parked it in front of our useless front door, which had frozen shut with ice on the inside as well as the outside. Although it was the most pathetic Christmas tree we ever had, it remained one of the most memorable. We were thankful for it, and Santa found us anyway.

CHAPTER 7

Called by the Light

They say that the northern lights are our ancestors watching over us.
—Yarii Walker, Alaskan Yupik

My first January in Fairbanks, 1977, coldness came to visit, like a disagreeable relative from a distant side of the family. With polite welcoming, the interfering company could be tolerated for a few days, but after that, the incessant arguing, criticizing, and consternation led to only one resolution: this visitor left, or I left. When the uninvited cold snap arrived, it introduced itself at a dreadful thirty degrees below zero. After a day or two of this intrusion, it disintegrated to a freezing sixty below. Finally, it fell to seventy-five degrees below zero. I couldn't think about it anymore. This now unwelcome caller had control of my life. And it stayed for two weeks.

Because of my seasonal guest, I couldn't dawdle outside anymore, or it would bite me in the face. I developed a direct route to follow, like a dog who patrols his yard every morning, never wavering from the tried-and-true path. My itinerary: house to car, car to building, building to car, car to house. But just getting outside that door became a challenge.

The front door had betrayed us. It froze shut with ice that had formed from the outside to the inside. No matter how much we chipped away at it, the ice remained a living, growing thing that didn't want to die. We finally gave up, let it have its life, and waited for spring when it would melt. Until then, the only exit available to us was through the garage.

I had lived with snow growing up in Pasco, Washington. Every winter, just in time for Christmas, the snow would fall and stay for a couple of weeks. Then it melted. During those two weeks, we took full advantage of it—sledding, making snowmen, and having snowball fights. I caught the snowflakes on my gloves and looked at their individual shapes before they melted. They were amazing.

But this snow in Fairbanks felt brutal. In fact, it snowed very little because it was too cold to snow. It was too cold to run outside to catch a snowflake on my glove, and too cold to make a snowman. It was not the snow I had grown up with in eastern Washington. This drier, bitter, freezing cold penetrated our bones. And it lasted eight months. This snow scorned fun.

Yet the snow did provide some pleasure. People in Alaska cross-country skied and snow-shoed, in the past, from the necessity to travel from place to place in the winter. But now they cross-country skied on the weekend for pleasure and to exercise during the few hours of sunlight available; it was a perfect winter sport for the hardy and suitably dressed. There weren't any downhill ski resorts; it was too flat for that. But I didn't mind. I had no interest in venturing outside in the Alaskan winter.

Unfortunately, Bill did. Sure enough, he bought cross-country skis, and sure enough, I begrudgingly went along despite how much I hated the idea. Every time I tried to be a good sport, it was so freezing cold I couldn't get warm enough to enjoy it. I preferred skiing at thirty degrees Fahrenheit above zero, not thirty degrees below. After doing my best to go along with this Nordic activity, eventually, I had to say *no*, I don't want to go. It was as simple as that. Why had it been so hard for me to say no to all the other activities I wanted no part of? The winter may have been brutal, but it was its brutality that chopped more chips in my bubble, that was teaching me to speak up, to save myself from freezing.

Alaska taught me that everything was relative. As the temperature started to rise from seventy-five below, sixty below became suddenly tolerable, and thirty below mutated to downright warm. Some high-schoolers astonishingly started wearing shorts with their snow boots. By the time it reached zero degrees, even I didn't need to wear a coat every moment I was outside. It was amazing how my body adapted to the temperature.

Then one night, Alaska gave us a present—a beautiful present that I never tired of seeing, but I only *heard* it this once: the aurora borealis, the northern lights. As soon as I saw them out the window, I bundled up and ran to the backyard, gleefully yelling at Bill to come and see. The sky was alighted with a spectacular display of red and green ocean waves made of light that seemed close enough to touch. I was mesmerized.

Then I heard them. They made the sound of snap, crackle, and pop, like milk just poured on a bowl of Rice Krispies. As if they were talking to me, they affirmed that I was in the right place at the right time, that life was beautiful and miraculous. I stood in the yard as long as I could, just a few minutes, and received their blessing on that cold and colorful night.

Once back in the house, Bill stayed downstairs watching television, and I went to bed. Alone with the magical wonder I had just witnessed, I thought about the spellbinding lights. Fascinated by them, I couldn't get enough. After that, I looked for them every night. They reminded me of that time before entering fourth grade, when I was charmed by similar amazing lights, those inner private lights inside of me, not outside.

Had that inner, swirling light of compassion years ago awakened me to the awareness of the importance of communication? Did it inspire my compassion for people who had difficulty communicating, like Rose and Stanley? Had it given me the strength to help them, even if my own communication needed help? Would I ever have the opportunity to use my training and experience as an SLP again? It had been a year already with no work.

But that night in Fairbanks, light had not only come to life in the sky like the ocean—in front of my opened eyes—it had spoken to me. What did those lights ignite in me? They reminded me of my calling. They illuminated my own darkness, reminding me of how many children I had already helped in Los Angeles, Seattle, and Vashon Island. They highlighted how much I had learned to become an SLP and told me to be proud of how hard I had worked to get my master's degree, even though Mr. Carlton had predicted in front of the whole sixth-grade class that I wouldn't finish college. One bad teacher can undo one good student.

I had internalized that belief that I wasn't smart enough, wasn't good enough, even years after I had graduated from college, then graduate school. Yet in a single night, alone in our bedroom, Bill watching television downstairs, the northern lights of Alaska had awoken me to the light inside my soul. It was time to heal my heart, be brave, and start to dissolve the fear and sadness locked inside. It was time to get to work.

CHAPTER 8

There's No Place Like Nome

Education is for improving the lives of others and for leaving your community and world better than you found it.
—Marian Wright Edelman

"Bill, look what came in the mail today," I said, chock-full of happiness.

"What is it?" he asked. The poor guy had just walked in the door. I didn't even say hello.

"It's an offer from an agency in Anchorage. They want me to sign a contract to go to Nome and screen some preschoolers for speech and language disorders. Can you believe it?"

With his arms crossed, he asked, "How much are they going to pay you?" Bill always thought about the money.

"They'll pay all my expenses and two hundred dollars for the day. This is so great. I need to get all my materials unpacked and organized. I'm going next week. Will you be able to take me to the airport?"

"What about the school district?" Bill scowled. "Don't they have any openings yet?"

"No. There's just the one position, and it's still filled. I've checked in with them." My hiring streak hadn't held in Alaska.

He looked through the rest of the mail and said he could drop me off. He worked near the airport, so it was on his way. We sat down to dinner and watched two-week old TV with no further discussion about my trip to Nome.

It was a good thing, I told myself, that I was emotionally self-contained. I noticed that if I felt too happy, Bill turned cranky. Instead of complaining, I took care of my duties and went along with his moods. He worked full-time, after all, and expected me to do the same. Since I had always done that, this one-day job was not enough. He let me know it by ignoring my enthusiasm.

It felt so good to unpack my speech therapy materials and tests. Would I remember everything? I didn't need to take it all. These were just preschoolers. But I decided to review it all and be prepared, not wanting to miss anyone with a problem. Children in this age group can be tricky because they are early in their speech and language development. What might seem on the edge of normal could, in reality, be abnormal. Many factors needed to be considered. I had to take tongue depressors, cotton swabs, gloves, toys, forms, and so many other things. I won't leave anything behind, I thought. Better to have too much than too little.

# # #

As I stepped into the plane to Nome, I realized this would be the first time I had ever performed my job alone, going to a legendary town for a one-day contract job as a professional speech-language pathologist. And it seemed so remote, as if Fairbanks wasn't remote enough. There wouldn't be any other SLPs there to confer with. My education, training, and experience would be put to the test. I felt proud, nervous, and happy.

I departed to a town just a few hundred miles south of the Arctic Circle, which had only four hours of daylight in December. The Alaska Airlines 707 fight path crossed over Denali, so I took a seat on the left side, hoping to get a better view of the mountain. Soon, the pilot made an overhead announcement. Like a tour guide, he mentioned the name, the height, and the statistics of the mountain. Then he told us that he would make sure everyone could see it, no matter where they were sitting. Suddenly, the plane started to bank left and flew in a half-circle, at a deep slant. The view was tremendous, majestic, and awesome.

Awesome. Awesome is the best word of all to describe Denali and Alaska. *Awe*: a mixed emotion of reverence, respect, and wonder, inspired by authority, genius, great beauty, sublimity, might, or dread. The mountain went on forever. I couldn't see its edges. Time had created an astounding mountain, beautiful to look at, symmetrically lovely, yet jagged and bumpy. Its weathered peaks were covered in snow, and the sun reflected off their icy faces. Shadows revealed the depth of each valley, large and small. Within a minute, we had crossed its expanse.

Later, we flew over the Alaska Range, which had at least two still-active volcanoes, and the Kuskokwim Mountains. For the next ninety minutes, flying over untouched wilderness, I surveyed only a few small, remote villages that interrupted the land. Stunned by the vast territory and changing terrain, I couldn't look away. No human had stepped on ninety-nine percent of it. It was beautiful and terrifying.

When we flew into Nome, reality registered. I saw the small and drab town. I immediately felt out of place, dressed in my black wool gabardine three-piece suit with a pink blouse and a bow that tied at my neck. And in place of snow boots, I wore my expensive black leather boots. After all, I was a professional.

Before I had left the university, I received the lecture on, among other things, how to dress professionally. My generation wore jeans and "waffle stompers" (hiking boots) to college in the early 1970s. Miniskirts and hot pants with sandals that laced up to the knees were also in style during hot weather. The chair of my department counseled me to leave these clothes behind and always look "professional" out in the world. I welcomed that message into my closet. I expected to dress professionally at work. There was no question about that. The advice served me well when I worked in Los Angeles, Seattle, and Vashon Island, but then came Alaska.

As I walked off the plane in Nome and looked around, I tried to dismiss my fears that I had overdressed and reminded myself that I was finally back to work. I had the first sense of myself as a strong, responsible, and professional woman, free in the world, traveling to the hinterland of Alaska.

After retrieving my bags, I spotted a couple of taxis in

front of the small terminal. I waved at the driver in the first one and asked him to take me to my hotel. I had never been in a taxi, so I sat in the front seat with him. He didn't say anything like, "You should sit in the back," so I stayed there. Looking at the town as we drove, in the background sat a small mountain with active gold-mining equipment. That surprised me. There were several streets with old and small homes. A few hotels, restaurants, and businesses—nothing over two stories—were on the main road.

I checked into a hotel and had a bite to eat. My work started in the morning, then I would catch the evening flight back home.

The morning light came early. I ate some breakfast and walked to the preschool. I soon learned a local word for "spring" in Alaska: break-up. Break-up is the time of year—in this case May—when the snow melted, the ground surfaced, and green emerged. In Fairbanks, the snow was long gone. But as I headed to work, I saw it was break-up in Nome. The sides of the streets were still lined with snow, leaving the middle of the road saturated with pure, deep, sloppy mud. The roads weren't paved, and my boots sure weren't made for walkin'.

After just a few steps, both my boots and the bottoms of my wool gabardine pants were covered in mud. What a mess. Luckily, I had brought my snow boots with me. I hurried back to my room and changed out my boots and wiped off my pants.

As it turns out, Nome is a white-man hub, which is a town in any region of Alaska that has more white people than natives. Nome has hotels and restaurants, and jets can land there. Villages weren't like that. The hub endured as a place for villagers who lived remotely to come for supplies or to catch a jet to Anchorage or Fairbanks. This remote Alaskan town turned out to be yet another male domain, one where a woman dressed for success sure didn't seem to belong.

I met the director of the preschool, a preacher, and started screening the children, who were mostly white. After I completed my assigned work, a concerned woman from Child

Protective Services found me.

"Are you the speech therapist from Anchorage?" she asked.

"Yes," I smiled.

"We have a six-month-old baby boy who has just been taken into custody. Would you be able to evaluate him before you leave?"

"Absolutely." I replied. "What's a good time for you and where is he?"

Specialists like me were rarely in town, and when we were, we had to do everything we could to help. And while a six-month-old baby is preverbal, by six months of age the formation of speech has begun. All those babbling sounds are speech and muscle patterns being formed. This is the stage where speech recognition begins. If a baby isn't showing the normal responses to verbal cues or babbling as babies normally do, then there's a looming speech problem. Another reason a speech pathologist might be called in is because of a cleft palate or some other physiological abnormality. Someone, or something, looked out for this baby to call me in at such an early stage in his development.

"I'll have him ready at three o'clock," she assured me. "Our office is right across the street." She gestured to the state agency, a small office tucked among the saloons and hardware stores.

When I returned that afternoon, I saw that the infant remained in his crib. His attendant left the room so I could work uninterrupted. This baby appeared clean, chubby, and happy. I started interacting with him as I would with any baby. I made babbling sounds—"bu bu bu" and "da da"—to determine if he would imitate me. Suddenly, he haltingly started to say a throaty, guttural sound, "gu gu gu." Babbling begins between the age of three and eight months. Not only did he watch me, smiling, holding my finger, moving his gaze to see a toy, but he also babbled. He was normal. It delighted me to make this report to his caseworker.

After we finished, I contemplated why he babbled "gu"

instead of "bu." All the tables of consonant-developmental norms I had read indicated that the lip and tongue-tip consonant sounds developed first. *Dada,* much to the disappointment of *Mama,* is often the first word babies said. But these norms are based on English speakers, not Iñupiat speakers. Then it dawned on me. Of course "gu" would be one of the first consonants to evolve with this language. Guttural sounds are prevalent in Iñupiaq. Thus began my recognition that many of the norms for speech, vocabulary, and language I had learned in college didn't necessarily correlate to indigenous Alaskan speakers. I wondered how many young children may have been diagnosed by Western social workers or teachers as developmentally delayed because of these linguistic differences. No doubt far too many.

Everything had gone well during my short visit to work in Nome, except for the mud. I had screened the preschoolers and evaluated a baby. Comfortable with my knowledge, I sensed a confidence in myself. I hadn't felt that confidence in ages, especially during my unemployment, when I only saw myself through my husband's eyes. Now back to work, I started to grow into my role as a specialist, no longer the beginner.

My work done for the day, I decided to walk around a bit before my flight home at seven in the evening. Studying the street map, I strolled to the end of Front Street, where the town met the sea. On this bright and sunny late afternoon. I stood on the boardwalk and scanned the horizon. The ocean bordered Nome. There should be ocean shores here. I remembered stories of the beaches filled with thousands of miners finding gold nuggets in the 1898 gold rush. Now that I stood on the edge of town, I couldn't find any shores—or ocean for that matter. As far as the eye could see, only snow existed. I looked at the map again. It should be here. Slowly, it dawned on me. The ocean was right there in front of me, frozen and covered with snow as far as *my* eyes could see.

A frozen ocean—only in Alaska! I couldn't believe it. I had learned about the polar icecap, but I had also been taught that ocean water didn't freeze. I couldn't connect those two dots until I studied it with my own eyes. Because of the salt, seawater freezes at twenty-eight degrees Fahrenheit. Temperatures ranged from sixteen degrees to thirty degrees at night in May. During the day, it might warm up to thirty or forty degrees. The snow on the land started to melt, causing the mud. On the ocean, however, the snow rode on the frozen salty sea and took longer to melt.

I had looked at the ocean hundreds of times in California, and it was nothing like this. Another concept bit the dust. Even the ocean was different in Alaska.

I had bought a camera to take photos of my travels. As I view my pictures now, I realize how much white and gray I lived with. Snow covered the rooftops and blanketed the ground. Overcast filled the sky. It all blended into a blank canvas, making it difficult to observe the horizon—where the land stopped and the sky began. The visual deprivation could be dangerous when flying because the pilot, especially a bush pilot, couldn't see it either. He had to rely on his altimeter (which sometimes froze) and not be lulled by the lack of definition, which went on for miles and miles between villages on the treeless tundra.

Even the frozen ocean, muffled with snow, could be mistaken for land. Rumor had it that if you were an Alaskan native, you had thirty different words for snow. I asked an Iñupiaq man if that were true. He told me, "No, just a few. We have snow on the ground, falling snow, drifting snow, and snowdrift." I set that rumor to rest in my mind—although there are twenty different native languages in Alaska, so if you add them all up, they could total even more than thirty.

I turned away from the ocean and walked to the Board of Trade, just a few blocks back toward town. Many Alaskan natives sold their arts and crafts at the Board of Trade, which doubled as a bar. I had heard that Wyatt Earp, a famous Old West lawman, gambler, and saloon keeper, had owned this bar during the gold-rush times. One side of the Board of Trade contained an ivory trading post. A bar resided on the other side. With a small door in between the two, a native person could come in from a local village with artwork, sell it on the trading side, walk through the little door, and spend his or her profits drinking on the bar side.

I entered the ivory/artwork side first. Since this might be my only contract job and I might never be here again, I wanted a souvenir from Nome. That shop had the finest scope and selection of native Alaskan artwork I had ever viewed. There were baleen baskets, scrimshawed ivory pendants, mastodon ivory jewelry, beaded necklaces, and dolls dressed in authentic Iñupiaq costumes. I decided then that if I ever went to a village, I would buy a piece of art, not only to have a souvenir of being in that place but also to support a local artist.

After buying a mastodon ivory bracelet, I hesitantly stepped into the bar side. I argued with myself and concluded that I had to get one drink in the famous saloon. At four in the afternoon, only the bartender and one customer, a woman, were there.

Amazed by the bar top, made from a humongous slab of a very thick, wavy-shaped tree, I took a seat near the middle of it. I ordered a Stoli and water over ice with a squeeze of lime. They didn't have any limes in Nome, so they substituted a lemon squeeze instead.

Soon, the woman at the end of the bar stood up, staggered over to me, and started calling me names that I couldn't understand. From the sound of her slurred speech and her angry voice, they weren't welcoming. All I could grasp was the word *gussuk*, which she practically spit at me again and again. I did my best to be polite but started to feel threatened. As her boring eyes came closer, I thought she might haul off and hit me at any moment. Finally, the bartender stepped into the fray.

Calling her by name, he told her, "Go sit down or I'm gonna throw you out."

That was the first time I had been called a *gussuk*, a generally derogatory term for a white person used by some Alaskan natives. In some locations, the word is spelled *kass'aq*. (There could be other spellings as well.)

After I heard that word, *gussuk*, I thought how much it resembled *Cossack*—a Russian who had occupied Alaska before America bought it. Since the Russians were here before the Americans, I surmised that *Cossack* had morphed into a word to describe white people. I had been in Alaska for only a year, but I already understood why she may have had such contempt toward me because I was white—because I descended from the colonizers, who had taken her culture and dignity away.

I had grown up white in a world that privileged me, but now I lived in a world where whites were sometimes unwelcome. Knowing the history of how white people had invaded North America, seized its land, impoverished its people, even stolen their children, I understood how that woman could see me, a white stranger, and be filled with rage. While I came to help, not to hurt, I couldn't escape the legacy of my race. I finished my vodka and left, my heart hurting for the people my race had so damaged, and for myself for being on the receiving end of their pain.

Unbeknownst to me, segregation—known also as apartheid or Jim Crow—had been enforced by law in Alaska. The Dreamland Theater in Nome had a section for "Whites Only" and a section for "Eskimos." One evening, a white soldier invited a woman to the movies. Her father was white, and her mother was an indigenous Alaskan. The soldier led her down the aisle, and the couple sat on the white side. Within moments, the usher quickly approached them and told her that she had to sit in the Eskimo section. Her soldier date told her to stay put. Soon, the manager stomped down the aisle, forcefully took her by her shoulders, marched her up the aisle for all to see, and threw her out of the theater. It was a common discriminatory practice against the people who were there first.

Signs such as "No Natives Allowed" and "We Cater to White Trade Only" were posted on the windows of many businesses and restaurants. Within a few weeks, the young woman—well known and well liked—was voted Queen of Nome at the city's annual winter festival. The town supported her to help relieve the shame and humiliation she had felt for being thrown out of the theater.

This incident is one of many that led to the famous testimony given during the debate on the Anti-Discrimination Bill in Juneau. It failed in 1943, but it came up for a vote again in 1945. People had changed. With World War II over and Hitler defeated, the Alaskan Native servicemen and women weren't willing to live with segregation. Thanks to Elizabeth Wanamaker Peratrovich, a Tlingit woman who attended a teacher's college in Bellingham, Washington, things would change. She had met her husband in college, and they returned to Alaska to become active in native rights. The bill passed in the House, but two senators were violently opposed to it: Senator Allen Shattuck from Juneau and Senator Frank Whaley from Fairbanks.

Shattuck argued that whites, with five thousand years of recorded civilization behind them, should be kept apart from these people barely out of savagery. Whaley said the Eskimos smelled, and he didn't want to sit next to them.

When the offer of public testimony was made, Ms. Peratrovich rose from the gallery. She sat next to the president of the Senate and stated: "I would not have expected that I, who am barely out of savagery, would have to remind gentlemen with five thousand years of recorded civilization behind them of our Bill of Rights. When my husband and I came to Juneau and sought a home in a nice neighborhood where our children could play happily with our neighbor's children, we found such a house and arranged to lease it. When the owners learned that we were Indians, they said 'no.' Would we be compelled to live in the slums?"

When asked by Shattuck, "Will this law eliminate discrimination?" Ms. Peratrovich replied: "Do your laws against larceny, rape, and murder prevent those crimes? There are three kinds of persons who practice discrimination. First, the politician who wants to maintain an inferior minority group so that he can always promise them something; second, the Mr.

and Mrs. Jones who aren't quite sure of their social position and who are nice to you on one occasion and can't see you on others, depending on who they are with; and third, the great superman who believes in the superiority of the white race."

She reported that discrimination against herself, her friends, and her people "has forced the finest of our race to associate with white trash." Her words packed a punch, for after a two-hour questioning, the bill passed, and the gallery burst into applause. From then on, Alaskan natives had full and equal accommodations in hotels, eateries, soda fountains, soft-drink parlors, and roadhouses. The penalty for violations included a $250 fine, thirty days in jail, or both. In Alaska each year, February 16 is celebrated as Elizabeth Peratrovich Day.

Shortly after returning from Nome, I received a call from the same agency in Anchorage that had sent me to Nome. They liked my work. My education had been put to the test, and I had left Nome a better place as a result. Now, they wanted me to go to St. Lawrence Island, where I would work for a week and make one thousand dollars. Finally, I was back to work.

CHAPTER 9

Searching for Siberia

Your journey is not the same as mine, and my journey is not yours. But if you meet me on a certain path, may we encourage each other.
—Author Unknown.

My first day of work as a speech therapist in Alaska had transpired as a one-day contract job in the gold-rush town of Nome. Now the same agency had hired me for a week to evaluate children of all ages in the oldest culture in the United States. I'd pack and dress differently this time. The wool gaberdine suit I wore on that first trip just didn't cut it.

This job raised the stakes. I planned for a journey into an ancient culture, filled with personal meaning for me to serve the people who had learned how to survive for over ten thousand years in a polar climate. How intelligent and strong they must be. I would come prepared this time. It would be a trip to remember for the rest of my life. My heart cried out for documentation, for a photo. I packed my camera. I wanted to capture this moment of self-discovery.

Since there were no hotels or restaurants in villages, I fretted about eating and sleeping. On this trip, I carried my food and a sleeping bag. I could buy school lunch for four dollars and sleep on the gym floor for fifteen dollars a night. I had use of the kitchen to cook my canned food.

When I learned on my trip to Nome that a wool gabardine suit might look polished and professional but floundered in an Alaskan winter, I developed a warm, village-traveling outfit. First, I slipped on my silk long johns, both top and bottom. Dang, those things were tight, but that is what I needed to keep out the cold air. Then I added a flannel shirt and a pullover wool sweater, along with a pair of corduroy pants. Over that, I slipped on a pair of insulated bib overalls made for skiing, what I called Farmer Johns. Thick wool socks and Sorel boots with felt inserts made in

Canada, rated to fifty below, tried to keep my feet warm.

Next, I surrounded myself with my warmest, royal blue, down coat with a big hood, rated to 40 below zero. I kept a red wool face mask handy, in the pocket, just in case I needed it. I adjusted a stocking cap on my head so that my ears were covered.

Finally, a pair of lamb's wool–lined leather gloves, covered by a pair of mittens, kept my hands warm. I looked in the mirror. Wow. Picture a big blue Michelin man. I could hardly walk. It was a far cry from what I wore in Los Angeles. None of that mattered. I felt warm and ready for the coldest cold.

My cold weather flying outfit, 1977. Photo: Unknown.

This was my first trip to an Alaskan native village, and I imagined how everything would be and look. Excited and honored, I journeyed to the only two villages on St. Lawrence Island—Savoonga and Gambell. During the Alaska Native Claims Settlement Act of 1971, the people in these villages claimed the island as their own. The island itself is only twenty-two miles wide and ninety miles long, resting in the Bering Sea, as close to Russia as to the Alaskan mainland. It is thought to be part of the land bridge that once existed between Asia and North America, where prehistorical Asians are believed to have migrated, evolving into the Native Americans who settled here. I agreed to enter this ancient, yet modern world.

Once again, I flew to Nome on an Alaska Airlines jet, where I switched to Mung Airlines. After I transferred my baggage to this noisy, two-propeller engine bush plane, I realized that I was the only passenger. Our departure had been delayed by lightly falling snow. As we eventually vibrated into the sky, I reached into my shoulder bag, dug out my earplugs, and stuffed them in my ears. I stared out the window, enjoying this first and unforgettable flight to St. Lawrence Island.

As we crossed over miles of ocean, I saw the sea ice breaking up. Gigantic and paltry clumps of ice, outlined in inky-black water, were everywhere. As we approached the island, I gazed at even more open water—the Bering Sea—the blackest and most terrifying water I ever saw. When I reached the isolated and mostly unoccupied St. Lawrence Island to screen their schoolchildren in 1977, my curiosity was piqued, for these were the most remote villages I ever visited.

Located less than forty miles from Russia, many indigenous Alaskans who lived there had relatives in the old Soviet Union. They routinely took their boats back and forth to visit their Russian relations. FBI director J. Edgar Hoover, however, decided to stop that practice in 1948, making it almost impossible for them to keep the family ties.

But where there is a will, there is always a way.

The International Date Line runs along the Bering Sea, halfway between Russia and St. Lawrence Island. The courageous natives on both sides, Siberian Yupik and Alaskan Yupik, motored out in their boats and met in the middle. They weren't allowed to enter each other's territorial waters. Because they spoke the same original language, they still understood each other.

As the elders died, the window started to close between families: another blow to indigenous Alaskans. But with the advent of video chat computer programs in the new millennium, some relatives have connected again. That is a blessing.

Northern Yupiks live on St. Lawrence Island. Unlike the southern Yup'iks, they don't use the apostrophe. Their traditions include passing *qunruyun*, or wisdom, from one generation to the next. The first and foremost *qunruyun*/wisdom passed from parents to children was *compassion* for others, something one feels. It might entail helping, protecting, sharing, or assisting others. When a person did something compassionate and filled with kindness, it would come back to him or her.

Never boasting or acting superior denoted *humility*. Because of humility, one might wear old clothes when visiting others in another village to avoid embarrassing them. One wouldn't tell others what to do if they weren't relations. Humility prevented one from flaunting their wealth or exhibiting their finery in public places. One spoke with shy humility so as not to disturb another's mind.

Gratitude is expressed daily with the word *Quyana*, which means "thank you." This gratitude is focused on the sentient universe as well as people. Expressing gratitude toward someone brings good fortune back to the expressor. As an example, this story was told: After a man shared a whole box of .30-.30 shells with a poor man from another village, he found his traps full of mink and muskrat on the way home. Because the poor man felt grateful, the sentient universe repaid the compassionate man with game.

If one acted with compassion, humility, and gratitude, they could attain *peacefulness*. Children were instructed on its high value. The ideal couple lived in peace. If one followed instruction, went about his work, and didn't provoke people, then he met the goal of being in relationships with humans—living in peace. Gossip and anger destroyed the peace. Acting as one family, cooperating and speaking with care, maintained peacefulness. On my first trip to a village, I would see for myself how the people of St. Lawrence Island lived these noble values.

**Mung Airline plane landing on the muddy, deserted airstrip in Savoonga to take me to Gambell,
May 1977. Photo: Kit Roberts**

As we circled Savoonga before landing, it seemed small, insignificant, and isolated. About four hundred people lived in the village of six square miles, located at sea level. Other than the snow and wind, not much existed there: houses, a school, oil drums, Quonset huts, shacks, sheds, dog houses, boats, motors, Ski-Doos, and parts. No roads into it, no police to protect it, just frozen ground undertaken by the Yupik People in this godforsaken place.

When we touched down on the deserted strip of gravel covered with mud and snow, I realized there weren't any buildings in sight. School had finished for the day, so I wouldn't be working with children until the morning. I had plenty of time to get settled, which was a relief.

The pilot helped me unload my bags, walked around the trusty plane, and checked its vitals. He said goodbye and took off down the half-frozen, half-muddy strip, lifted off with a flurry of blowing snow, and disappeared into the distance, leaving me at this outpost on the edge of the world, open only to a matchless few, closed off to the rest of humanity, including the military.

I caught sight of a wind shelter, where I waited for my "taxi-man" to come and get me. The "shelter" consisted of eight boards nailed together in a row, with a little roof sticking off the top, like an upside-down L. There were no sides or seats. This ramshackle lean-to, meant to protect me from the wind as I waited, missed the mark. Nothing blocked the stinging cold of the Bering Sea's arctic wind.

I watched for a truck. I planned to hurl myself into that warm cab. None of this lady-like, derrière first, knees together, swing your legs in stuff. Grains of dusty snow blew across the land in sweeping gusts as I kept my head down.

I had no means to contact anyone in the village to let them know I had arrived. And now that I had landed, I couldn't spot any structures. The grey-white sky stretched as far as the grey-white ground. While I plastered my back to the windscreen, I hoped that someone had relayed the vital message that I needed to be collected. As I tightened my hood, stamped my feet, shoved my gloved and mittened hands deep into my pockets, and squeezed my arms into my torso, I woke up, more awake than I had ever been in my life.

After several minutes, which seemed a heck of a long time, I caught sight of a man in the distance driving placidly toward me on a snowmobile, towing a homemade wooden sled. I prayed he was coming to collect me. My face was so frozen now that, even with the face mask on, my eyelashes had frost on them, and I could barely speak.

As I watched him coming closer, I realized that this was the first Alaskan native man I had seen in a real Alaskan native village. Sitting with his back straight, he calmly and slowly drove the snowmobile toward me. He wasn't in a hurry, he wasn't anxious, he wasn't cold. Just by watching him, my own body relaxed, as if a reflection of him had merged into me. I expected him to be wearing a fur coat and traditional native clothing. Instead, he dressed in traditional American clothing, down to his mirrored aviators, which protected his eyes from sunburn off the snow. Clean-shaven, with a toss of his head, he indicated I should stash my gear in the yellow sled with a red stripe that he pulled with a rope.

Taxi-man, Savoonga, end of May 1977. Photo: Kit Roberts

I quickly loaded my four bags and sat behind him. He drove serenely on the cold ride back to the village as I clung to him for warmth. I could never have imagined this when I was commuting on the Seattle freeways to get to school.

As we rode into Savoonga, the village appeared in the whitewashed distance. My imaginings of what it would look like soon gave way to reality. Many small houses, some of them made from plywood, were sprinkled here and there. I shuddered at the thought. *In this weather? How does a family stay warm in a plywood house?*

Laundry hung in one yard. Plaid shirts and pants appeared hard as boards. The cold and dry air must have completely evaporated the moisture out of the clothes. The garments had to be rigid when they were taken off the line, probably softening as they warmed. Again, everything was different in Alaska.

Clothes drying on the line, Savoonga, late May 1977. Photo: Kit Roberts

My driver came to a smooth stop at the school and helped me take my bags inside. I thanked him for the ride and for bringing in my bags. He raised his eyebrows and smiled, no need to talk. Gathering my shoulder bag and audiometer, I walked through the double doors at the arctic entry, an anteroom to reduce heat loss. After pushing through the second set of doors, I found the school secretary. She led me to the principal's office. I introduced myself, and Eric asked me how my flight went.

"It was amazing," I told him, eager to share my experience venturing into this frozen world. "The Bering Sea is in break-up. I've never seen ice floes like that before. I couldn't stop staring at them." Even more eager to get to work, I asked, "Is there a good spot to put my gear that's out of your way?"

"You can put your things in the back of my office. Let me give you the schedule," he said.

"Thanks. Does everybody know I'm coming?" I wondered.

"Yes, but we never really know if someone is coming until they actually arrive. The weather around here can delay both the coming and the going of specialists like you," he offered with a smile.

"This is a very nice school you have here. I'll plan on testing the lower grades in the morning and the higher grades in the afternoon. I'll give you a quick report on my findings before I leave. After I get back to town, I'll write up reports and treatment plans as needed and send them to you. I'll be catching a flight to Gambell after school tomorrow."

"Okay. I'm sorry we don't have a room for you to work in," he said.

"That's alright. I just need a couple of desks. I'll put them in the hall and take the children, one at a time, for testing. Where will I be sleeping tonight?"

"You have a choice. You can have the gym, or you can use my back office. Did you bring a sleeping bag?"

"Yes, and my favorite pillow," I smiled. I always traveled with my childhood pillow, a comfort I couldn't sleep without.

"Feel free to use the kitchen. I'll see you in the morning." With that he left, and I stayed alone in the school.

I'd use his office. It felt cozier than the gym. I took off my parka, hat, gloves, Farmer Johns, and boots. I changed to my inside shoes and arranged my gear in the small conference room behind his regular office. It was warm in there, and the hour was already getting late.

After the principal left, I found the kitchen and cooked my dinner: a can of chili. I cleaned up after myself and went back to the principal's office. Now it was even warmer in there.

I unfurled my sleeping bag and threw my pillow on it. I found the girl's bathroom to wash my face, brush my teeth, and use the toilet before bed. After I shut the door to the principal's office, changed into my pajamas, and crawled into my sleeping bag, I realized it was too hot to sleep. Here I was in the coldest place on earth, overheated. For obvious reasons, I couldn't open a window. I just had to get used to it. I set my alarm early so that I could have everything out of the way before Eric came to work in the morning.

I lay back and let my head sink into my pillow and closed my eyes. I marveled at the reality that I was lying on the floor of the principal's office in Savoonga, Alaska, out on the edge of creation, invited to serve these kids. The stillness and quiet overwhelmed me. It reminded me of my childhood home in Pasco, where all was quiet at night. The noise of Los Angeles remained a distant illusion. Was there ever a quieter place than this? *Tomorrow will be a good day*, I thought. *I'll get to be a speech therapist again. I'll have someone to care for, to help if needed. It feels so good to care*. I lay awake until sleep finally overtook me.

When my alarm went off at six in the morning, I was the only person in the school. I hurriedly dressed and packed anything I wouldn't need that day. Taking my instant apple-cinnamon oatmeal to the kitchen, I looked in the refrigerator, which had an opened box of milk in it, and the freezer, filled with long rolls of meat, wrapped in plastic. After boiling some water in a pan, I cooked the oatmeal and ate it with some of the boxed milk, then cleaned up after myself. Soon after, the students and teachers arrived.

My job included screening grades kindergarten, one, three, five, seven, and nine for any speech problems. And I checked the students' hearing. Additionally, if a teacher had concerns about a student, I evaluated him or her in depth, beyond a simple screening.

When the time felt right, I knocked and quietly entered the first classroom, "Hello everyone," I said, introducing myself to the students. "My name is Mrs. Roberts. I'm a speech teacher and we're going to go in the hall and talk about some pictures, and then I'm going to check your hearing. You get to wear these big headphones"—I held them up—"like the airplane pilots wear. It will be fun. Who gets to go first?"

"Frank, you go first," the teacher said. A boy stood up, and I took him by his hand. We walked to the two desks just outside the room in the hall, butted together front-to-front. I listened as he said certain words and marked his responses on the articulation screening form. As he identified pictures, I noted if they represented things that were in his environment or something he had never seen. Television hadn't yet hit the island, so I wanted to be sure I didn't misjudge a student's cognitive/articulation skills based on cultural objects he or she might not recognize.

After Frank had finished the identifications, I put the large, noise-cancelling headphones on him and screened his hearing. He followed directions well, remained calm, and responded gently. Reaching for my stickers, I peeled off a gold star and put it on the back of his hand. He looked at it with delight, touched it with his fingers, and took a quick sniff.

"You did a very good job, Frank," I said, smiling at him. "Time to go back to class now. Thank you for talking with me." I took him back and called the name of the next person on my list. And so, one by one, I finished grades kindergarten, one, three, and five in time for lunch. Without exception, all the children were calm and respectful.

Smells of lunch permeated the hallways, and aromas of meat cooking and rolls baking filled the air. Although I had built up a great hunger, I held myself back from being first in line. The elders of the village had already arrived and were eating from the standard lunch trays with compartments for the spaghetti with ground beef, canned green beans, canned mandarin oranges, fresh, homemade rolls, a cookie, and a carton of milk. The discovery that lunches were always good in the villages relieved the necessity to bring my own. And I delighted in the fact that the elders were being taken care of as well.

I screened the older children during the afternoon, and by midafternoon, I finished my first school. My plane to Gambell would pick me up at four-thirty in the afternoon. I packed my bags, dressed for another snowmobile ride, and before I could slip on some ice, I returned to the airstrip, another successful day behind me.

The noisy flight to Gambell, at the most northwest end of the island, didn't take long. It, too, looked small and isolated. Its population mirrored Savoonga, around four hundred people. In Gambell, I found it possible to lodge with the resident teachers for twenty-five dollars a night. Their home, supplied by the school district, functioned as a local Bed & Breakfast. It was clean and warm, and I appreciated staying with them. The couple, a principal and a teacher, were happy to have an itinerant worker as a lodger and someone new to talk with.

By morning, my enthusiasm to work had increased, for I would be seeing another group of children for the first time. Just as in Los Angeles, where I went to a different school every day of the week, the work was always fresh. Driving on the freeway, however, leaving the house daily by 5:45 in the morning to beat rush hour, quickly got old. But I had another problem in Gambell, and it wasn't a paved highway.

Deep gravel formed the base of Gambell. The residents, young and old, transported themselves by snowmobiles, four-wheelers, or their own two legs. I used the latter. As I lugged my heavy bags of materials to school across the gravel, my feet caught in the chunks of rock. I worked hard to get my boots out, up, and down again, over and over, until I reached the school, about ten minutes away on foot. By the time I arrived there, I had worked up a sweat and breathed a sigh of relief for some plain old floor.

Once again, I found the school to be overly warm. I arranged a couple of desks in the hall and organized my evaluation items. I finished screening the lower grades in time for lunch. After eating another delicious meal, I trudged through the same snow-packed gravel to the teacher's quarters in the old school building. I needed to take off my long johns for the afternoon. It was too hot in the school to wear them.

The old building stood close to the shoreline of the island. The porch steps were completely covered with drifted snow. I didn't even realize they were there. The snow had piled so high that it covered the large windows that were built all around the rectangular, wooden building, painted a dull tan. As I reached the porch, the man of the house—the principal—stopped me on the doorstep and pointed behind me.

"Do you know what that is over there?" he asked,

Curious, I turned and glanced toward the ocean. Beyond the end of the island, I saw a patch of water as black as tar—the Bering Sea. After that, I saw more land covered with snow. "No, I don't know what it is," I said, vaguely curious.

"That's Siberia," he said. "It's sixteen miles away."

What? Siberia. The most desolate place on earth as I had learned it, growing up during the Cold War. Being "sent to Siberia" was a punishment beyond reckoning. And here it survived. Alaska looked just like Siberia! Now I recognized what people meant when Russians sent a political prisoner to Siberia. Here in this village, we had warm dwellings and good food. But on the other side, I imagined it wasn't as nice.

How far I had come from the bustling cities of Los Angeles and Seattle. It hadn't hit me so hard until I found myself gazing at Siberia. I felt bewildered, in the middle of nowhere. The Yupiks had lived on this island for two thousand years. How had they done it? I was stunned. Until my travels to the bush commenced, I didn't realize that a developing country existed in America. But it did, in Alaska. Some of the conditions that Alaska natives lived with angered me, but I didn't have any solutions to fix the problems that other people, who were much more knowledgeable than I, were already trying to implement.

Looking out from the teacher's quarters in Gambell, I could see the shore of St. Lawrence Island, the blackness of the water of the Bering Sea, and the land on the other side. Only sixteen miles away, it was Siberia. May 1977. Photo: Kit Roberts

"Wow. Are you kidding? It looks just like here," I exclaimed.

In reply, he asked, "Would you have sex with me?"

"No," I said, our momentary camaraderie having come to an end, my frozen voice instinctively rising to full expression.

Entrance to the teacher's quarters in Gambell, where I got my first proposition in the bush. It was from this porch where the school principal pointed out Siberia behind me, May 1977. Photo: Kit Roberts

I finished my screenings by the end of the day, but I had a couple of children who needed full evaluations. I stayed over another night and finished their testing before lunch. After eating lunch, I waited in the teacher's room for the chartered plane to land. There were several photos of an igloo pinned to a bulletin board. Every winter, the men of the village taught the schoolchildren how to make this traditional dwelling. They told me how they cut chunks of ice from a nearby lake, shaped them, and packed them with snow. What an amazing skill to create a perfect dome of ice in which to live temporarily. My visit to nearly-Siberia drew to a close, and in those few days I felt I had learned so much.

Igloo with a Coleman lantern inside, Gambell, Alaska, February 1977. Photo: A local man.

I had met so many friendly people on St. Lawrence Island. Isolated from the mainland, the ravages of urban life hadn't influenced them as much. At that time, they had only one communal phone available, television didn't exist, and there were no medical personnel of any kind. No doctors, dentists, or nurse practitioners. Successive installments of a two-channel television—one channel instructional, and the other one with news and programming selected by a native committee—began in the rural villages in the late '70s and early '80s. How soon your village obtained television depended on where it was on the list. It took many more years to get satellite television to the villages, not to mention the cities in Alaska.

Though my stay had been brief, I never heard a raised voice or spotted children fighting. In Savoonga, the people were joyful and strong, even though they, too, lived an isolated way of life. I felt honored to serve these First Peoples, who had great hearts and loved their children.

I had felt the compassion, gratitude, humility, and peacefulness embodied by the people on St. Lawrence Island.

These qualities of humanness were in the air. They had an electricity to them, a wavelength of delight that traveled beyond the body, and they felt good. What if all parents actively taught these feelings and made them important in their communities? Imagine how great our world would be, how civilized. I felt my bubble thawing just a little more.

CHAPTER 10

The Great One

I hope that in the bill you will call it 'Mt Denali National Park' so that the true old Indian name of Mount McKinley (meaning the Great One) will thus be preserved.
—Charles Sheldon, 1916

It had been an eventful May. I had worked in Nome, Savoonga, and Gambell. I had felt the serenity, stability, and exceptional ancient goodness of native Alaskans. I also felt the isolation, the blank landscape, and my own concerns for what they didn't have—especially medical and dental services. About their subsistence lifestyle, which they had honed over centuries, I was proud—proud of the ingenuity of humans.

Although I had only worked a short time in Alaska, I had been welcomed as a person of knowledge with skills that others needed. The people treated me with respect, and I felt safe at all times. The adaptive behaviors I had developed as a child—deferring to males, trying to make everyone happy, and keeping quiet—weren't on display. I worked in harmony with people and felt a comfort with complete strangers that I didn't feel with my own husband.

Communication with Bill was more about his power over me, following his ideas, and maintaining the superior-inferior role that he had adapted to as a child. Unknowingly, I kept my bubble strong around him and deferred to him so I wouldn't be hurt. As adults, we hadn't learned any other way to be and were now maladaptive in our communication. But there wasn't anything obviously wrong. We were like most couples.

Being in a professional environment allowed me to adapt to a more grown-up way to communicate, where people were equal and the same as each other, neither person playing the inferior role while the other played the superior. I felt relaxed, flexible, and open instead of frozen. I appreciated that.

At the end of summer I checked in with the local school district, and the only speech pathologist job they had was still filled. Then Bill came home one day and said, "The FAA is sending me to a school in Anchorage this fall. I'll be gone for seven weeks. Maybe you can come down for a visit."

Heck yeah, I'd be down for a visit. I wanted to see Anchorage and all it had to offer. I had learned that I was more of a city girl than I'd thought. I still didn't have a full-time job. The contracts I had with the agency in Anchorage hadn't turned into full-time work.

A few weeks later, the feeling that something holy and momentous was about to happen filled my heart as I planned the 350-mile trip from Fairbanks to Anchorage on the Parks Highway. Although I thought it would be exhausting, with its fifty miles of gravel road, I was eager to see Denali. At 20,310 feet, the highest mountain in North America, it had already been given a superlative name by the indigenous Alaskans before white men had named it Mount McKinley after our twenty-fifth president. I longed to see Denali—"The Great One."

I had drooled over pictures of it in the *Rand McNally Guide: Alaska*—pictures about one by three inches, which couldn't do it justice. If Washington's Mount Rainier was the Prince of Mountains, then Denali was the King. He sat in regal repose with his consort, the Queen, Sultana ("The Woman"), beside him. The creator made them to be together, side by side, not alone in the world of ice and snow. All who saw the King bowed before him because of his longevity, his strength, and his presence.

His handsome peak was substantial, and when his ridges receded into foothills, the peak vanished behind them. Even the foothills were towering mountains, which, when near Denali, obscured his snow-covered crest. Unlike Denali, their snow melted. The foothills diminished into a grubby mud brown—no beauty, just jagged, lone dirt and rocks.

Not Denali proper—oh, no. His towering, glacier-clad, dreadful, commanding peak was unmatched in its intangible sacredness, snow never melting, men and women dying to climb it, some never to be found again, like a young firefighter I knew personally. He was only thirty years old and lived in a beautiful home with his young wife. It was spring break, and even though a severe storm had been predicted, he and his climbing buddy had planned this weeklong trek for months. They weren't going to miss it.

By Friday, the worst of the storm hit, and it was estimated that the two of them were caught in an avalanche and fell over a thousand-foot drop. Their bodies were buried forever. His mother flew up from the Lower 48—the contiguous United States—for a celebration of life in his home. I started to tear up as I told her what a wonderful man he was in every way, and how much he would be missed. I didn't expect to cry, but it was so tragic.

Multiple times on my trip I pulled to the side of the highway to get out of the car and look at Denali in his snowy robes and crown of eternal, glacial ice. I was grateful he was "out." Since he created his own weather system and frequently shrouded himself in mist and clouds, he was visible only fourteen days a year during the summer. Luckily for me, this was one of them.

I showed up that evening at the door of Bill's trailer, provided by the FAA. The cats and I moved in, tired but wired. We had some dinner together, and I tried to tell Bill about my wonderful drive and seeing Denali and Sultana so clearly against a crisp blue sky. Some people are more impressed by mountains than others.

After some private time with Bill, exhausted, I fell asleep thinking of Denali. I had been in its presence, its solidarity, its might. Driving the highway alone with the cats, it felt as if some of that majesty had seeped into me. We had received the grace of the Great One on our trip from Fairbanks to Anchorage. Another adventure in Alaska, and I'd only been there several months. I had no idea of how many more adventures were ahead of me—nor of how those months would turn not into years, but into decades.

CHAPTER 11

Hoping for a Call

I had a speech impediment as a child. . . . I had a problem with saying all the /r/ sounds.
—Amanda Gorman, Youth Poet Laureate and Inaugural Poet 2020

In November, the phone rang. "Hello, may I speak with Kit Roberts please?"

"Yes, that's me," I answered.

"I'm calling from the Fairbanks school district. Our speech-language pathologist has given us notice that she'll be leaving after the Christmas break. Are you still available for work?"

"Yes, I am." I held my breath, ready to burst with joy.

"Could you come to the district office for an interview and to complete the paperwork?"

"Absolutely." The only SLP job in town would be mine in January. Finally, I would be a full-time SLP again. It felt good to walk into the school building on Monday morning, January 1978. I could work here indefinitely. Good things come to those who wait.

It's cold—no, freezing—and dark in January in Fairbanks. Bears are hibernating, and humans don't want to go outside much either. We tire early and are compelled to go to bed by eight in the evening. Without a job, it is isolating, humdrum, and expectant. But this winter I would have a job, a place to focus my energy, to use my education, and to be with people.

I cheerfully dug out all of my speech therapy materials, including the cards I had made for Genie. Most of them addressed articulation. Articulation is how we put sounds into words. With words, we express our concrete and abstract ideas, feelings, and imaginings. When we speak to other people, our ideas are fleshed out, and we discover amazing things we didn't know were in us.

An articulation problem, like not being able to make

the /r/ sound, may seem trivial to some, but for the person who can't articulate, it can be frustrating, embarrassing, and demoralizing. Most problems are easily correctable with stimulation. If they aren't, we work to make it the best we can and encourage the person to be proud of themselves no matter what.

I loaded my car with all my speech therapy tools and let it warm up for ten minutes. Starting my drive to work, I noticed the temperature—sixty degrees below zero. I moved slowly through the cold, ice-fogged roads, more excited to be back to work than concerned about the cold. After the thirty-minute drive to Eielson Airforce Base, I checked in at the gate and proceeded to the elementary school, where I was escorted to a nice room set aside for me. There were only fifty-four children on the caseload. Now that seemed much more civilized than the mandatory ninety students I had to have on my caseloads in Los Angeles and Seattle.

I looked through the files and materials left behind. It's a good thing I had the experience that I did. The materials were paltry, but I had my own. I found out that I had a budget of only 150 dollars a year. No wonder they didn't have anything. A couple of tests could eat that up right away. Additionally, there were no therapy notes. I had been taught to chart everything I did as I went along. My clinical notes were thorough, if you could read my handwriting.

My previous school district experiences had given me the knowledge and background to pick up the caseload in Fairbanks and carry on with business as usual. What I hadn't experienced before, however, was recess duty. In Fairbanks, I was hired as full-time faculty, not itinerant. The faculty and staff supervised recess, something I didn't have to do as an itinerant. Now, I couldn't get out of it. Recess cut off at twenty degrees below zero. So, at nineteen degrees below, out we shuffled to supervise the kids. Brrr!

When I answered the call to work at a school, I couldn't help but compare it to the adventurous traveling I had done.

This position had the distinction of being the fourth school district I worked for full-time. It had a decent caseload and a nice staff. It felt familiar. But I left home in the dark and left school in the dark. It was too cold to do anything outside. The effort it took to maintain my enthusiasm surprised me. I could lie in bed, under the warm covers, until March, when we finally had twelve hours of daylight instead of six. On the other hand, I had a job to do, even if it meant driving thirty minutes in the freezing dark over to Eielson Airforce Base and back again each brutally cold, dark day. Mother Nature had invented hibernation, and now I understood why.

CHAPTER 12

A Room with a View

Between individuals, as between nations, peace means respect for the rights of others.
—Benito Juarez

"The FAA is transferring me to Anchorage," said Bill. "We will be moving in three weeks."

"So does that mean we are staying in Alaska?" I asked. "We only have six months left on our obligation."

"Let's see how it goes," he said. "We can decide after we have lived in Anchorage for a while."

Here we go again. And I had the school position in Fairbanks. Luckily it was summer, but we had planned to live in Fairbanks for two years, then decide if we wanted to move back to Vashon Island. Now this. It was an opportunity and a curse.

We had both been through Anchorage, and we liked what we saw. We considered this opportunity to leave the extreme cold, the tiny fir trees, and the limitations of Fairbanks behind. That part I liked. But leaving SLP again, not so much. That's what I was born to do.

I had to admit that the isolation of Fairbanks made my job, well, isolating. I never got to talk to another SLP as I had in Seattle or Los Angeles. A "speech department" didn't exist. The budget was abysmal. Clearly, every other therapist had to make her own materials and took them with her when she left. Even if a job didn't work out right away, at least I would be in Anchorage. There were clinics, agencies, hospitals, and schools there that could be potential employers for me.

Anchorage had beautiful, 360-degree scenery all around. Enthralled at the immensity of Denali to the north, I couldn't wait to gaze at it, uninterrupted. To the east were the vast, heaven-reaching Chugach Mountains. When the setting sun was just right, the alpine glow on their slopes kindled a bewitching pink and purple light, worth as much time to admire as possible.

The Cook Inlet lay to the west. As a part of the ocean, it emptied out every day to reveal a bed of mud, so much like quicksand that both humans and animals had become stuck and drowned in it. Because of that inlet, air temperatures in Anchorage rarely dipped below zero degrees Fahrenheit. *Yes!*

When school started in the fall, I made an appointment with the director of the Anchorage speech department, a real department with other speech therapists. There weren't any jobs at the time. Once again, my application would be stored in the file drawer.

In the cool of October in that peaceful year of 1978, our house in Fairbanks sold, and we started looking for another house to buy in Anchorage. A realtor showed us a couple of homes with terrible floor plans and lacking the three things we wanted: a fireplace, a garage, and a view. But then one day, after leaving a main, paved road south, up to the Hillside, and turning onto a mud and rock road for a few miles, he showed us a house abandoned on an isolated slope.

The sun revealed every treeless inch on a dome of dirt, at the 1,100-foot level on the Hillside, holding a forlorn house. I couldn't imagine living there. But when we went inside—oh, on the inside, with the fragrant cedar tongue-and-groove walls, the chocolate brown carpet and kitchen cabinets, and the floor to ceiling rock fireplace—all was warm and wonderful. It wasn't a forlorn house, after all; it was our dream home.

Outside, the sun still touched every clod and rock of the muddy mess on the ground, and it radiated through the triangle windows at the peak of the open beam ceiling, streaming into the living room, dining room, and kitchen. Light, wonderful light in a land so dark, filled the space like air in a balloon. Standing there on the quiet, dark carpet, looking through windows that began at my knees and climbed to fifteen feet high, I thought, *This light will warm my soul and lift my spirits every day*. Certain this was the place, I turned to Bill and said, "I want this house."

He liked it too, with the double car garage, the fireplace,

and the view. It wasn't on city water and didn't have a sewer. Instead, we had a 150 foot deep well with good water and a septic tank/leach field. Trash pick-up wasn't available either. It was our responsibility to get the trash to the dump in town. But it did have a trash compactor in the kitchen, a new invention I had never seen before. That would reduce the number of trash trips we had to make.

Even though it was extremely expensive for us, we were ready to sacrifice everything for this home. My spirits lifted with the knowledge that I now had the chance to get out of the basement floor we had been renting for three months after moving to Anchorage—a basement with window slits for light, too high for me to see through, with the sound of the upstairs family walking around from morning until night on the noisy linoleum floor.

We made an offer on the house, it was accepted, and we moved in November. The snow had already fallen and stuck, but not the inhuman, painful ice of Fairbanks.

Once frozen, the snow never melted until May at our place. It packed down as hard as cement, but it was easier to drive on than I imagined. As I drove at night during snowfalls, a magical scene took place. The flakes of snow shimmered like crystals in the headlights, turning to sparkling diamonds as they touched the ground. My world in Anchorage transformed into an enchanted, bewitched fairyland, as if any number of amazing things could happen at any moment. I wanted to be the only driver on the road so I could take my time and enjoy the wonderment.

Our home in Anchorage, November 1978. Photo: Kit Roberts

Alone in my living room, facing the picture window, I looked across the bay and scanned the Aleutian Range for volcanos—Mount Redoubt at ten thousand feet and Mount Spurr at eleven thousand feet. Cold weather magnified them, and they appeared to be right in front of me, as if I could walk out the door and touch them. I marveled at the phenomenon, my good fortune to see them, and the feeling of greatness that swelled within me.

At the same time, I faced the great American dream—the dream to have my own business and be my own boss. I had never before thought about going into business; I was accustomed to looking for a job, not creating one. But women were becoming entrepreneurs and starting their own businesses. Why couldn't I step out on my own? I had plenty of experience. Since there weren't any jobs available, at least I could give it a try.

Naturally, starting my own business would mean a lot of pressure and a lot of work. But there were numerous people with communication disorders who were not being served—in short, everyone but the kids in school. I could help them. But I soon learned that I had to rely on a professional network to be successful.

The people I had met and worked alongside in Alaska,

all manner of working people, worked without complaint. If the weather was bad, we didn't grumble, we prepared. If the temperatures dropped, we didn't cry, we put on warmer clothing. Alaskans did things, for there was much to do. We worked hard and we played hard. First work, then play.

The Yup'ik elders knew that the world and everything in it is sentient: humans, animals, plants, and seas. All beings have their own way of living, eating, and dying. *Ellan Yua*—awareness, world, universe, sense—is the unseen force that watches over everything. The ancestors took good care of their surroundings because they understood that everything is *ella*, conscious and perceptive.

Perhaps something was watching over me, I considered—something constant, like the mountains giving me strength, the volcanos giving me fire, the ranges stretching me to new situations greater than my individual self. As I looked through my living room window, I remembered looking through the window at Crippled Children's Services. My first conscious awareness of someone with a communication disorder being helped now became a beacon for me to emulate.

I had a decision to make. Like an avalanche that crossed the highway, I could wait for others to come along and clear my path, or I could find another way around. How long do I wait for other people to hire me? How long do I wait to fulfill my calling? How long do I wait to contribute to the family expenses? An idea started to take form, to bubble up inside me. Frozen, like the snow, scared to even think about it, I let it hibernate for a couple of months as I checked out Anchorage and its opportunities. Were my imaginings feasible, or would they be like planting palm trees in our empty yard and expecting them to grow? Would Bill support me in this endeavor or slap it down like an irritating mosquito? There was only one way to find out.

CHAPTER 13

The Folly of Guns

If all my possessions were taken from me with one exception, I would choose to keep the power of communication, for by it I would soon regain all the rest.
—Daniel Webster

We now lived in the thriving city of Anchorage in an incomparable setting. We loved our cedar home with the stunning views. We led adventurous lives, so different from the tranquility of Vashon Island. We both wanted to stay in Alaska. Opportunity was everywhere and for everyone. We made our final decision: we were not going back to the Lower 48, even if the move would be paid for.

I should have suspected that whatever force drove me to become an SLP would assist me in my new venture into private practice. I quietly stepped into the belly of the whale, ready to dive deeper into my intention. I contemplated the steps ahead of me and decided which ones to take.

Then, as if by coincidence, a step came before me in the form of Holly, the nurse from Vashon and Fairbanks who had moved to Anchorage with her husband Darrel, shortly after we did. I told her about my intention to open a private practice. She recommended that I talk with Deanna. Deanna directed a facility that provided skilled nursing, short- and long-term care, and rehabilitation services. It had a good reputation.

I met with Deanna, an RN, BS, and Licensed Nursing Home Administrator in her office at the facility. She sat behind her desk in the middle of the room, facing the door. I walked in and saw a woman about my age, with shoulder length brown hair, dressed in a navy-blue suit. I had a letter of introduction and credentials with me, referencing Holly, who had taken a job at the facility. The three of us were about the same age. It seemed that most of the people in Anchorage were in their late twenties and early thirties. She was very kind and spoke with a gentle, but professional voice. She placed her faith in me. I signed a contract to work up to fifteen hours a week. That gave me some steady income but kept my time freed up to launch my business. It also confirmed my decision to open a private practice.

Holly and Deanna quickly became my allies. By supporting me, by hiring me to work with their patients on the rehabilitation floor, they facilitated the restoration of my calling. These two intelligent and capable women positioned me back on my path.

The work at the facility was interesting and flexible. It allowed me to earn enough money to travel Outside (as Alaskans referred to the rest of the country) for specialized training. It gave me the opportunity to continue to travel to the bush. With that additional income, I was able to open a private office only a few miles from the facility. However, I needed to re-create myself from an SLP with a degree and public-school experience to an SLP in private practice—two vastly different therapists.

To be a part of speech-language pathology in the 1970s and '80s, to learn the incredible information that was coming from the field, from researchers, from inventors—not to mention our sister profession, audiology—was marvelous. Programs for people with fluency, voice, laryngectomy, and swallowing disorders, known as dysphagia—a completely original branch of SLP that didn't exist when I was in college—were highly instructive. I was a generalist; I had to know it all.

I didn't want to be caught off guard. When patients arrived at my door, I wanted to be what they expected: an SLP who knew what she was doing. I sought out training to help me improve. Outside, in the Lower 48, there were all kinds of seminars and specific workshops being offered. But in Alaska, most classes pertained only to children, and they were usually presented for one to two hours at an annual conference. Needing to address adult communication disorders, I started with weeklong immersion training for people with aphasia, laryngectomy, and neurological disorders such as head injury and autism.

Something told me the patients would be coming.

Speech-language pathology is both a science and an art. The art involves how to apply the science to each individual. The art cares for the client as a person more than anything else. It observes each tiny response: a facial expression, a tone of voice, a defeated breath, an elated smile.

Simply applying research is not enough. Knowing how to speak to *this client*, pace their therapy, take her or him to the finish line, even if it is not the end of the line I wanted them to reach, is essential. In therapy, art is not more important than science; it is equal to science.

Private practice wasn't a *thing* when I graduated in 1974. Schools, hospitals, and clinics were the main employers. I never heard a lecture on how to start and manage a private practice. I couldn't find any books written about it. I figured it out by doing it.

I met with the first SLP in private practice in Anchorage a few weeks before she closed and moved south. As I prepared to open my office, she refused to tell me anything about anything. She wished me well on my way out the door and didn't give me any encouragement. She didn't offer any information or give me any tips. I was surprised by this.

I never understood people who wouldn't share information. There was so much work to do. So many people needed our services, and there were so few SLPs to provide those services. With over seven percent of America's population exhibiting speech/language/hearing problems and 175,000 people in Anchorage, that meant there were over 13,000 clients right there in town who needed our skills. SLP positions always went unfilled.

Whenever SLPs in school districts got together, we traded information back and forth. We talked about all kinds of cases, materials, and new methods we found useful. We supported each other, like the people of Alaska in snowy weather. Allowing others to flounder, without offering assistance, was anathema.

Assistance was always offered. And anyway, at the very least, shouldn't women help other women? What was that all about? Sure, I felt snubbed, but preparing me for private practice was not her job. I got over it. As usual, I would figure it out for myself. I had learned to be resilient back on the farm, and I found it to be useful still.

Then I spoke with an audiologist in private practice before she packed up and left town. (Was everybody leaving?) She gave me one of her simple billing sheets. It had two codes on it—one for evaluation and one for treatment. That was enough to get me started. I'm forever grateful to her for sharing.

My drive to open a private practice, to serve people with communication disorders, empowered me to keep my enthusiasm strong and figure it out. Unprepared but determined, like the gold miners on the Chilkoot Trail, I was the second SLP in the city to open a private office and among the first to provide services all around the state. Like everyone who comes to Alaska, I would be a pioneer.

Visiting the University of Alaska, Anchorage (UAA) library, I read magazines and books on how to open a business. I decided to incorporate as Dynamic Communication, Inc., because as I thought about it, communication was dynamic. It was always changing.

Incorporating gave me some legal supports that being a sole proprietor did not. Did I fully understand it or consult a business attorney? No. I sent fifty dollars to Delaware and became a corporation of one person.

Bill and I had divided our money into his, mine, and ours. We contributed money to a joint account to pay bills, food, and the mortgage. Then, with the money we had left over, we had our own accounts for personal expenses. In my case, that meant my office. I attended a workshop at the Small Business Administration in Anchorage about financing opportunities. I discovered that they would loan me thousands of dollars at eighteen percent interest. I passed. The interest on our home mortgage was bad enough in 1978, at over nine percent. I wasn't a "big business" that needed heavy equipment, a big building, and employees to cover. I was a one-woman band.

Needing a professional place to work, I rented an 800-square-foot office in the "medical ghetto" part of town, to be close to the medical/dental buildings. The front half of my office was open space. The back half was divided into two rooms. One had a door and a large window, which was perfect for parents to observe their child in therapy. The other room had a door, but no windows, and worked as a treatment room for adults. The beige walls and thin brown nubby carpet fit right in with my brown desk, brown folding rectangular conference table, and brown folding chairs. I had a sign made with my name on it and taped it to the door. It wasn't the most attractive office in town, but it was all I could muster with the five hundred dollars of savings I used to open it.

Placing an ad in the *Anchorage Times*, I notified the town that Dynamic Communication, Inc., had opened for speech therapy with children and adults. I sent letters to the pediatricians, physiatrists, and neurologists informing them of my practice. Then, just like it is supposed to happen, people started to call.

The first caller had an office across from mine. Her three-year-old daughter had a head injury at the age of eighteen months when a wooden door, waiting to be hung, fell on her and cracked her skull from ear to ear. She wasn't talking and needed help.

All the materials I had made years before came out of the closet. The comprehensive evaluation and treatment manuals I had saved from Los Angeles were dusted off. I shopped locally for appropriate toys and materials. I purchased a child-size table and two chairs through a catalogue. The price was outrageous, but I had to have it. It reminded me of the fear I had when I first bought food in Fairbanks. Trusting it would all work out in the end, I came to the same conclusion with work-related purchases —if I needed it, I would buy it. When the three-year-old came for her first appointment, I was ready.

Meanwhile, I started to see clients at the nursing facility. One day, a nurse's aide wheeled a nice-looking young man in his late teens into my tiny treatment room for an evaluation and introduced him as David. David slumped in his wheelchair, securely strapped into a sitting position. His head hung down to the left and his slackened jaw nearly touched his chest. A towel draped under his chin absorbed the continuous trickle of saliva from the corner of his mouth. Thank the Lord that I had volunteered at Crippled Children's Services while in college, or I would have been stunned.

Even so, I saw that his problems were devastating. With a smile on my face and a heartfelt "Hello," I introduced myself to David and welcomed him. I met every patient with the assumption that they were worthy of dignity and understood everything I said.

Since David had little to no muscle control, he couldn't swallow, talk, or vocalize. Tragically, he had no facial expression and no gestures, but he did make eye contact. His disability was the result of placing a pistol to his right temple, pulling the trigger, and the bullet exiting his left temple.

The gunshot to his right and left temporal lobes destroyed his verbal and nonverbal communication. The abilities to make and understand sounds, words, and sentences are located in the left temporal lobe. The abilities of facial expression, intonation, and prosody (pitch and intensity of voice) belong to the right temporal lobe. As the bullet traversed his brain, it also ripped through the cranial nerves that controlled his facial, arm, and leg muscles. Effectively, he was a quadriplegic, tube fed, and unable to communicate. I diagnosed him with both a severe-profound communication disorder and a swallowing disorder. I arranged to see him three times a week, but his prognosis was poor.

As he left my office, I asked the aide to make sure David had a head strap from now on. The pain of having his head slumped over like that must have been excruciating, but he had no way to tell anyone and no way to independently lift his eleven-pound head.

I wondered what had caused his attempted suicide, but the topic never came up during patient planning meetings. Why would a teenager feel the need to kill himself? I had met his parents. His mother was as sweet as could be. His father was the quiet type. They seemed to be nice. As far as having a gun in the house, everyone in Alaska had guns. It was normal. Pistols, shotguns, and rifles were common because most people went hunting or fishing, and yes, you have to shoot a large halibut before you pull it on board or it can break your leg. I don't know why we never discussed the reason for David's injuries at our weekly rehabilitation team conference. With no psychologist on the team, emotions were left out of the conversation.

Another important diagnostic item I never saw was his brain scan. Certainly, he'd had one. But he was my first brain injury client, and I didn't know that I had the right to ask to see it. It would have given me valuable information about the status of his physical brain and help me to plan his rehabilitation. It is one thing to read the radiologist's report and another to see the scan with my own eyes. As time went on, I learned to go to the radiology department at the local hospital and look at the actual brain scans of my clients. Eventually, I could predict where the brain damage was going to be, based on my functional evaluation.

I understood that David's inability to communicate left him locked inside himself. He couldn't tell his aide to shift his position, to adjust his catheter, or to wipe his mouth. Like so many of the people lined up in their wheelchairs along the hallways in long-term care facilities, with staff and visitors whizzing by, I wondered what they would say if they could talk. Help me? Move me? Say hello to me? Acknowledge me?

My goals for David were to have him be able to swallow and eat again and, of course, speak. If ignorance is bliss, then those goals I had set were ecstatic. I hadn't worked with a patient with a bilateral gunshot wound before, but I proceeded with all the confidence of a seasoned therapist in this area.

I designed relevant materials directed at adults instead of children, on color-coded pastel paper instead of construction paper. There were exercises to stimulate the jaw, the lips, the tongue, diaphragmatic breathing, vocalization, posture, and relaxation. I used my electric typewriter, mimeographed copies of the handouts, and included them in patient's folders.

To initiate David's treatment, I took the little bit of the reflexive swallow he did have and attempted to shape it into an intentional swallow. This required repeated stimulation of all the oral-motor musculature: the lips, tongue, and jaw. I gave him instructions. "Open your mouth. Close your mouth. Stick your tongue out. Push on this tongue depressor. Keep pushing. Stop. Curl your tongue up. Touch your tongue to the right corner of your mouth—here (I tapped the tongue depressor there for extra stimulation with each command). Touch the left corner. Touch your upper lip, now your lower lip. Stick your lips out, squeeze your lips together, smack your lips, push them on this tongue depressor." These exercises were like asking a little boy to repeatedly lift a 250-pound weight over his head.

I put David through his paces as if he were going to succeed. Curiously enough, his resistance to swallowing made him vocalize, which was his second goal.

Rolling him in front of a large mirror, he saw himself sitting in the wheelchair with his head supported by the strap around his forehead. He saw his blond hair, blue eyes, and pale skin and smiled at himself. Then, I held a small paper cup with a little water in it to his lower lip and lifted it as if I were pouring a sip of water into his mouth that he had to swallow. He resisted this idea, turned his head away, and vocalized "uh" to stop me. He reflexively made a sound. I had found the way to begin vocalization through swallowing therapy.

Week after week, he practiced with me, occupational therapy, and physical therapy. Sometimes, when he was upright in the standing box during physical therapy, I would practice with him. This helped his breath support, which strengthened vocalization.

Finally, after voicing and shaping thousands of "uhs," over a few months, he was using real words. We practiced phrases, sentences, and conversation. His shattered prosody hadn't returned. Like Genie, he couldn't master the timing and intonation. He spoke a few words at a time, phrase by phrase, quickly and softly—but he talked. He could get his point across with words. He could direct his life again.

Proudly, David also learned to chew and swallow again—eventually, he even ate hamburgers. I was thrilled that his brain had been able to regain these skills. I had renewed insight into what was possible for people with traumatic brain injury.

I intuitively developed a program for him that stimulated his brain over and over and involved the emerging science of neuroplasticity. The fact that David reacquired most of his speech and swallowing skills was due to neuroplasticity. Neuroplasticity is the ability of the brain to change, which it does all the time. A Polish neuroscientist, Jerzy Konorski, coined the term in 1948.

At first, neuroplasticity related to childhood. Over time, scientists discovered that the brain's neurons could be altered through stimulation in adulthood as well. In his 2013 manual *Neuroplastic Transformation*, psychiatrist, pain management specialist, and professor Michael Moskowitz, MD, stated three rules of neuroplasticity: 1) What is fired is wired; 2) What you don't use, you lose; 3) When you make them, you break them; when you break them, you make them. With mental, visual, auditory, and motor stimulation, your neurons create additional connections. Therefore, you break the old, impaired connections. When you break your old habits and make new neuronal connections, this strengthens your brain and your cognitive skills. These are the principles that underlie our brain's ability to change with repetitive stimulation.

Seven years to the day that David shot himself, he walked again. He used braces and a walker, but he walked. That was the criteria for being discharged back home, and home he went. He had lived at the facility that whole time and got a great send off from the staff.

While David required assistance when he moved back home with his parents, the skills he recovered, considering the amount of damage to his brain, were remarkable. A rehabilitation team, when allowed the time, can stimulate great changes in a person. They can even overcome the folly of guns.

During this time, in addition to providing therapy, I instinctively expanded into the arena of training. I developed staff and family handouts and started giving talks at orientation meetings for new nurses and employees. This felt like the perfect place for me to begin again. Although I was doing speech therapy, I wasn't in a school. The setting was challenging and interesting, and I was appreciated.

My business was doing well, but it hadn't replaced my full-time school salary yet. Bill didn't like that, but I avoided the subject. I was doing the best I could, thriving on learning and polishing my skills. It took an average of five years for a new business salary to grow large enough to replace a full-time salary job. The money I earned went right back into improving myself and my business. Cognizant of our money issues, I made sure I paid my share of the household bills.

Once Bill discovered he could attain a lucrative position on the North Slope, at Prudhoe Bay, in the oil fields, he left the FAA. As an electronic technician, he calibrated the equipment sent down into the drill pipes. He worked one week on and one week off. During the week he was gone, I lived alone, developed my own routine, and took care of everything. When he came back from the Slope, it took a few days for us to get used to each other again. I'd be restless. I wanted to go out to dinner and do something for entertainment. But he wasn't interested in going anywhere or eating out. He had been eating out for a week, fed gourmet meals by the oil company chefs. Slowly he had gained thirty pounds and wasn't happy about that.

Sometimes, when Bill was in town and could tend to our pets, I took the opportunity to schedule a trip to a village. Some months, we might only see each other one week. We started to joke about how long we had been married but that we had only been together fifty percent of it.

While I continued to work, he had a week off. Although he could have offered to cook for me, I still went to the grocery store after work, came home, and cooked dinner. Unless I had planned to take a week of vacation, Bill was alone. Since all our friends worked full-time jobs, they weren't available either. Our lives were out of balance.

Even though he had made a lot of money, we hadn't spent it on anything yet, like a cabin or a boat. We were like two ships passing in the night. We noticed each other, ate together, watched television, and went to bed. Eventually, he realized that he was a homebody. He quit the Slope and took a job with the local power company. He was much happier with that, and he tried to lose some weight.

CHAPTER 14

Gutted

Don't wait to have your children.
—Kathleen Pendergast, Director of SLP Services, Seattle Public Schools

Within a year, I had more than four clients a day coming to my first office. Since I still worked at the nursing facility and traveled to the villages, I couldn't keep up with referrals. Therefore, I contracted with several SLPs to treat some of my patients. I didn't want to hire employees because business fluctuated so much, and the thought of having to learn about payroll and the complexities that went along with it overwhelmed me.

Bill and I discovered one of the best possible pastimes in Alaska, fishing for salmon in the summer. He had a friend with a boat on the Kenai River, famous for its red salmon runs. Red salmon are unique to Alaska, taste incredible, and freeze well. Bill spent the weekend combat fishing and trucked home dozens of fish packed in ice. Since he had already gutted and cleaned them, he saved me from that messy job. After I vacuum packed them in the newly available Foodsaver, we stored them in another required appliance in Alaska, a stand-up freezer. We dined on salmon all winter, just like Alaskan natives.

As everything rocked along at work, I decided to get a routine checkup with a gynecologist. My last one had been in Los Angeles when I was nineteen years old. That's when I received a diagnosis of endometriosis. I had been dealing with its painful side effects for years. The treatments for it were limited, and none of them worked for me. At the time, the doctor told me to have a baby as soon as possible or I might never have one. I was single, in college, and on food stamps. But he put the fear of God in me that I'd better have a baby soon.

How could I do that? I wanted to finish college before I had a baby. Bill was in the Philippines. Then we started moving—to Vashon Island, to Fairbanks, and to Anchorage. With each move came new challenges that weren't optimal for having a baby. Every couple of years we started over. Now I had opened my own business. How was I supposed to keep that going and have a baby? Our discussions around having a child were nil. Until . . .

Back in Anchorage, a physician's assistant did my pelvic exam and then excused herself for a moment. She came back and introduced me to the doctor who owned the office. He did another pelvic exam then asked me to get a pelvic ultrasound right away. It showed that I had an endometrioma, which is essentially a balloon of blood. In my case, it had grown off my left ovary to the size of a grapefruit.

The doctor explained to me that the endometrioma might burst at any time and cause internal hemorrhaging, which could be fatal. The two of them hadn't seen such a big one before. I had noticed a bulge on the left side of my abdomen, but I just thought I must be fatter on that side. I had also noticed my left leg ached after jogging, but the sensation went away after fifteen minutes. Having lived with this stabbing disorder for eleven years, I had learned how to repress pain. Unless it was something major, I just ignored it.

The ultimate cure for endometriosis—a total hysterectomy—included removal of the uterus and the ovaries. After discussing my history with me, the doctor suggested I have a hysterectomy. He wanted to remove my uterus and ovaries, not just the endometrioma.

At thirty-one years old, not only would I never have children, but I'd be going through menopause. I hadn't read the September 21, 1975, article in the *New York Times*, "Hysterectomy is the second most frequently performed major operation. Should it be so frequent?" If I had, I might have challenged the doctor's recommendation, but I didn't understand the controversy around it and expected the doctor to give me a complete picture of both sides of the situation. After all, he was the man and the expert on everything related to female sex organs.

I talked it over with Bill. I knew he would be a great father. I had seen him play with Holly and Darrell's girls. He threw them around, swung them in circles, and played tag with them. They loved "Uncle Bill." But Bill, concerned for my health, knew all the pain I'd been in for so many years. He assured me that if we couldn't have children, he'd be fine with that, and if we wanted children, we could adopt.

"Well then, will you come with me to my next appointment?" I asked. I wanted his support when we discussed this plan with the doctor. Back then, most doctors were men, and sometimes a male doctor said things differently when he talked with a man. At the end of the appointment, we agreed with the doctor that I should have the endometrioma removed and have a total hysterectomy at the same time. He assured me that hormone replacement would take care of any issues resulting from hormone loss, including osteoporosis and heart disease. The misery would be over, finally. So, with my usual no-nonsense approach to myself, we scheduled surgery for Thanksgiving week. I had my operation on Wednesday, and a friend of mine brought me turkey dinner in the hospital the next day. I felt fine.

On Friday, the doctor came to my hospital room. He held my uterus in a jar in one hand and the pathology report in the other. My uterus and right ovary were completely normal. My left ovary had a hole in it, which was unique and something he hadn't seen before. My heart sank and I thought, *If my right ovary and uterus were perfectly normal and my left ovary was the issue, why didn't you just take the left ovary and leave everything else alone?*

Apparently, a plan is a plan; there is no room for flexibility when new information presents itself. He didn't botch the job. I came through the surgery well. What else could I ask for? He couldn't put my organs, now soaked in formaldehyde, back into my body. But he did put me on hormones. He told me, "Take two weeks off and don't do any heavy lifting." I assured him I wouldn't, and I didn't say a word about how I felt to see my perfectly normal uterus and ovary floating in a jar. My frozen bubble wouldn't let me express that anger and sadness.

Two weeks after my surgery, I flew to the coastal village of Chevak for a couple of days of work. Chevak is 518 miles west of Anchorage as the crow flies, but it's not possible to fly there like a crow. I flew west to Bethel on an Alaska Airlines jet, changed to a small plane, and proceeded northwest almost to the Bering Sea, landing in the village, which had a population of about 450 lovely people.

I have fond memories of Chevak. My time and experience there clearly taught me the difference between a communication *disorder* and a communication *difference*. This concept was just beginning to be defined when I attended college. Speech-language pathologists worked with people with communication disorders. We didn't consider people with communication differences to have a disorder.

Communication disorders stem from impairments to receive, process, or transmit symbol systems. Speech, language, reading, and writing are symbol systems. Words transfer information about things; words are not the things themselves. Words are symbols for things and ideas. Communication disorders manifested as disorders of hearing, language, or speech processes.

Communication differences are not disorders; they are speech and language characteristics common in a population. For example, people on Long Island, New York, have a communication difference compared to people in the Midwest. Their accent and pronunciation were distinctly different for some sounds as well as intonation. A Southern accent varies from a Minnesota accent. SLPs may choose to work with people who want to change their accent or grammar variations, but their communication wouldn't be considered disordered.

Communication differences are common in groups of people who have a native language, then learn a second language. The second language would often be a blend of both languages. Some of the grammar, pronunciation, or prosody of the first language were adopted into the second language. In the case of English as the second language, back in 1970s it was sometimes referred to as "Pidgin English."

Pidgin English still has rules. It isn't that people speak some random version of English. It has sounds that follow rules from one language to the next. If students have difficulty pronouncing a sound in both of their languages, for example, the /r/ sound, we will want to help them. That would indicate a disorder. But if the residents of the whole village spoke that way, it was not in our domain. There were TESL programs for that—Teaching English as a Second Language.

Perhaps there is a third and larger group of people like me, with my communication in a prison of my own making, wanting to experience deep connection yet protecting myself from the fear of rejection by staying silent. Or Bill, craving tenderness but stuck in a strong man, tough guy persona, unable to give me the tenderness I desired but could not ask for.

There are people in advertising who use words to manipulate us into buying things to feel happy, as they, themselves, are in their own bubble of fear, sadness, and anger.

Clever politicians use their primal fear, anger, and sadness to move our society backward or forward, depending on how oblivious they are to their own cruelty, shame, and guilt. With their speech, they separate us instead of unite us by creating negative images that increase our stress and fear, causing us to look for danger, rather than promoting positive outcomes to allow us to engage in a meaningful life.

Aren't we all on a continuum of disorder? I wondered. If we don't recognize our pattern, we become manipulated chumps, not knowing our worth, bereaved, helpless, and hopeless.

As a child, I was taught to be polite, not to contradict my elders, and if I couldn't say something nice, don't say anything at all. But how did that serve me as an adult? I had to learn to do every one of those "taboos" if I was going to self-actualize and reach my full potential—oddly enough, the same goals I had for my clients, to reach their full potential.

These kinds of communication problems were not within the domain of SLPs. Psychologists treated these problems. The only psychologist I met in Anchorage put me off when I called him about doing a joint project together on sexual harassment. I had just returned from Hawaii, and the first thing he said was, "Did you get a good tan in your bikini?"

I couldn't believe my ears. First of all, I didn't wear bikinis, and second, it was none of his business how I looked with a tan. I decided to be brave and use this as a teaching moment for myself and for him, to use my voice.

"That's not a very professional thing to say," I said.

I don't remember what happened after that, but I immediately put all psychologists in his basket. They had the same societal stereotypes as any other group of people. Women were sex objects first, ditzy second, then human beings who deserved respect last. I would have to continue to work on myself by myself, by reading new books on sexism that were just being published in the 1980s.

Communication breakdowns and barriers happened everywhere, at every level. Personal relationships, family relationships, professional relationships, cultural relationships, societal relationships, and political relationships were continuous stressors. Why? Because like me, other people likewise didn't realize that we all lived in our own minds and had repressed our ability to communicate fully as human beings. We had much to learn and implement as a species.

In Chevak I screened children in several grades for speech, language, and hearing. It started with the Photo Articulation Test. I showed the children some pictures and asked them to name the test items. If they didn't recognize the picture, I had them repeat it after me. I tested all the sounds in the English language in the initial, medial, and final positions of words. I noticed that the boys and girls were saying the /s/ sound with a bilateral lisp. In other words, instead of the air coming out through the front of their tongues with a skinny air sound, it came out the sides of their tongues, with a fat air sound. This had to be a communication disorder. However, that diagnosis did not last long.

After testing a whole room of first graders with the same "lisp," I had figured out that I had just documented a communication *difference*. They all spoke that way, including the adults. I naively thought that the indigenous Alaskans would speak Midwestern English as I did. But they spoke a dialect of English, which was not a disorder. Luckily for me, I didn't have to declare that an entire village had a speech disorder. I would have been extremely busy correcting all of those bilateral lisps, and terribly embarrassed at my lack of understanding.

Concerning the hysterectomy, I felt well in Chevak. All the endometriosis pain disappeared. But I was unprepared for the hormone replacement therapy side effects. Premarin, made from horse urine, was the only option presented to me and the only option I knew about. Within a few months I started to experience severe and chronic migraine headaches. Within another few months, I had stomach aches, nausea, food sensitivities, an extreme sensitivity to smells, and tight muscles. Salt became intolerable, I stopped sweating, and I had 24-hour-a-day migraines. I had never experienced constant, unrelenting headaches comparable to these. I usually had a great appetite. I ate everything. Now, even drinking water made me nauseous.

The gynecologist didn't schedule any follow-up with me after the first two weeks, so I had switched to a general practitioner, another male doctor, this one smelling of cigarette smoke. I told him about the headaches and reported that I never had them before taking the hormones.

He lectured me. "The headaches have nothing to do with hormones. Keep taking them, and I want you to exercise more."

He was the doctor. So I believed him, but I had a nagging question in my mind. *Okay. Yes, sir, whatever you say, sir. But I already have a great exercise routine. How will more of that make my headaches go away?*

After a year with him and no improvement in my health, much less in his lectures, I decided to find a female doctor. I thought a woman would be more cutting-edge for women's health problems. I sure hoped so. If the pain didn't relent, I'd have to close my business. All because a perfectly normal uterus and ovary had been plucked out of me and pickled in a jar.

From now on, my maternal instincts of compassion, care, and concern would be used for other people and their children. It was my calling, and I had felt that way during my entire career.

It will be all right, I told myself. If there is one thing I'm good at, it's blocking out pain by keeping busy and stuffing sadness by helping others to be happy. All I had to do was smile when I walked into my office or a new village, and happiness would fill my body. Any other options never occurred to me.

CHAPTER 15

The Fear of Repetition

I used to stutter really badly. Everybody thinks it's funny. And it's not.
—President Joe Biden

I had been flying to the Lower 48 for training in a variety of communication disorders for three years. I didn't go for fun (although I occasionally did some shopping); I went for knowledge. My decision to master private practice remained crucial, but my confidence wasn't high enough. I had a great fear of meeting a client whom I couldn't help. My inner drive to do better, to be better at my profession, never stopped.

At the most recent conference, on the topic of voice disorders, I met a speech-language pathologist who specialized in fluency disorders. The first time a client with a fluency disorder, sometimes known as stuttering or stammering, came to me for help, I didn't feel confident in the treatment strategies I had learned in college. Dr. Dunlop introduced himself to me during a break and we started to chat. "Where are you from?" he asked.

"Alaska," I replied. "I have a small private practice up there. How about you? Where are you from?"

"I'm from Ann Arbor. I'm a professor at the University of Michigan, and I have a private practice too. I specialize in stuttering."

"Really?" Immediately, my interest piqued. "I'd like to know more about the treatment of stuttering. Do you do any workshops?"

"Well, Kit," he said, "I've developed a weeklong program to train SLPs how to work with people who stutter." He continued, "I'll also be publishing a program I developed for clients soon."

Wow. That was exactly what I wanted. He could take me and my contractors, and any other SLPs in town who wanted to learn, from start to finish. A week would be enough time to thoroughly learn his program. I told him I was interested, but wondered if he would have the time to travel so far during the academic year.

"I'm available over the summer when I'm not teaching at the university," he said. "I've heard Alaska is amazing in the summer."

So he wanted to come to Alaska. This was April. If he was available, he could teach us that summer. But when the idea of inviting him to Alaska popped into my mind, I simultaneously thought about the expenses. I'd have to pay him a daily rate, get him a hotel, pay for his meals, and buy his plane ticket. I had learned how costly and tiring it was to fly Outside twice a year. The plane ticket alone was eight hundred dollars.

It would be expensive, and I had never done anything like that before, inviting an expert to come to my place of work. Excitement filled my heart as I decided to bring him to Alaska. There was something about him—he was funny, yet compassionate; relaxed, yet professional. He was Irish, with red hair, and liked to have a beer after work. That was fine with me. My great-grandfather was born in Belfast. Heck, we could have been related.

I hoped that what I was going to ask him next would have the answer I wanted. If it did, everyone would benefit. "What's your schedule like this summer, and how much do you charge?"

Three months later, in July, I greeted him at the airport.

In June, I had run an ad in the newspaper announcing the weeklong training at my clinic for people with fluency disorders. I also notified all the speech therapists in the area. I didn't charge them anything. And I didn't charge the clients either. This was something I could do for the whole community and learn at the same time. I love it when everybody wins.

On a Monday evening, Dr. Dunlop met with the several men and one woman who answered my ad and showed up at my clinic. They dressed in sportscoats and slacks, or nice shirts with slacks. They seemed to be professional working people.

Dr. Dunlop, wearing a gray suit, sat at the head of the folding conference table. They all conveniently fit perfectly. The SLPs sat in chairs around the room and listened as he talked.

I introduced Dr. Dunlop to the attendees and sat down. He had obviously done this before. He spoke sincerely, but with humor, to the group of people, all of whom stuttered. He started by telling them about his own struggles to speak.

"I developed stuttering when I was twelve years old, by imitating a friend of mine who stuttered. I continued to stutter throughout college until I received treatment from some of the best SLPs who specialized in stuttering at that time."

He continued, "This was in the 1960s. My speech therapist told me to wear a clown-size bow tie, stand outside, and collect the names and phone numbers of a hundred coeds. This was supposed to desensitize me and make me more accepting of my stuttering problem." I was horrified to hear this, but it immediately gave him credibility with the group. Who knows what they had been subjected to, or if they had even had any treatment?

"I decided I wanted to study treatment methods that created a positive change and acceptance of that change," he explained. "Since then, I have spent my career studying what fluent people do when they speak, and that is what I'm here to tell you about tonight." Because of his experience, he knew that people who stuttered could become fluent.

Sitting back with the other SLPs. I thought about this group of people sitting at the table. I guessed this was the first time in their lives that they had been together with other people who stuttered, at least in Alaska. *They are with their tribe,* I thought. *They don't have to hide or pretend. What a relief it must be.* I dared myself to be proud of what was happening—that I had brought this specialist to Anchorage, that these people were there because I had taken a chance by investing in this man's visit. And now he was openly talking about a topic that had filled so many with shame.

It is terrible when a person cannot talk about their

stuttering, like it is something so horrible that it is unspeakable. When parents pretend it is not happening, and their child knows something is wrong, it's confusing and shaming.

We had all been afflicted with struggles to communicate, and this was probably the first time that any of us had heard this new information about the research and science behind stuttering. I took copious notes, thinking that I would be telling this same information to other people in the future.

Dr. Dunlop spoke to the group like he was their equal, like he knew their frustration, their anguish, and their hope. He went on, "Eighty percent of people with fluency disorders become normally fluent with treatment. Another fifteen percent improve their fluency but aren't completely fluent. The final five percent have too much neurological interference to change their fluency at all.

"We found in our research that to improve fluency, the typical client needs about thirty-two to thirty-four, one-hour sessions of speech therapy. Treatment begins with daily therapy for the first one to two weeks. Subsequent sessions are spread out over time, starting with three times a week, reduced to two times a week, once a week, twice a month, and then once a month. Consistent, daily practice on the part of the client at home is a must for automaticity to take place." He was relying on neuroplasticity to improve fluency, which required daily stimulation. That meant the client needed commitment more than anything.

When he opened the table for questions, they wanted more basic information about their problem—what had caused it, why some people outgrew it, and whether it could be passed to one of their children. Dr. Dunlop answered all of their concerns.

"It's normal for young children to stutter on two to three percent of their words for a few months. Their motor-speech skills are developing, which is to be expected. Overall, four percent of children stutter, but only one percent of adults stutter. So there's some truth to the saying that most children will grow out of it. But if children stutter on more than nine percent of their words at any age, they need professional help. The earlier these children receive therapy, the better. New neural pathways can be stimulated, and any psychological problems that may appear can be addressed."

At the time, Dr. Dunlop reported that while psychological factors can play a part, stuttering is mostly a physical problem, caused by immature development of the central nervous system. Additionally, there is about a fifty percent genetic component, passed on through the mother's genes. Then he noted a few comments about new research.

PET scans had found that in addition to areas lighting up in the left hemisphere of the brain during speech, which is normal, hot spots were noted in the right hemisphere of people who stuttered. Even when the person imagined they were speaking, the same hot spots showed up on the scan. If the right hemisphere was fighting for control, it could throw off the timing. "Only one side of the brain can control the tongue for speech," he explained.

He brought up cluttering, a cousin of stuttering, which I had never heard of before. Cluttering has a strong connection to cerebral dysfunction, namely: dysfluent speech, rapid speaking rate, short attention span, auditory processing difficulty, and unawareness of the disorder. It is a central language imbalance disorder that frequently affects reading performance, speech articulation, and word finding. Cluttering can occur concomitantly with stuttering, and both emanate from organic causes.

"If anyone here would like to participate in the program this week," he announced, "you're all invited to make appointments in the afternoons or evenings for fluency training. I'll be training the speech-language pathologists in the room, and all of us will be working with you."

Then he added, "Gaining control of the vocal cords is part of the treatment. Ninety-seven percent of all stutterers have no problem when they sing because the vocal cords are perpetually together. The same is true when they whisper because the vocal cords are apart. It's when they talk, and the cords open and close sporadically, that their voices get stuck. My program helps people to use their vocal cords in a new way, almost as if they were singing. It's how fluent people speak."

The next evening, I watched Dr. Dunlop as he modeled the first contact with a client. He asked Edgar, "What's your name?" He listened patiently.

Edgar's throat locked up and his jaw jerked up and down as he tried to get the /e/ sound out. When he couldn't voice it, Edgar took another breath and tried again. He did this over and over for a full minute; then he finally said his name, "Ed."

Dr. Dunlop watched Edgar with a calm face and never took his eyes off him. He didn't tease him or joke with him. He didn't imitate him or laugh. He didn't say Ed's name for him. In this way, Dr. Dunlop built a strong bond with Ed, one based on respect, in just one minute. This is how gentlemen and gentlewomen act around people who stutter: respectfully.

Dr. Dunlop's knowledge bowled me over. He generated an impressive body of research on stuttering and cluttering. His training gave me great confidence in how to diagnose and treat people with fluency disorders. I had found the right person for the job of mentor. How he had fallen into my lap was a mystery.

Adults who have stuttered since childhood have suffered through terrible verbal abuse, mocking, and shaming for their speech. As adults, they are stressed during job interviews, while making phone calls to someone they don't know, and when starting new relationships. They often vacillate between accepting themselves as a stutterer and giving up on improving their fluency or trying, yet again, to improve.

Some people who stutter belittle other stutterers who want more fluent speech. They claim the others are "using techniques," as if doing so is something phony and not real. Using techniques actually changes the brain, again through the process of neuroplasticity. Techniques aren't phony and can make lasting changes if done correctly and long enough. But the techniques used must be based on validated research, not some random distraction device. This is how jaw-jerking gets started.

A person who stutters might pause and jerk their jaw one time to get out a sound. Then their brain remembers that pattern. *Remember when you jerked your jaw, and the sound came out? Do that next time*. All this is happening subconsciously, and through neuroplasticity it becomes a pattern. The treatment I learned from Dr. Dunlop uses neuroplasticity to develop fluent speech. In just one week, Dr. Dunlop had changed the lives of many people, and he had changed mine as well.

The concept of neuroplasticity opened up new directions in my work as I began to see the many ways that the brain can change. And I came to see that by overcoming my own fears and inviting Dr. Dunlop to come to Alaska—rather than just assuming he wouldn't want to or that I couldn't pull it off financially—I was changing for the better as well, at work.

At home, I remained in my subservient role of wife. My needs for tenderness and warmth were ignored because I didn't even know I needed them. That's how it was. Bill planned our macho activities, which I enjoyed as well, so what did I have to complain about? I don't know. The busyness was relentless.

Since women's liberation, we women went to work, opened businesses, and became corporate leaders. When we got home, nothing had changed. Songs were written about Superwomen who did it all, with one hand tied behind their backs, figuratively. In reality, stress took its toll if we didn't ask for help. And sometimes when we asked, we didn't get it. The transformation of society with the women's movement continued at a slow pace. It would take another generation or two for the men to catch up, if they were willing. In the meantime, we did do it all.

To help my headaches, I enrolled in a hatha yoga class. I thought maybe the stretching would relieve the migraines. It did reduce some muscle tension and stiffness, so I stuck with it. Unfortunately, it didn't help my headaches.

Thinking my nausea was food related, I changed my diet

to the new craze, macrobiotics. Although both Bill and I enjoyed the food, it had no effect on my headaches. Always in the back of my mind, the hormones remained the culprit. But even my new female doctor hammered into me that it wasn't the hormones, and if I didn't want heart disease and osteoporosis, I'd better keep taking them. I did as I was told.

The one thing I wouldn't do was give up on my life. I would keep my business, keep moving forward, and keep my positive attitude toward helping people with communication disorders. It was the main thing in my life that made me happy. If I had to do it with a headache, so be it.

CHAPTER 16

The Runaway Boy

Everyone you meet is fighting a battle you know nothing about. Be kind.
—Robin Williams

"When I was little, I lived with my mom and dad and my older brother. They used to beat me, and sometimes they tied me up and left me in a dark closet for a long time."

"Go on," I replied calmly, but horrified.

"They would make my brother fight with me. He was a lot bigger, and I tried to defend myself. But they cheered him on no matter how much I cried or begged for him to stop. Sometimes they didn't give me any dinner or any breakfast. They told me I was evil and going to the devil and that's why they had to do it." He paused, eyes looking at the ground. "I got whipped with a belt when I did something wrong, but I couldn't figure out what I did," he continued. "They would tell me to go take a bath, then they would come in, add hot water, and try to drown me. They told me if I ever told anyone what they did, they would kill me."

Alaskans are rightfully proud of their military residents. Anchorage is home to Elmendorf Air Force Base, and occasionally I received a referral from one of their doctors. One such referral was Robert. The psychiatrist at Elmendorf airbase had referred Robert to me for stuttering, as I had become somewhat of a specialist in that area following my work with Dr. Dunlop. Robert had recently developed a stuttering disorder, and it is rare for stuttering to develop in adulthood. I was intrigued.

Robert was an airman. Quietly proper, he sat up straight in the blue velvet wingback chair in my office. He dressed in street clothes—clean and neat, with a short haircut. He wore regular sneakers because it was summer and boots weren't needed anymore.

During his evaluation, I asked Robert if he had ever stuttered as a child. He revealed to me that he remembered being five years old when he first started to stutter. It coincided with the age he recalled his abuse began.

Concerned both professionally and personally, I had asked him for more detail about his abuse. For some reason, he was the scapegoated child in the family, the one who took all the abuse from those sick and twisted people—physically, mentally, emotionally, and spiritually.

He stopped stuttering after a couple of years, which is normal for children who go through a developmental dysfluency pattern. His abuse, however, continued.

When he was twelve, he decided to tell his teacher about the trauma he was still enduring at the hands of his parents, even though he had been told by them that they would kill him if he ever said anything to anyone. But he never secured the opportunity to reveal his situation, because his family left for Africa on a mission. His parents were fervently religious.

"What happened in Africa?" I asked.

"We lived in a tent. My parents kept me tied up in there, and I wasn't allowed to go out. I had to be quiet, and they wouldn't let me go to school." He shook his head. "Sometimes I could go out at night with my brother, as long as no one else was around. Pretty much nobody even knew I was there." He hesitated. "My parents still beat me, just because I was there. Then we came back to America."

"What did you do then?" I asked.

"When I was fifteen years old, I ran away from home and lived on the streets. When I turned sixteen, I had grown a lot. I lied about my age and joined the Air Force."

"I'm so sorry this happened to you. What your family did was terrible, wrong, and sadistic. I'm so glad you were able to get away from them. I can't imagine how hard it has been for you. I'll do everything I can to help you," I replied with empathy.

The military was the right decision for him. He eventually

married, and he and his wife had a son. They were transferred to Anchorage, far away from his past and his parents. When I met Robert, his little boy had just turned five. This was the age when Robert had started stuttering. This was the age that he only recently remembered being abused. Suddenly, and unsurprisingly, his stuttering reoccurred. All the past that he had buried somewhere deep in his mind came flooding back too. Psychologically, he was in a crisis.

I gave Robert the battery of tests recommended by Dr. Dunlop. After we had finished, I scheduled Robert's first treatment appointment and said goodbye. While analyzing his scores and preparing his therapy, I kept the referral in mind. His psychiatrist wanted me to treat Robert's fluency so that he could attend group meetings on the base. These meetings were for people with substance abuse problems, mainly alcoholism.

Robert reported that in these meetings everyone sat in a circle and took turns talking. Each person spoke about their substance abuse and how their treatment was unfolding. But Robert wasn't a substance abuser. He was an abuse victim. His problem didn't relate in any way to this group. He didn't feel comfortable talking to these people about what had happened to him, and I supported him in that.

Additionally, people with a fluency problem tell me that one of the worst things that can happen to them is to be positioned in a queue to speak. Their tension tightens as they wait their turn, which increases their odds of being dysfluent. Robert didn't need this group therapy, and in fact, it was hurting him. He needed help with a skilled professional, someone who understood childhood abuse and trauma.

I worked with Robert five days a week for the first two weeks. This was the standard protocol when initiating fluency treatment. It helped him with his fluency immediately. I taught him the components of fluent speaking, which gave him the knowledge and experience to stay that way. The psychological issues were another story.

Bewildered and stunned, I had listened as he recounted

his abuse in childhood. Robert had had one of the most terrifying experiences I'd ever heard; only Genie's story was more horrific. His cause of stuttering was *not* typical. Given his abuse, I considered that he might have had neurological damage caused by being hit in the head. In all probability, however, his childhood stuttering was a response to the abuse he was enduring, which impacted his still-immature nervous system for developing speech. When he was five, he was afraid to talk, and he became dysfluent.

Dr. Dunlop had taught me how to use the delayed auditory feedback machine (DAF) with his treatment protocol. This machine helps the dysfluent person to break the tension-filled habits associated with speaking. It helps them habituate continuous phonation, which is keeping their vocal cords *on* while speaking. Robert practiced with it for a few minutes at the beginning of every treatment session until he no longer needed it.

I put the DAF head set on Robert and asked him to speak into the microphone attached to it. About the size of a cigarette pack, I adjusted the two dials, one to control the volume, and the other, the rate of his speech. He heard his own speech through the headphones, but I had slowed it down to a level 10, which was extremely slow. Eventually, I asked him to speak at a level 2, which was considered optimal. His job was to keep continuous phonation, no matter how slow the dial was set, and not talk any faster than he heard himself.

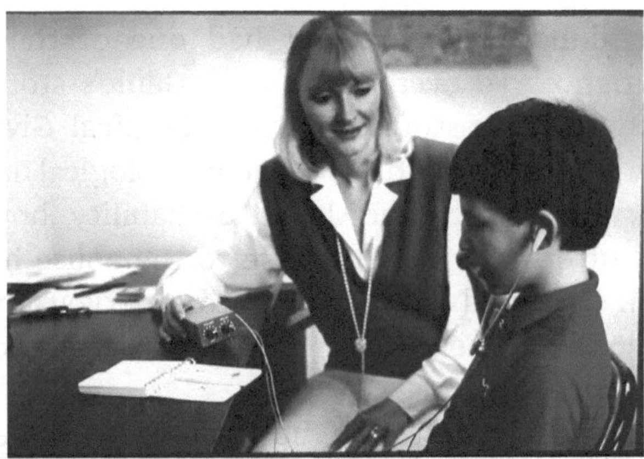

Kit Roberts using a delayed auditory feedback machine with a boy, 1984. Photo: Unknown.

Treatment continued with several parameters: breath control during speaking, gradually increasing the amount, complexity, and rate of speaking with continuous phonation; reading (which was more difficult because the client could not substitute a word on which they thought they might be dysfluent); making phone calls; and speaking to others. Once Robert reached a normal, calm rate of speech while remaining fluent, he was ready to practice his new skills outside of the treatment room. This is called carryover.

Ultimately, Robert was asked to make a carryover contract to apply his new fluency skills in public. No, I didn't make him wear a clown-size bow and collect girls' phone numbers. He decided what to say to a specific person, where, when, and the difficulty level. The difficulty level ranged from zero to ten, with zero extremely easy and ten quite complex. To begin carryover, he wrote down several speaking situations to complete each day, no higher than a level three, and signed the paper. After speaking, he evaluated his fluency and noted the results, which we discussed at our next appointment. The procedures involved in fluency therapy were done in baby steps, ensuring built-in success.

I also made a cassette tape for him using relaxation, visualization, and positive suggestion as it related to speech.

I instructed him to listen to it every day. Research shows that visualizing a motor activity perfectly stimulates the same parts of the brain that perform that activity and leads to improvement.

Robert made excellent progress. Once he became a fluent speaker, which didn't take long, I discharged him back to the base. For some reason, he had been sent to me, and I gave him some relief, compassion, knowledge, and fluency. If we follow our calling, the people who need us will find us. We will have the skills to help them if we listen to our intuition and get the additional training that we need to deliver the best treatment.

One thing that bothered me was insurance companies that didn't pay for stuttering treatment. They had singled out stuttering as not being a medical condition and wouldn't pay for it. I decided to call three big-name insurance companies and ask what they did when they received a speech therapy claim.

"Hello, this is Kit Roberts. I'm a speech therapist, and I would like to speak with a representative in your claims office, please."

"One moment."

"Claims. My name is Mary. How can I help you?"

"My name is Kit Roberts, and I'm a speech therapist. I have a question about how you handle speech therapy claims for stuttering. What do you do when you receive that kind of a claim?"

"We automatically deny it."

"What about the report I send with it? Do you read it to determine if it is associated with a medical problem or a functional problem?"

"No, we automatically deny it," she said.

"I have sent in a speech therapy claim, with a doctor's prescription for speech therapy, for an eight-year-old girl who started stuttering after being hospitalized with a stomach problem. It clearly had a medical cause. She had treatment in school for a few months, which didn't help. She was brought to our clinic, and with our intensive treatment program, her stuttering resolved. Her parents have speech therapy coverage in their plan. Legally, it should be covered, which was all detailed in the report I sent. The claim has been denied. What do I need to do to get this covered?"

"You have to send it to the next level for a review."

"So are you saying that you automatically deny the first claim, and to get it considered, I have to write another report and send it to another person for a review?"

"Yes."

"Thank you. Please give me the name and address for the claim review."

I called two other insurance agencies and got the same answer. I was incensed that they automatically denied the claim. I spent time and energy writing comprehensive evaluation reports, only to have to send them again, for no other reason than the insurance company didn't want to pay. It took six to nine months to be reimbursed for these services. But if I didn't take my time to send the additional report, the parents would have to pay. The fact that three of the biggest insurance companies were doing the same thing seemed illegal, like price fixing. At the very least, it was systemic discrimination against a group of people with fluency disorders.

My intuition had brought Dr. Dunlop to Alaska, which served me and my clients well. It prompted me to follow up with the insurance companies. For so long, I had ignored my intuitions, telling myself others knew better, downplaying my gut feelings. I was learning to trust my gut where work was concerned. I was compassionate, helpful, and aware of others' needs. The same thing was not happening at home.

There was no compassion, help, or self-awareness left over for me. For the most part, I kept those feelings down. What good would it do to ask for compassion or help? Who would give it to me? I never reached my father, and I couldn't connect with my husband. It was a classic situation that I didn't understand. For now, I worked harder, tried to earn more money to make Bill happy, and pretended everything was fine. *Me* was a painful word.

CHAPTER 17

Failure to Thrive

A child that's being abused by its parents doesn't stop loving its parents, it stops loving itself.
—Shahid Arabi

In the dead of winter one year, I boarded an Alaska Airlines jet from Anchorage to the isolated town of Bethel. The local hospital had hired me to evaluate an Alaskan native boy with a diagnosis of failure to thrive. All I knew was that he was eighteen months old, and he needed a communication disorders evaluation. I'd have to find out the rest when I met him.

In my readings about Alaskan native culture, I had learned that traditionally, the Yup'ik women talked to their babies when their little ones were in the womb. The mothers lifted the collars of their blouses, tucked their chins down, and spoke underneath the fabric to their babies. They used a loving tone of voice, especially during the first two years of life, before the child became aware. They talked and talked to their infants, even while breastfeeding. Although the little ones could not understand, they learned to listen, and one day they would know how to behave from all they had heard from their mothers.

Those mothers understood that a child's mind was delicate and that speaking with affection prevented injury to it. They had learned by experience that giving children instruction as early as possible made it easier for them to speak when they were older. This perspective and the resulting customs are as beneficial now as they were in the past. They have been scientifically proven to stimulate speech and language development in children. What a loving culture they have created, and what a great teaching to pass on from one generation to the next.

As I flew to Bethel, I wondered what I would see there. The

town had a population of 3,500 people, with 2,400 indigenous Alaskans, mostly southern Yup'iks. Having a hospital, a paved runway, hotel, and restaurant, Bethel was a hub, not a village. It was even bigger than Nome.

From the air, the town resembled many of the remote places I had worked, just bigger. The land was flat as a pancake and covered with snow. I had let my thoughts drift to what was ahead. Although I was getting ready to see a little boy with failure to thrive, I wondered how Bethel was thriving. I knew the people in the town had an alcohol problem and had tried to curb it by voting to be "dry." That meant that alcohol could not be sold there.

I had also learned what happened in a dry village when people wanted to get alcohol for an event. All they had to do was buy it direct from Anchorage. They called the Brown Jug Warehouse—from the one and only public phone in town—ordered a small planeload with about twenty-five cases of alcohol, and had it flown to Bethel.

During the celebration, the partiers drank until every bottle was empty. This might take three or four days. So, depending on how many people were involved in the drinking and whether or not they had children, the kids may or may not have made it to school on Monday or Tuesday. The children had to climb over their drunken, passed-out parents and fend for themselves. I shuddered at this profoundly disturbing problem. It replicated the era of Prohibition, when efforts to control alcohol led to the production and consumption of alcohol no longer being controlled.

I had only experienced this effect once, when I arrived in a village on a Monday and many children were absent. I was told that there had been a drinking party over the weekend and that's why the kids weren't in school. I wondered if the same thing happened in Bethel.

As we circled the airstrip before descending, something distinctive caught my eye. A series of curious yellow piping crisscrossed the landscape, as if we were entering a giant Tinker

Toy world. But my curiosity didn't linger long on the image because my mind was somewhere else. I was thinking of the little boy who needed my help.

As I walked down the stairs wheeled over to the plane, the now-familiar exhilaration of Alaska's crystalline air reached my face and penetrated each pore. My lungs suddenly chilled as I inhaled the vitalizing oxygen. I loved that first breath of invigorating Alaskan air after a plane ride. It felt like home and health.

The sun hadn't gone down yet, and the afternoon was clear and bright. There wasn't much activity as I waited for my luggage, picked it up, and went outside the small building. Parked at the curb was a white airport shuttle van. I asked the driver, a local man with a weathered face, if he could take me to the hotel and then to the hospital the next morning. He nodded. When he stepped out of the van to get my luggage, I noticed that he wore jeans and a winter jacket with a hood. He didn't have his hood up, but I did.

He drove slowly on the snow-packed road into town. With the warm heat blowing on our feet, he didn't say a thing. The town seemed far away. After a few minutes, a big sign welcomed us to the Bethel National Forest. I scoured the landscape for the forest, but only one lone fir tree in the distance appeared. With a grin on my face, I concluded the people of Bethel had a good sense of humor.

Bethel also had a nickname, "the Armpit of Alaska." I couldn't imagine what that referred to. As we rode into town, I asked my driver what those yellow pipes were that I'd seen from the air.

"That's our sewer system," he said. "The pipes are covered with heated insulation and wrapped in yellow plastic to keep them dry. We didn't put our sewer pipes underground because of the permafrost. They might break under there; it's too unstable. They connect from house to house and building to building like usual water and sewer pipes."

Since the pipes were heated, any snow that fell on them

melted away, and they remained cheerfully visible all year long. Brilliant ingenuity.

My driver dropped me off at a two-story hotel on a snowy road in the middle of town. "Here's your hotel," he said. "I'll help you with your bags."

I thanked him and paid him and asked him to pick me up in the morning so I could make it to the hospital by nine. He smiled and waved as he drove off, and I checked into my room.

My dingy room had two double beds. The furnishings were a bit worn, and there hadn't been a fresh coat of paint on the walls in a long time. Being in the middle of a distant and meagerly populated part of Alaska, I didn't expect a four-star hotel. And it was better than sleeping on the gym floor like some of my other jobs.

I started to unpack my clothes and get my materials arranged for the morning when I heard a woman shouting in slurred speech, "Get up! Be a man!" The voice was coming from the other side of the paper-thin wall. Worried, I leaned toward the wall and listened. "Get up," she screamed again. "You told me you weren't gonna get drunk."

Then I heard a man's voice make a moaning sound: "Uuuuh." A different man then griped, "Don't yell at him. Stop kickin' him."

As my gut tightened, I stepped away with concern. I wondered if I should call for help or tell the man at the check-in desk what was going on. Finally, I decided not to interfere. The low arctic sun had descended into dusk, and at 4:30, I left to get an early dinner.

While I ate—at an equally dingy restaurant—I remembered a TV show I had recently seen. ABC's *20/20* had done an exposé on dirty hotel rooms. They showed rooms with bedbugs, urine-coated mattresses, and filth. When I got back to the hotel, I decided to check out my mattress for myself. I lifted the sheet and gasped. Dried, crusted, yellow urine trails covered the edges. Astonished and unsettled, I didn't even want to lay my body on that bed. That night, I slept with my clothes on.

The next morning, I packed early and prepared for my ride to the hospital. I carried everything with me because I was going straight to the airport after I finished. The taxi driver arrived on schedule, and I arrived right on time. The hospital was a nice building, clean and modern.

I was the first member of a team of rehabilitation professionals flown in from Anchorage to evaluate this little boy. After finding the treatment room, I talked to the nurse's aide. I introduced myself, and she left to get the boy. Quietly, I watched as she gently placed and propped him on an old, comfortable couch in the evaluation room. He looked like a ragdoll, a thinly stuffed pillow, sitting lifeless on the sofa. I'd never observed such an empty boy before. I felt sickened by the thought of how he had become that way. I imagined alcohol may have had something to do with it.

Chronologically, he had survived eighteen months. Yet he didn't seem that young to me. He resembled a miniature person. He was so thin and pale. His eyes stared vacantly from his expressionless face. I searched for his presence but found only absence. He had vanished.

As a member of his rehabilitation team, I evaluated his speech development to determine if it was within normal limits or impaired. Sadly, it didn't take a degree in communication disorders to know that he was severely delayed in verbal and nonverbal communication skills.

He was nicely dressed in a long-sleeved T-shirt, blue overalls, and little socks and shoes. He smelled clean, and his black hair was cut in a cute style. But he hadn't been so thoughtfully cared for in the past. Child Protective Services had custody of him now, after he had been removed from his home for neglect and abuse.

I read the medical diagnosis of this sweet boy: failure to thrive. While this disorder can have different causes, his cause was the worst I had seen. It could have been prevented.

Fundamentally, he had learned in the first few months of his life that survival meant disappearing. Don't cry, don't whimper. Don't babble, don't try to talk. Don't make eye contact, don't move. Don't laugh, don't play, don't giggle. Don't call attention to yourself, don't respond to another human. Don't hear, don't see, don't feel, don't taste, and don't touch. Although he had a normal body, he was clearly undernourished, and *hadn't* learned how to thrive, like other eighteen-month-old children.

I opened my bag of evaluation tools, including developmental scales and a variety of objects. I tested everything. I presented him with the cutest stuffed animals, the funniest noisemakers, the smallest rattles, the tastiest animal crackers, and the easiest balls to hold. I blew bubbles, sang songs, and made sounds. I said words and played peek-a-boo. "Where's the ball?" I asked him. "Touch your nose," I coyly commanded. "Let's clap hands," I playfully asked, inviting him to join me. But he didn't respond to anything.

I picked him up and sat him on my lap. He had no weight to him. He wouldn't hold my finger or make eye contact. I couldn't get him to point at an object or hold anything in his own hand. He wouldn't even imitate a smile. I never heard him make one sound. I'm not talking about making a babbling sound—"ga ga ga"—I mean generating a noise of any kind coming from his throat. Some evil spell had turned this human boy into a ragdoll.

Alone in the evaluation room, I held him to my chest with his head resting on my shoulder, as any caring individual would do. I patted his back, rocked him from side to side, and told him what a good boy he was. I felt so much love and compassion for him. I could have held him for the next three hours, but I had to lay him down. I had been with him for forty-five minutes, and he needed to be evaluated by the next therapist.

A baby who isn't stimulated for speech and language before the age of two acquires irreversible brain damage. The brain prunes itself from a lack of interaction, and cognitive development declines as a result. Time was running out for him.

The diagnosis in my report stated that this frail boy was functioning below a three-month age level: a profound disorder.

Infants cried; he didn't even do that. The behavior of one or more adults had caused him to be this way. He couldn't run around, speak in single words, or follow simple directions. He didn't play with toys, giggle, or laugh when I blew bubbles. When I gave him animal crackers, he couldn't say "More."

He should have said "More."

I left copious notes and detailed activities to stimulate his communication development. He needed constant treatment woven into his day, and he needed it now. By the age of two, his brain would eliminate any areas left unused. He had six months to make up for one and a half years of neglect. He had six months to say "More."

On the flight home, with the droning sounds of the jet engines, I opened the tray table and dropped it down. I rested my elbows on it with my head in my hands. Filled with overwhelming sadness, incredulity, and helplessness for what I had seen that morning, I rubbed my forehead, already hot with a headache, and wondered how things like this could happen.

My clients' problems were confidential. I couldn't talk to anyone about them, not even Bill. I had learned to stuff my feelings, not express them. So that's what I did. I had to stay professional. What I wanted to do was break down and sob, to wail like he was my child. I needed to heal him, to make him whole again. I tucked the memory of him inside myself, under my blouse, where I could talk to him sweetly, if I ever had the chance.

As I looked out the window at the blank landscape, my mind wandered back to my childhood. I could see how great it was growing up on a farm, having three wonderful meals a day, and three brothers to wrestle with, yell at, and play with outside. After seeing this little boy, I thought to myself, I had nothing to complain about, not a thing in the world. What a lucky child I was. What a lucky girl.

Given the fact that he had eventually been evaluated by a team of professionals—occupational therapists, physical therapists, social workers—all of whom diagnosed him with severe developmental disabilities, I expected some follow-up visits for treatment. That never materialized. I never knew who, if anyone, used my written activities to stimulate his speech and language or if they had any training or support, even over the phone, for how to do it. This frustrated me to no end. I kept wondering about him. But I was hired to evaluate him, not treat him. The hospital knew where to find me if they wanted follow-up.

If you can't serve the smallest and the most helpless of your people, then your system is not working. Alaska's systems for service delivery to the disabled needed direct interventions. I didn't work at the systems level for the state. I worked at getting my own business system to work, hired contractors, billed insurance, and paid bills. Since I didn't hear anything from the hospital after a couple of months, I knew nothing was going to happen, at least with me. Although I wanted to call them, I didn't; it just wasn't done. Instead, I sat back in my office chair and felt defeated for him, for me, and for so many others who weren't getting the help they needed. I just decided to do more, to see more clients. This wasn't the time to give up. It was the time to get moving. But sometimes one step forward was followed by two steps back.

CHAPTER 18
Goldilocks and the IRS

Nothing is certain except death and taxes.
—Benjamin Franklin

Alaska had existed for millennia, and her laws were natural laws, created by her. Don't go outside in the winter without proper clothing, or you will get frostbite. Don't drive into the wilderness without enough gasoline to reach your destination, or the State Patrol will surely find your jackets and boots on the side of the road, then come upon your dead body frozen from hypothermia. Don't go into the bush in the summer wearing shorts without mosquito repellent, or the sluggish, spring B52 bomber mosquitos and the zippy summer F15 jets will surely suck your blood dry like a million vampires. Yes, she has natural laws that are at the level of life and death.

Once she had been discovered by white men, Alaska attracted adventurers, misfits, and what we called the *end-of-the roaders*. They came to Alaska, trekked as far as possible, and remained where the road retired. They didn't like man-made laws. While she had already taught me her natural laws, I was now about to experience a man-made law, the kind of law that the end-of-the-roaders detested.

By 1987, I realized that I needed a larger office. Gazing at my minimal, tan space, I felt the loss of an old friend. I had gotten my start here, but it just wasn't big enough anymore. Bill had set up my first computer in this office, an Apple Macintosh. He plugged it in and left. At the time, he was more of a hardware guy than a software guy. It was supposed to be user friendly, but it took me about ten minutes to figure out what the blinking square was and how to move it.

I thought the Mac was going to save me time from having to type everything in triplicate and deal with carbon paper inserts and Wite-Out correction fluid for mistakes on my Remington electric typewriter. But no. I soon learned that writing a report on the computer took me two hours instead of one. This little box gave me the option to change my wording, an option that I found unbearably irresistible. Once typed on the electric typewriter, that's the way the report stayed. But now on the computer, I could rewrite, move whole paragraphs, and erase. While it consumed my time, at least it was small and would be easy to move to the new place.

I found a larger suite a few blocks away. As I left my first office, however, I did some measuring in preparation for moving shelves, tables, and other furniture. I discovered that my 800-square-foot space was actually 550 square feet. When I had signed the lease, the landlord told me it was an 800-square-foot office. It never occurred to me to measure it. This guy cheated me out of 250 square feet—for three years.

Business space in Anchorage was awfully expensive and customarily charged by the square foot. There had been a time when I would have said nothing and silently fumed about being cheated. But Alaska was teaching me to be strong, to speak up. So I confronted the landlord as he came to do a final check for damage.

After we exchanged hellos, I composed myself and said, "You told me this office was eight hundred square feet." I spoke in the strongest, yet still professional voice I could muster. "But I measured it, and it's only five hundred and fifty. I want a refund for the overpayment of two hundred and fifty square feet for the last three years."

"The number of square feet wasn't written on the lease, and there's nothing you can do about it," he replied. "I'm not refunding anything."

I checked my old lease. He was right. I was screwed. I had nothing in writing to prove I'd been told it was larger. I felt like the femme fatale in an old-timey melodrama and was surprised that he didn't have a handle-bar mustache. But I had spoken up for myself. Even if I hadn't won the argument, I had taken a step forward. And after that, I measured every office myself so I wouldn't be swindled again.

Many Alaskan companies hired contractors. Construction workers, pilots, fishermen, loggers, and the like were regularly contracted for their services. These people were qualified, were licensed if necessary, and paid their own taxes. I, too, contracted with at least three or four SLPs who were certified and had their own businesses. I needed them to help my private clients, work in a hospital or other facility, or travel to a village for me. That's why I needed a bigger office. There just wasn't enough room for all of them coming and going at the same time. But these jobs were spotty. The SLPs had to have their own materials, write their own reports, and be independent. I genuinely appreciated their work, and so did the clients. Their treatment helped many people.

Contracting, hiring employees, and billing insurance companies required knowledge and experience, which I didn't have. As I worked, I learned and wanted to do everything accurately.

In the midst of this big move to a larger office, the IRS came to town. I had recently read an article in the local *Anchorage Times*, which reported that the IRS had sent a cadre of fifty agents to Anchorage to "crack down" on contractors. I didn't think it had anything to do with me, so I ignored it. I couldn't figure out why they were doing it anyway. Summer was short. All kinds of construction, as well as road and sewer repairs, got completed then. It didn't happen year-round; the ground froze. Contractors were hired because if you had employees, they would all have to be fired when winter arrived. Didn't the IRS get it? We weren't breaking the law. That's just how we did it in Alaska.

Within a couple of months, however, I received an audit notice from the IRS. According to them, I owed $60,000 in back taxes for my contractors, which had to be paid immediately. They contended that my contractors were definitely employees, making me responsible for the last three years of their taxes.

Period.

Panic set in. Bill and I always paid our income taxes. I always paid my business taxes. My contractors always paid theirs. Where was I going to find $60,000? I talked to Bill, and he offered some choice words describing the IRS. He was angry, but that didn't help me. I was scared. It was like the time Bill and I were walking on an animal path in the forest (all paths in Alaska's forests are animal paths), and we ran into a bear. There was no place to run and no place to hide. I talked to Kathleen, an SLP who had done contract work for me, and she suggested I hire an attorney and fight it. Here ensued another issue, this time legal, that I wasn't taught in college.

I made an appointment with a dually certified accountant/attorney. Since he had worked for the IRS, I thought he would be perfect. Carrying the IRS paperwork in my briefcase, I entered his small office in a strip mall and introduced myself to his secretary. Within a few minutes, the accountant came out of the room behind her and introduced himself. He was at least ten years older than me, slightly balding, and dressed in a dark suit. He invited me into his office, which was mostly a large conference table with several chairs around it. File cabinets and shelves of books lined the walls. "Please have a seat," he motioned. "How can I help you?

Pulling out my IRS paperwork, I handed it to him and told him what was going on. He nodded. "Here's what's *really* going on. The IRS wants their money sooner, rather than later. They don't approve of this whole contracting business. Here's a list of nineteen things that differentiate a contractor from an employee. Read it over and let me know if you still think your contractors are in fact contractors and not employees."

Tipping my head, I fixed my eyes on the list and read the nineteen criteria carefully. Eventually, I looked up. "Yes, I think they are contractors, not employees." I hoped that meant I wouldn't have to go through time-consuming and expensive auditing. I started to feel hopeful. "Now what do I do?"

"We'll have to take it to arbitration. Get copies of all your contractors' back taxes, showing the taxes have been paid. Be prepared to address the nineteen items. Then, if you decide to hire me, we'll meet with the agents. You'll be there, but I'll do the talking," he instructed.

"What do you think my chances are?" I asked.

"I think you have a good case, but it's hard to know what they will do."

I was happy with that answer. I did not want to pay sixty thousand dollars to the IRS. If I had done something wrong, it wasn't intentional. That's when I learned that ignorance is not a defense. Darn it.

"Okay," I told him. "I'll get all the information from my contractors. What do you charge?"

"My fee is ten thousand dollars."

That was quite a stunning number that just entered my ears. As I suppressed a choke, I thought, *Hmmm. Sixty thousand or ten thousand?* I hired him.

A couple of weeks later we met in his room with five suits —men from the IRS. We sat around his large conference table, squeezed in by the shelves of books and filing cabinets. He did most of the talking. I was a nervous wreck. After all was said and done, I won my case. I paid him, not the IRS. Still, I had been right from the start, and paying $10,000 to prove it—ten thousand 1987 dollars—was no small punishment for a crime I'd never committed. But I had won.

Shortly afterward, I received a "safe haven" status from the IRS on the contracting issue, meaning that I couldn't be audited on that issue again. But after living through all the stress, I reluctantly decided to let the contractors go and transferred the clients they were seeing for me to them. Now, because I had no contract therapists, I became limited in the number of clients I could serve. I had faced the bear and turned around. I went backward. At least I knew where to find a good business attorney and accountant in the future.

Dealing with all these intricate laws was dizzying and overwhelming. I now felt a kinship with the end-of-the-roaders, my new comrades. I had a better appreciation for their desire to retreat and simplify. The KISS principle came to my mind: Keep It Simple, Stupid. Now the only person's work I was responsible for was mine. Just follow the natural laws and the man-made laws, and everything will be fine. Or will it?

CHAPTER 19

The Sly Lady

Being here in Alaska, so richly endowed with the beauties of nature, at once so rugged and yet so splendid, we sense the presence of God's spirit in the manifold handiwork of creation.
—Pope John Paul II

First, we work, then we play. Playtime arrived into our lives in Alaska, in a big way.

In addition to skiing (and falling) at Alyeska, a local ski resort, in the winter and fishing in the summer, Bill and I turned our sights south, to the Prince William Sound, thinking we might invest in a boat.

On a sunny but cool Saturday in June, we woke up at five-thirty in the morning, dressed warmly, and had a quick bite to eat. For this scouting mission, I loaded the pickup with our cooler filled with water, lunch, and snacks, which I had made the night before. We didn't know if there were restaurants at our final destination, Whittier. We heard they had incessant rain down there. I threw a trash bag with rain gear, rubber boots, and bug spray in the bed of the truck. Bill drove out our dirt road, turned onto the newly paved street, and dashed 1,100 feet to sea level and the Seward Highway. We turned south, heading for Whittier. But to get there, we had to catch a train first.

As we turned onto the highway, our view opened onto the Turnagain Arm, a thrilling inlet south of Anchorage. I rolled down my window. The fresh morning air, alive with pure health, brushed my face and filled my lungs.

When we reached the highway where it met the water, I sniffed the fishy ocean, the mired mud, and the crispness of the air swirling in my nostrils. Being June, the early morning light made it possible for me to view it all—on the left, the sturdy Dall sheep climbed the jagged mountains; on the right, the water swelled where white beluga whales gathered each summer; and near the end of the Arm streamed the mouth of 20-Mile River, where the silver salmon ran in July. The whole bay, now filled with sea water, would empty and refill daily with the tides, revealing the quicksand mud below. I loved this drive.

The further expanse of spectacular, snow-covered mountains surrounding Turnagain Arm in the distance filled me with awe—the snow never melted, like a bridal veil for the third lover in our triangle: Bill, me, and Alaska. She had many surprises for us along this route, sometimes filling us with beauty, sometimes shrouding us in thick fog, and displaying always the awesomeness of Alaska. As one of the most scenic drives I had ever taken, I never tired of it.

Our first destination was the train at Portage. After forty-five minutes of driving, we pulled off the highway onto the bumpy dirt-and-gravel parking area. From a tiny hut that opened a few minutes before the train left at seven-thirty in the morning, Bill purchased the tickets for us and our truck. This train had a few passenger cars, a couple of open baggage cars, and several flat cars that carried vehicles with their drivers. Bill drove our truck onto a flat car, pulled it as far forward as possible, and shut off the engine. Not knowing what to expect, we settled in for the ride.

After we departed, still in the open air, we passed the ageing Portage Glacier in the near distance. It had already receded a couple of miles since we moved to Alaska. It had melted out of the water and onto the ground. Soon, we entered a long, dark-rock tunnel that led to Whittier. As we moved deeper into the tunnel, all went pitch black. There weren't any lights in the tunnel, and the engineer made good use of that. He shut off all train lights except for his headlight and the dim emergency lights on the floors of the passenger cars, which were far ahead of us. When we saw everyone in front of us, turn off the cab lights in their vehicles, we followed suit. I literally couldn't see my hand in front of my face. It felt eerie and exciting. Fifteen minutes later, when we reached the end of the tunnel, the train emerged from inky obscurity into the bright golden sunlight, a crystal-clear sky, and the enormous blue water of the Prince

William Sound. It was spectacular. The magical ride had taken us from one planet to another.

I haven't been on every waterway in the world, but I have been on what must be the most breathtaking one, filled with fjords, inlets, and arms that terminated at ancient glaciers. Saturated with mountains, islands, and bays, its vast water is home to waterfowl breeding grounds, whales, and porpoise. It is protected from the Gulf of Alaska by the variety of land masses in it, much like the Inside Passage in Southeast Alaska. When we caught our first glimpse of the Sound, named Port Wells, and saw small whitecaps lapping many miles away to the horizon, we knew this water was imposing. Yet if we respected its massive magnificence, these powerful waves would respect us in return.

Bill had been in the Navy during the Vietnam War. His ship, the USS *Wichita*, an AOR-1, provided ammunition, oil, and replenishment to ships at sea. Bill told me how during his deployment in the Philippines he saw the 50-foot-high bow of the 659-foot *Wichita* go under blue water during a typhoon. When it came to boating, I felt safe with Bill. He was well educated, experienced, and competent in the roughest of waters.

In Whittier, we drove off the train and discovered that a car was unnecessary. We could walk everywhere. We went straight to the harbor to look at the boats. We spent the afternoon accruing information from the harbormaster about fees, walking the docks, and looking at every type of boat from commercial fishing boats to small personal craft. We scrutinized the boats with "For Sale" signs taped to their windows and contemplated what kind of a boat we wanted. After considering all our options, we decided on a twenty-four-foot cabin cruiser. We definitely needed an enclosed cabin in Alaska. We also needed a name for our boat, and we were about to get one.

Every trip through the Turnagain Arm is sacred, and our next trip was no different. After a couple of intense months of work, we made the journey to Whittier once again. This time, to take possession of the cabin cruiser we had bought after our prior trip. When we turned onto the Seward Highway, my heart swelled in recognition of the natural cathedral we had just entered. The glassy, mosaic floor of tidal waters and mudflats were surrounded by imperial, protecting walls of mountains, which opened to a radiant and beneficent canopy of a living sky.

I swelled with thankfulness and gratitude for the opportunity to behold its divinity, to receive its rich blessing, and be enveloped by its protecting and affectionate arms. Like a grandmother who has been separated from her long-lost grandchild, waiting to engulf her in all the love she had been storing up for that child for hundreds of years, the sacred grandmother who lived eternally in that cathedral gathered me in a reassuring hug. Loved and secure, I could relax.

As time went on, we developed our routine. It was all hurry-up, hurry-up until we boarded the train. Then we could relax in the black tunnel. For days before a trip, I cooked, packed, and loaded—our food, dog food, dog bowls, water, coffee, half-and-half, life jackets, boat shoes, rubber boots, mosquito nets, guns, USGS maps, nautical charts, dehumidifiers, money, and of course, our frantic excitement. Instead of two rugged individualists, alone in the wilderness of Alaska, we became "us."

When we were on our boat, Bill was the captain, and I was the first mate. At the helm, at his best, Bill surveyed the water, checked gauges, analyzed the maps, and anchored the boat in various bays. Once we were out to sea and all was stowed away, he let me drive through the bottomless blue water. We both watched for floaters, like tree trunks, and deftly motored around them. The porpoise rode on our wake. He prepared the dingy and took our dogs—Sugar Bear, an Australian Shepherd, and Cinnamon Bear, a Sheltie—to shore to do their business.

After a few days at sea, we returned to the harbor. I jumped off the boat onto the dock and tied it up before it drifted into another boat (except for the time I fell into the water and Bill had to pull me out by the nape of my collar). He took care of all things mechanical and electrical, like gassing up the boat and checking the propellers for tangled ropes or seaweed.

I took care of everything else. I cleaned, stowed whatever we brought, and I prepared the bed in the forward cabin. I poured Bill a cup of tea as he drove. "A clean boat is a happy boat," he used to say. He made a departure list and taped it inside the back door. Every time we left the boat, we consulted that list. Working together, we were a well-oiled machine, and it felt good.

For years, we spent every weekend and a couple of summer-vacation weeks in the Prince William Sound from mid-June to September. Before and after that, all the bays were frozen, and we couldn't ensure anchor. Exploring for remnants of old gold mines built in the early 1900s became our favorite pastime. Visiting glaciers and picking up chunks of glacial ice for our cooler was a must. Awed by glaciers and their beautiful, blue color, I couldn't get enough of them.

When we drifted near a glacier and shut off the engine, we heard great explosions as the ice moved down the mountainsides. They were, after all, moving rivers of ice. The Prince William Sound is beautiful, peaceful, and safe if you honor the weather and respect the seas.

When we tried to think of a good name for our boat that first weekend, we decided on *The Sly Lady*. We had seen that name on a boat when we were on a vacation and liked it.

One Sunday afternoon, as we motored back to Wittier, we turned into the looming Port Wells, which was wide and deep. The wind had kicked up to about twenty-five knots, and there were small to medium white caps on the waves. Bill told me to stow anything not tied down. Then we saw a man in the water, holding onto his jet ski.

We looked through our binoculars and watched him being knocked around as his craft floundered on the waves. He wore a wet suit, but in that extremely cold water he was probably already going numb from hypothermia. I called the Harbor Master on our CB.

"Harbor Master, Harbor Master, this is the *Sly Lady*."

"Harbor Master to *Sly Lady*, go ahead."

"We're on our way in and there's a jet skier floundering out here. We're going to assist him as well as we can. Over."

"Copy that, *Sly Lady*, let me know if you need help. Harbor Master out."

A few minutes later, another voice broke in. "*Sly Lady*, *Sly Lady*, this is the *Klondike Express*. We have spotted the skier as well. If you will stand by, we have the equipment to hoist the jet ski and we'll get the skier as well, over."

The *Klondike Express* was a well-known tour boat that took hundreds of passengers on a twenty-six-glacier tour. We had enjoyed the excursion ourselves more than once. They monitored the cross-talk and had heard my call to the harbor master. Now, coming up behind us, they had spotted the jet skier as well.

"*Sly Lady* to *Klondike Express*, copy that," I replied. I appreciated that they would be assisting too.

Bill went to the back of the boat, hailed the man as we came closer to him, and threw him a life ring. The man's jet ski had run out of gas and he had been hanging onto it for about twenty minutes, with no life jacket. With hypothermia, the life vest wouldn't have mattered, but at least his dead body would have been recovered.

Bill pulled him up to our swim step and into the back of our boat. He told him that the *Klondike* was coming for him and asked him if he could hold on a few more minutes. He nodded. We threw a blanket over him, and I helped him sip some hot tea from a thermos we had in the cabin.

Then we backed off a bit so the *Klondike* could get closer. They sent a dingy for him. We helped him climb in, and they took him on board. His jet ski secured, they continued to the harbor. All the passengers were watching this rescue at sea.

We, too, watched the rescue at sea. In fact, we had rescued him, on a cold, windy, and gray afternoon. If we hadn't come along at that time, he might have died. It is amazing when *ella* puts us in the right place at the right time for her own reasons.

We were humbled, serious, and thankful that we were there to help in the *Sly Lady*.

Bill and I had great communication on the boat. We knew how to focus on a certain goal—to reach a specific bay, to hike the brushy land, to find artifacts from the early 1900s. Bill was in charge of the boat; I was in charge of everything else. We were a team, and that communication felt right. There was so much to see and do that talking wasn't a priority, unless a decision had to be made. This was our style. I never analyzed it. It felt right given the circumstances.

Our communication was compartmentalized, like the organization of our time. It ran on the cultural system that men were smarter than women, that one department dominated the other, and as in a well-oiled machine, feelings were stuck in psychic prisons. Allowing for flux or the rarity of transformation could only jeopardize the profits, the bottom line of a good organization.

In the evenings, at night, at home in my cedar sanctuary, Bill and I would meet, both worn out from our chosen fields. He stayed himself, and I was his. Bill, the story-telling, co-worker insulting, yet jovial strong man. And I, my stories inside, my gaze fixed on his face, as I listened with interest about his day.

Once, after a couple who had been visiting us left the house, he turned to me and said, "I'm so glad that woman is gone. She talks incessantly. I can't stand women who talk so much. That's why I like you. You don't talk that much." Around him, it was true. I didn't talk that much. I was afraid. And once I knew that was the way he liked it, that's the way I kept it, like the silence of the open tundra.

Our conversations were dutiful. "What do you want to eat for dinner?" I would make him anything he wanted. I wanted to please him, like a beautiful Alaskan sunset.

"I don't care" was his familiar answer. He never cared. I could open a can of chili, heat it up, and serve it to him with saltine crackers. He was happy as long as he didn't have to open the can and heat it himself. That was my department.

Our conversations were utilitarian. "When do I need to be ready to leave on Saturday morning?" I'd ask, whether we were going to the boat in the summer or skiing in the winter.

We spent more time with our sweetheart, Alaska, than we did each other. With both of us working and both of us traveling, we met on the weekends like good neighbors. And as the saying goes, "Good fences make good neighbors."

We would briefly meet to eat together, watch television together, and sleep together. Our life was on the surface, and we never dared to go beneath it. Don't dig into the permafrost; there might be something rotten down there. Or maybe there was a gem, waiting to be discovered.

I noticed that Bill gritted his teeth constantly. To me that indicated he was worried about something or that stress had built up inside him. But as his jaw muscles visibly popped under his cheek, I never asked him why he gritted his teeth. I never knew what was underneath him, and he never knew what was underneath me. Maybe we didn't know ourselves.

Once, we tried to break the fence down. A friend of his from work told him about a weekend workshop that his church was sponsoring. We never went to church. Bill didn't believe in it. The workshop was for couples' communication. Surprisingly, he agreed to go, with my enthusiastic support. We were taught how to write a letter to one another every day for fifteen minutes and then trade letters. We could talk about them if we chose. But that usually led to a disagreement.

The letters are long gone now, in reality and from my memory. They only lasted a couple of weeks in our hidden desire to tear down the fence. So back we went to our usual modus operandi. He went to work and traveled; I went to work and traveled. We met in the evenings and on weekends—he with his teeth-grinding stories of the day, and me with my headache and questions about dinner.

CHAPTER 20

Everybody Wins

Humankind has not woven the web of life. We are but one thread within it. Whatever we do to the web, we do to ourselves. All things are bound together. All things connect.
—Chief Seattle, Duwamish (1780–1866)

Like a traveler with a nameless longing, an inner voice within me would say, there are more people who need your help. I had gained tremendous experience with patients on the rehabilitation floor at the long-term care facility. Now I needed to coax my courage and introduce myself to the administrators at the hospitals. People with strokes, brain injuries, and swallowing disorders had no speech-language pathologists to help them. So, with some inherent bravery, I signed contracts with both of the largest hospitals in Anchorage and in all of Alaska.

When I summoned my courage and phoned the first hospital, I knew they had patients with stroke and traumatic brain injury. I felt for those patients as I called and set up an appointment to discuss a contract.

The local hospital had recently been taken over by a national chain, and it had been expanded and refurbished. As I walked in, I noticed they had placed slip-resistant industrial flooring in the entryway, a practical choice for Alaska's climate. The main carpet was soft and colorful. I noticed the soothing light-gray paint colors and mauve accents in the hall and looked out the large windows, north toward the Chugach mountains. Everything was sparkling clean. It looked like a modern, brand-new building.

I took the elevator up to the administrator's floor and walked down the brightly lit hallway to his office, thinking it must have cost millions of dollars to make all of the improvements. I announced myself to his assistant, and she asked me to take a seat. I settled in one of the beautiful hardwood chairs with mauve upholstery. While I waited, I thought about how I could convince this man that he needed my services and what I should be paid.

The door to his office opened. Here was a pale man in his late thirties, slim, with dark hair. He wore casual clothes, something I had gotten used to in Alaska. Some doctors even wore jeans. I never got used to that. Administrators in the Lower 48 always wore suits.

"Please come in," he said.

After we introduced ourselves and shook hands, I took a seat in front of his desk. "What a beautiful facility you have here. It's a great asset to the community," I began.

"Thank you. It has been quite an undertaking," he said. "It takes a lot of money to keep this place going."

He laid his cards on the table early. The insinuation was *we don't have any money to hire you.* At least, that's what the nervous me thought.

"Thank you for meeting with me. I'm sure you're very busy. I wanted to find out if you need speech-language pathology services for your patients. I have experience with people who have had strokes and head injuries, among other things. Have you been thinking about hiring an SLP?" I inquired.

He knew why I was there, but honestly, I couldn't get a read on whether he was considering hiring an SLP or not. We still had to educate administrators back then about what we did, who we served, and how they could bill for our time.

"You have a rehabilitation floor here, right?" I asked, as he fumbled with some papers. I don't know. The whole thing was awkward. Maybe I was supposed to schmooze more instead of getting right to the point of my visit. I didn't want to waste his time, so I might have seemed too forward. Finally, he answered.

"Well, yes, we do," he said. "But we don't need anyone full-time. What are you proposing?"

Now I knew what was holding him back. He thought I

wanted to work full-time. I knew that the hospital couldn't keep a full-time SLP busy. That wasn't my intention.

"I'd like to contract with you on an as-needed basis. I would basically be on-call and bill you by the hour. I'd provide all my own materials. That's what I do at the long-term care facility," I said, handing him my résumé and credentials.

He looked at my paperwork and agreed that the hospital did need the services of an SLP. We talked about money and settled on forty dollars per hour to start, with a yearly review. He told me that he would run it by his supervisor and get back to me. If the supervisor agreed, he would call, and I'd come back to sign the contract.

I got the call a few days later. My contract had been approved. I drove to the hospital, went to the administrator's office, and signed it. I was excited. The rehabilitation floor here was beautiful.

"I'll walk you out. I'll show you the staircase at the end of the building. It's a shortcut to the parking lot," he offered, as he was leaving too.

We went to the end of the hall and walked through the exit door. Still inside the building, it led down one story. It was the corner of the building, with light streaming in through large windows that revealed the outside parking lot. On the way up the stairs came a man in a very expensive looking suit. He was tall, tan, and healthy, like a general.

The administrator stopped him and said, "Let me introduce you to our new speech therapist. This is Kit Roberts. Kit, this is John Anderson. He's in charge of our operations for Alaska and the west coast. He's visiting us for a few days."

I was standing above John and reached my hand out to shake his. I had recently bought the book *Speaking Up*, by Janet Stone and Jane Bachner. They coached women to speak effectively and included how to introduce yourself. At the time, women were still trying to figure out if we should shake hands or not. To eliminate the awkward confusion, they recommended that we offer our hand first, to man, woman, or child. They reported that with a firm but brief handclasp, while maintaining eye contact, we established ourselves as friendly and serious.

I extended my hand down to John. "It's nice to meet you," I said with a friendly smile. He took my small hand with his large, muscular hand and put it in a vise grip. As my bones started to crack, he slowly squeezed it up and down, and to the side, so that his hand was now on top of mine, like we were having some kind of an arm-wrestling contest. I continued to look at his eyes and hoped he couldn't see the pain on my face, which I was desperately trying to hide. I wondered why he was doing this to me. Surely, he knew that he was crushing my hand. He finally let go and I continued down the stairs.

After I left the building, I rubbed my hand and shook my head in disgust. What was wrong with that guy? I knew that by turning his hand over mine, he was demonstrating power. And also, why didn't I say something to him? Why didn't I call him on it? Feeling afraid that if I had spoken up, possibly insulting him, he might have canceled my contract, I kept my mouth shut. So much for speaking up. My fear-generating bubble didn't stop me from thinking; it stopped me from talking. Thankfully, I never saw him again.

Still, I was proud of myself for initiating the contract meeting and landing the opportunity to work in the hospital and serve more people with communication disorders. And sure enough, it wasn't long before they started calling me to see patients.

After working at the hospital for a couple of years, however, I grew frustrated with the lack of new diagnostic methods available for people with dysphagia. Concerned, I pondered how to get the hospital to spend thirty thousand dollars on new equipment. I counted on my credibility.

Swallowing disorders, known as dysphagia, had become a new area of research and treatment for SLPs since the late 1970s and early 1980s. At my office, we were treating children with severe disabilities who lived in group homes. Several of them had swallowing problems.

Some children had chronic lung infections resulting from the inability to control their food or liquids when they swallowed—at least, that was our opinion. Instead of food moving down their esophagus into their stomachs, it slithered into their trachea, then into their lungs. Because they couldn't speak to tell us something was wrong, it was difficult to prove that the "rattle" sound in their lungs was from dysphagia—and potentially fatal. It could be treated with swallowing therapy, and the children's diets could be modified to stop the problem.

For example, we might restrict thin liquids, recommend a mechanical soft diet, and allow thick liquids only. The child must be in a full sitting position with supervised feeding and remain sitting for at least fifteen minutes after eating. At the very least, the situation required a proper diagnosis.

Adults with a head injury or stroke might also suffer from dysphagia. The musculature involved in swallowing could be paralyzed or weak, causing choking and coughing, with possible lung infections or complete airway obstruction. It was an important issue that needed to be addressed. Unfortunately, no one in the entire state of Alaska had a videofluoroscopy machine, which was necessary to diagnose dysphagia adequately. I wondered if I could change that.

Excited to make an impact at the hospital, in 1985 I flew to Los Angeles and attended the Diagnosis and Treatment of Dysphagia workshop, featuring the "mother" of dysphagia in our field. She had conducted most of the research for years. Her skills and knowledge were stellar. By the time the weeklong session was finished, I had the information needed to convince the hospital to get that equipment. I couldn't wait to get home.

When I returned, I wrote up a rationale for the dysphagia evaluation equipment and the justification for spending $30,000 on it, in 1985 dollars. After preparing a presentation, I showed the administrator the different kinds of swallowing studies. The most common is a barium swallow, during which a doctor has the patient drink a barium liquid, which lights up on an X-ray. The doctor notes how the barium traveled into the patient's stomach and how it emptied.

SLP studies were different. We used barium, yes, but that's where the similarity ended. We presented a thin liquid, a thick liquid, and barium paste on a cracker. Then, using videofluoroscopy, which records and shows real-time movement observed by fluoroscopy, we watched how the client chewed and swallowed each of the preparations. We watched what happened in the patient's mouth, nose, and throat. How long did it take them to swallow? Were they able to use their tongue correctly? Did any liquids or food items get stuck? Did material get into the larynx or the trachea? There were several parameters we were measuring. Videofluoroscopy was an important evaluation tool being used all around the country, and we needed it in Anchorage.

After the presentation, I submitted my request for the equipment to the administrator in writing, but he didn't give me much hope. He agreed to discuss it at his next meeting on equipment purchases. I tried not to get my hopes up. I was just an SLP, not a person with great influence. A few months had passed by the time I heard from him. He had discussed my information with other department heads and doctors, and they were more persuaded than he had been—they urged him to purchase the equipment.

The cardiologists needed one as well. Since they were on board, the hospital ordered all the items on the list I gave them, which included brand names and model numbers. I made it easy for them to spend that money, and what a boon for everyone.

Once the equipment arrived, I performed a few swallowing studies on patients with stroke and head injury. I brought in Janice, one of my contractors at the time, and showed her how to perform the evaluation.

She started educating the staff at the group homes about dysphagia and how to feed the residents who were under her care. One child had chronic lung infections and was being treated with antibiotics. She was under the age of seven and had moderate to severe cognitive and physical disabilities. Once the equipment was in place, Janice was eager to perform a dysphagia evaluation on the girl. She suspected that food and liquid were going into the girl's trachea, causing difficulty with breathing and possibly the reason for her lung infections.

When Janice came back from the evaluation, she had a tale to tell. Not only did food and liquid spill into this little girl's trachea, but her trachea was also almost completely compacted with matter. It was amazing she breathed at all. Janice watched the videofluoroscopy as the tiny amounts of barium-coated test items dribbled into her client's trachea. The girl required and received surgery to eliminate this rotting food.

Janice prescribed a feeding plan that addressed the girl's sitting position, the consistency of her food, and swallowing stimulation exercises. Her lung issues completely resolved with the correct diagnosis and treatment. This situation had evolved into a life-and-death dysphagia evaluation. The state-of-the-art evaluation tools were now available in Alaska to all who needed them, whether they suffered from a cardiac condition or dysphagia. I love it when everybody wins.

This scenario taught me that making an effort to improve the life of my patients with swallowing disorders had a ripple effect. It improved the diagnosis and treatment of many people in Alaska with a variety of disorders. Even if an improvement seemed too good to come true, it was important to make the effort to make it happen. I could have talked myself out of it because it seemed too daunting. But I had more power than I thought.

My knowledge on a variety of subjects and how they intertwined were at a high level. My power came from that knowledge, which I didn't fully appreciate at the time. I had the burning desire to make improvements happen, for the right reasons, so I pursued it. It was my calling, and my calling was teaching me to speak up, not just helping my patients to do so. Little by little, my calling penetrated my frozen speech bubble.

Eventually, I contracted with several hospitals around the state to evaluate and treat people with stroke, traumatic brain injury, laryngectomy, Guillain-Barre syndrome, and swallowing disorders. I flew to Kotzebue, Homer, and Cordova on an as-needed basis. All of these places rested in their own Alaskan beauty. They filled me with gratitude and awe. The many faces of Alaska are lovely to behold.

I couldn't wait to travel again. What wonders would I see next?

CHAPTER 21

Waiting for Break-up (Part 1)

There will be no child on the North Slope of Alaska who will be denied the opportunity to go to school.
—Eben Hopson

Thousands of years ago, a new epoch dawned: the epoch of the land of Beringia. She awakened before the pyramids of Egypt, before symbols were written, and before the land bridge to Beringia was swallowed by the sea. She covered the territory of what is now northern Russia, Alaska, and Canada. Fourteen thousand years ago, Beringia sprang to life.

Triumphant was the sun in his fiery heat. Mountains of ice from the Great Ice Age had dissolved. Laid bare, the long-lost land of Beringia appeared. She opened her presence to all who would dare to travel through her. Some who trekked were human newcomers, nomads traveling eastward from Asia, and they were enlivened by what they found. Roaming mastodons flourished in a countryside of grasses and herbs. Poplar, birch, and elder trees swayed in the breezes. People came, settled, and built their homes, such as they were. Tribes stayed near the water, for the sea provided sustenance.

Some traveled on, south, all the way to the Americas. For 4,000 years, the ice thawed and melted. The sea rose. The land bridge, which had conveyed the wanderers, eventually deferred to that rising sea. Ten thousand years ago, Beringia's land bridge drowned beneath the ocean. No longer able to cross, the people were cut off from their ancestors on the other side—unless they had boats to paddle in the summer waters before the sea froze again for the winter. To this day, the people on both sides of the sunken bridge share the same DNA.

Beringia, an ancient swath of planet Earth that still

exists today, was my next destination. Good fortune—or was it destiny?—impelled me to travel across the Alaskan portion of Beringia.

I received a call from the special education director in Barrow, the governmental seat of the North Slope Borough. "I need an SLP who can go to all of our villages, and I want to complete the work in two weeks. I'm hoping to get it done before break-up in May. Would you be available?" Phil asked.

Education in the villages had a checkered past. When the United States bought Alaska from Russia in 1867, the indigenous Alaskans were mostly ignored. That is, until gold was discovered in 1898. Suddenly, interest heightened. Catholic, Congregational, Episcopal, Methodist, and Presbyterian missionary groups were contracted as educators. They taught reading, writing, arithmetic, industrial skills, and citizenship in strict English-only classes.

In 1905, Congress passed the Nelson Act, which established segregated, dual school systems. Standard public schools were authorized for white children and a small number of "civilized" native children who lived in incorporated towns in the territory. Indigenous children in villages were consigned to the Bureau of Indian Affairs (BIA), which contracted with the churches. In Washington, DC, thousands of miles from Beringia, the fate of the children was sealed.

Using education to accomplish assimilation, civilization, and Christianization, the BIA slowly usurped the lives of the children. It dismantled the self-rule, self-sufficiency, and subsistence of indigenous Alaskans. For decades, this apartheid continued. When I moved to Alaska, it was in the process of being demolished.

If I took the job, I would fly the length and breadth of the largest county in the United States in a small plane. This land was above the Arctic Circle, which meant the sun never rose for over two months in the winter (a phenomenon known as polar night), and, likewise, it never set in the summer. Spring had come, and with it, abundant sunlight. However, it was still cold with snow, frigid with blowing winds, and tipping northward, causing the dreaded, but much anticipated, break-up.

During break-up, the frozen ocean, frozen rivers, and frozen runways melt and give way to savage chunks of ocean ice, deadly walls of rushing river ice, and soggy runways too dangerous for landing and take-off. This meant that for a few weeks in April or May, no one could get in or out of a village by plane (there were no roads), while waterways were opening for much-needed transportation of goods and fishing.

"Let me get back to you tomorrow," I said, not wanting to pass on business, but not sure it was business I wanted. "I'll check on some dates and see what I can work out."

Hearing his request, I sat back and let my mind wander. A calm, still, and capable feeling infused my body. The "real people," as Alaskan Yupiks called themselves—I would be with the real people. Outside in the sun, I saw their open faces and looked into their kind eyes. Raven black hair peeked from underneath their hoods or caps. Unhurried were the sounds of their boots as they walked on the squeaky snow. Under an endless sky, with the smell of that snow in the air, they had come to stay in Beringia. They had conquered it through cooperation, respect, and happiness. They had survived being conquered themselves, yet ghosts did remain. I valued their values and wished I could emulate them, using kind, quiet words to resolve problems. Yes, I do want to go to Beringia and see the real people again.

What about all those bush-plane rides? A gloomy, foreboding thought again drifted into my mind. Like a dike, I had shut out those waves of fear. I had developed a new attitude of acceptance thanks to a doctor I met waiting for the same plane in Anchorage. We were the only two people sitting in the boonies of the airport where the small chartered aircraft departed. I asked him, "Do you ever get nervous about flying in these small planes? Do you ever worry you might crash?" People crashed and died every year.

"I don't worry about crashing," he said, "because then I'd

be dead."

I thought about his answer. It had some logic to it. But what if your plane crashed and you lived, and you were out in the middle of nowhere and you couldn't be found, except by hungry bears? Those were the people I had worked with on the rehabilitation floors, the ones who crashed, perhaps on a glacier, and lived with serious head injuries. Rather than worry myself about it, I decided that his way of thinking was better than mine.

I became quite Zen about flying after that. If it was my time to die, then so be it. After all, this was my calling. If *ella* took me out, then it was meant to be. If *ella* kept me safe, that too was meant to be. After analyzing Phil's request, I chose to sign the contract for my longest journey yet into bush Alaska.

With my schedule cleared, approved by Bill, and my fortitude summoned, I called the director back the next day and gave him my answer: "Yes, I can take the job."

I knew from experience that this late in the school year there would be no fresh fruit or vegetables on the North Slope. All the food in the villages had to be ordered and shipped on barges, which arrived no later than August. The food needed to be enough to last the whole year, until the next barge could get through open water after break-up. Otherwise, they would have to buy from the local and limited store or fly it up from Anchorage—both very expensive. I usually took something fresh as a surprise. In this case, I asked Phil.

"Is there anything I can bring you from Anchorage?"

Rather than ask for fresh oranges or apples, he said, "A case of Budweiser Light."

But Barrow was dry at the time. People weren't supposed to have alcohol up there. I wondered if I was breaking the law by bringing it, but if it was okay with him, it was okay with me.

"All right," I said, not bringing up the subject of being dry. "I'll see you in a couple of weeks."

"I'll meet you at the airport," he replied.

"Thanks. Bye." That was easy. There were only a couple of flights a day, and he knew I would arrive in the morning. The town was so small, he could hear the plane land. I didn't need to call him from the airport—if they even had a public phone there.

A couple of weeks later, I spent Sunday preparing and packing for my trip. I brought my materials and audiometer home from the office. This time I had something new, an otoscope, a hand-held device used to look into the ears. Ear infections were prevalent in Alaska and the bush. These conditions required medical attention. If I discovered a child with an infection, I could get him or her some help. I couldn't stand the idea that a child would have to suffer because no one knew what was wrong. Conditions and services in the villages were catching up, but medical treatment was as sorely lacking as sunlight in the winter.

This trip was a milestone for me. I'd be traveling to places I'd never been before, and I was excited. While I had never been to these particular villages, I had been to enough other villages to know the ropes. I learned what to pack. Once there, I knew to take the time in the evenings to get my reports written up to the point where I could finish them on my typewriter when I got home. And on this trip, I'd have an extra weekend to write reports as well.

There were two historical landmark decisions taking place on the North Slope at the time I started traveling there. First, the Molly Hootch lawsuit in 1976 had stopped the practice of shipping native Alaskan children to faraway places, such as Sitka, Oklahoma, Oregon, and California, for high school. This meant that I worked with the first generation of native Alaskan children to go to high school in their own village, where they wouldn't be traumatized, punished for speaking their native language, and raped or killed. In fact, I was working with just the fourth generation of native Alaskans since 1900.

Second, the initial shipments of oil through the Alaska Pipeline from the great oilfields in the North Slope Borough had started in 1977. This meant that the North Slope had received millions of dollars from oil revenues to build the new schools and hire the new faculty to teach the new high school students in each village. The BIA was out, and the North Slope took over the education of its children. The borough spent its oil money to build new homes, fire departments, and community centers. Everything converged at just the right time. Indigenous Alaskans on the North Slope were well into their village upgrades when I arrived. As a guest, I absorbed the hopeful atmosphere and focused on my work.

The Alaska Pipeline, which is built off the ground, crosses the Tanana River, south of Fairbanks and close to Delta, AK, 1977. Photo: Kit Roberts

It was during this climate of renewal, regeneration, and respect in the late 1970s and early 1980s that I started flying to these villages. For the most part, it was a prosperous, enthusiastic, and welcoming environment. The oil at Prudhoe Bay started to flow through the pipeline at 1.5 million barrels per day. Over the next forty years, billions of dollars in oil revenues were allocated to state and local governments, such as the North Slope Borough.

As recently as 2020, new fields continued to be discovered. With money came autonomy. Indigenous Alaskans started to restore their culture with their children safe at home. Elders taught native language classes in the schools, and new laws protected their subsistence rights for hunting whale and walrus. As the days approached for my visit, my worries were replaced with excitement as I realized I was venturing into an anthropologist's paradise—a unique and vibrant culture in one of the most remote places on the earth.

Barrow

I had seen many beautiful lands—the lush paradise of Hawaii, the piney evergreens of Seattle, and the redwood forests of California. Now I headed for a different kind of beauty on the planet Earth, a beauty so cold, so dark, and so dry that fewer than 5,000 people lived on over 90,000 square miles of land, equivalent to the size of thirty-nine states. Scattered were its villages, and with the exception of one in the Brooks Mountain Range in the south, the other seven resided in the arctic desert known as the tundra. Endlessly flat.

I gazed in awe out of the Alaska Airlines jet window. There was nothing, yet it was full. It was noble, yet unrefined. It was stable, yet fragile. It was cognizant, yet thoughtless. It went on without interruption.

This is the tundra, primeval. But where are the trees that held the birds, and where is the land on which mastodon roamed? Frozen over with snow like dust, nothing is left but its permafrost—land and soil that remain frozen most of the year and only melt to a few feet deep over the summer. This thawing allows shallow plants to take hold in the boggy landscape. Trees cannot take root. Because it is a flat canvas, it allowed my mind to wander, to think about my work, my patients, and my skills. I imagined new plans and reaffirmed who I was and why I was here—on this plane, in this state, and in my profession. I realized how effortless it all was, if I got out of my own way, if I listened to my enthusiastic self.

On a cold and sunny morning, Bill had dropped me off early at the Anchorage airport. As he kissed me goodbye, I reminded him, "I won't be calling you for the next two weeks unless something really serious happens." He nodded and drove off to get to work. There was only one telephone in a village, and I didn't want to use it to chat. Long-distance phone calls were expensive, and I didn't want to prevent a local person from talking.

My jet approached Barrow in the bright sunlight that reflected off the snow. I saw that it was different from the other villages I had visited. It had masses of phone and power lines crisscrossing every corner. Houses stood built off the ground. There were trucks and cars driving on the snow-covered roads. I had only seen snow machines or snow-gos (the local names for snowmobiles) or four-wheelers in the villages. And they didn't have roads, they had "paths."

Soon my luggage started coming down the ramp in the bustling baggage area. Then came the case of beer. *Damn,* I thought, *I should have wrapped it in brown paper*. Everyone could see it. Several minutes had passed since landing, and I wondered if Phil was on his way. Suddenly, there he was, a tall, slim, thirty-something man scooping up the beer and quickly taking it to his truck. Then he came back and helped me with the rest of my baggage.

On the way to school, we exchanged pleasantries, meeting one another face-to-face. Then Phil asked me, "I have a boy in preschool I'd like you to test. Is that possible? He's got a lot of developmental delays and he's supposed to start kindergarten next year. His teacher doesn't know if she should advance him or not."

I didn't usually screen preschoolers unless a teacher had made a specific request. But it was fine with me. I had the rest of Monday and all of Tuesday for testing. "Sure. No problem," I replied.

Too big to be a village, Barrow had the largest population on the North Slope. Of the 2,200 residents, the majority were 1,700 native Alaskans, mostly Iñupiat. It had a hotel and a restaurant, and commercial jets landed there. People who traveled in Alaska hoped to stop in Barrow at least once. They could then boast that they had reached the northern-most city in the United States, and almost in the world. Situated near the Arctic Ocean, just 1,300 miles south of the North Pole, Barrow was built on permafrost, which had started to melt a little more than usual during the summer. This warming created concerns about the sewer system, built twenty feet underground in a series of heated tunnels.

Phil arranged for me to stay with an older couple. Both were teachers, and their home was attached to the school. I didn't need to go outside to get to their place. That was nice. It was below freezing and windy. As much as I was interested to be there, I wasn't motivated to walk around town, even though the skies were blue. I gathered my materials and got to work, starting with the little boy Phil had told me about.

I went to the preschool room and quietly nodded to the teacher. "Hello, I'm Mrs. Roberts, the speech therapist, here to see George. Is he here today?"

"Oh, yes," she said. "Thanks for coming. He's been with me since the age of three. He's scheduled to start kindergarten next year, but I don't think he's ready. I really appreciate you checking him." She was a knowledgeable and young teacher.

"Where is he?"

She pointed to him.

As soon as I saw him, I knew George was different. His face appeared flat, his eyes were short in width, and his upper lip was thin. He looked smaller than his peers, and instead of participating in the class activity, he was off to the side pounding toys on the ground. This is often an indication that the child can't follow the directions of a lesson, understand the words the teacher is using, or attend to the activity.

"How's his English?" I asked. Many of the elders spoke Iñupiaq. The younger people understood some of their native language and spoke a few words and phrases. English had become the language of the younger generations.

"He speaks English at home and at school," she replied.

"That's great. Could I borrow a few toys and books from the room that he likes?"

She gathered up a few things for me. I took George by his hand, and we walked to a back corner in the room. I laid out all the toys and books on the floor, and we sat down.

"My name is Mrs. Roberts," I told him with a smile. "Let's play with the toys." I waited a moment and asked, "George, what do you like? What do you want to play with?" I waited to see if he would point to something or pick up one of the objects. "Show me." I waited another thirty seconds. When he didn't move, I followed his gaze to the teddy bear and said, "Where's teddy bear? That's right. You hold it." I picked it up and handed it to him.

"Where's his eyes?"

George pounded the stuffed animal on the ground over and over again in rapid succession. Eventually, I stopped him. I held the bear in front of him and slowly said, "Where are his eyes?" He didn't respond. I asked him to show me the bear's ears, arms, and legs. He shook his head back and forth. He wouldn't point or couldn't point. It was an intellectual problem, a sensory processing problem, and/or a speech processing problem, which had become a behavior problem. He was showing me that he couldn't follow my command at that time.

"Where are your eyes? Show me. Here are my eyes," I pointed to them. "Show me your eyes."

He didn't respond then, but a few minutes later, he picked up the teddy bear, pointed to its eyes and said, "Eyes." He had a delayed response, meaning he needed more time to process speech and language. This indicated impaired sensory processing and executive function as well.

"Good thinking," I cheered him. "You showed me eyes. Let's look at your favorite book." I gently opened to the first page. "Where's the dog?"

George looked at the page, hit it, and knocked the book out of my hand.

"What does the dog say?" I picked up the book and prompted him, "Woof, woof, bark, bark."

He was silent. Then I got the teddy bear, a toy dog, and a

toy whale. "Give me the dog," I said.

He picked up the dog and said, "Woof."

So identifying the dog in a book was harder than identifying the object, the toy dog. The picture is more abstract than the toy, the toy being more concrete. And the word *dog* was the most abstract of all because he had to know the sound of the word and picture the dog in his mind to match it up with the picture in the book or the toy dog. He had to use both the visual and auditory parts of his brain, the right and left hemispheres, as we all do to receive and express language. He had to cross the corpus collosum. This was all good.

By hitting the book and knocking it out of my hands, he was telling me that the task was too hard. Most five-year-old children can listen to a book. His inability to do this indicated he had a poor attention span for auditory information—listening. He couldn't concentrate on one thing long enough to participate in a kindergarten class.

I gave him a yellow crayon and a piece of paper and got the same for myself. I wanted to observe his eye-hand coordination. "Let's make the sun." I started to draw a large circle on my paper. George scribbled back and forth on his paper and held the crayon like someone would hold a knife to stab something. He hadn't learned how to hold the crayon correctly. He had been in school for over two years, so he had had plenty of teaching, practice, and encouragement. At his age, he should have been able to draw a crude circle while I was demonstrating it beside him.

Suddenly, George got up and ran around the room. This indicated that he had a short attention span for sitting and performing cognitive tasks, like listening, talking, and drawing. He needed to move and complete tasks that involved his whole body. His nervous system wasn't mature enough to sit in one place for long. A kindergartner has a twenty-minute attention span. Then they need to move and change to a new activity or teaching skill. George didn't last more than a few minutes before he had to move, even though I tried to make my test items interactive.

Playing with a variety of objects and looking at the pictures in the books, I had checked his receptive and expressive language level. I had listened for the sounds he could make, how intelligible he was, and if his voice was normal and his speech fluent. Using the International Phonetic Alphabet, I had written down everything he said. I analyzed his mean length of utterance and his ability to follow a one-, a two-, or a three-step command. Watching how he played with selected items, I checked his developmental level of play. I observed his behavior and attention span. If he overreacted to sensory stimulation or was under-responsive, I noted it. I observed when he shut down, when he cheered up, and his general attitude. We were together about twenty-five minutes.

In those twenty-five minutes I concluded that George, an almost five-year-old boy, was developmentally two years old for speech and language development. He had intellectual disabilities, attention deficits, behavior issues, sensory-processing impairments, and poor executive functioning. He had the full range of fetal alcohol syndrome disabilities, and they were severe.

Alcohol consumption soared during the 1980s in Alaska. That's when I had first encountered a child with a fetal alcohol spectrum disorder (FASD). This totally preventable and devastating disability is caused by women consuming alcohol during their pregnancy. One session of binge drinking—a total of four alcoholic drinks in two hours—between days 17 and 22 of the pregnancy can damage the lower brain, the corpus callosum, and cause abnormal facial features in the baby. Women generally don't know they are expecting a baby until they are five to nine weeks pregnant. These mothers don't understand that alcohol is affecting their child in the womb because they don't realize they are pregnant. FASD is just one crippling consequence of alcoholism.

SLPs don't diagnose FASD. We diagnose the speech and language strengths and weaknesses of children with this birth defect. In the 1980s, they were labeled as children with fetal alcohol syndrome (FAS). Since then, the disorder has been further defined. It includes people with partial fetal alcohol syndrome (pFAS), who may have a combination of facial features, behavior and cognitive deficits, growth retardation, and neurodevelopmental abnormalities.

Children with alcohol-related birth defects (ARBD) can suffer from heart, kidney, and/or bone problems. Their vision and hearing may also be negatively affected.

Those with alcohol-related neurodevelopmental disorder (ARND) might present with intellectual, behavior, and learning disabilities. They don't have the abnormal facial features, but they do have brain damage. Without a confirmation of their mothers' alcohol consumption during pregnancy, these children may be misdiagnosed or missed altogether. Why does it matter? Treatment.

FASDs are lifelong impairments. Alcohol crosses into the baby during pregnancy through the mother's placenta and umbilical cord. It interferes with cell development and causes brain cells to die prematurely. Most of the children are born with smaller brains and specific defects in the frontal lobe, the corpus callosum, the cerebellum, the hippocampus, and the basal ganglia. These defects impact decision-making, planning and organization, memory and learning, motor control, attention, and behavior. As the children mature, their disabilities become more pronounced. Their damaged brains cannot keep pace with the more complex cognitive-language and behavioral skills that gradually develop as they grow into adulthood.

Native Alaskans didn't always have alcohol. The elders noted that when they first saw a person staggering with their arms seesawing and making loud noises, it was like being punched in the heart. They thought maybe that person was having a seizure; they hadn't seen this behavior before. When the men and women drank alcohol, they sang loudly and danced. Later, they would start to fight. When treaties were being signed in the late 1800s and early 1900s, Alaskan natives were plied with alcohol so that they would agree to whatever was presented. The introduction of alcohol into their culture has had devastating effects.

Alcohol is the worst teratogen—an agent that can induce abnormalities of growth in the development of an embryo or fetus. It settles in specific organs and concentrates in the brain. If a woman is pregnant, there is no known safe amount of alcohol, no harmless type of alcohol, and no healthy time to drink it. It is the leading cause of mental deficiency in the United States and Europe, and two to seven percent of all school-aged children are on the fetal alcohol spectrum. In the United States, one in one hundred babies are born on the spectrum. Alaska reports the highest documented prevalence of FASD in America and admits that its diagnostic system has limitations.

During the same years I traveled to the villages—1977 to 1992—143 cases of children with FASD were *officially* identified. Eighty-three percent of the children with FASD were born to just fifteen percent of the population, native Alaskans. Alaska's system for dealing with this preventable and lifetime damage to a human being faltered in its support for indigenous Alaskans.

George was one of these casualties of Alaska's history of conquest through alcohol. I wrote up a program for George that included simplifying his goals and objectives, eliminating negative consequences, and modifying his environment to make things easier for him. His treatment focused on reducing anxiety and calming his nervous system so that his frontal lobes, which handled information processing and executive functioning, could be accessed.

For communication, I recommended a picture exchange system. He could access or select a photograph of an activity to indicate his wants or needs to his teacher or peers. It could be used to organize his day as well, so that he would know what was coming next. Ensuring no surprises or unexpected changes would help to keep his nervous system calm. I spoke with his teacher and parents about this plan before I left. Loving him was the final, and most important, recommendation. He needed a safe harbor and quiet time.

When I finished screening Tuesday afternoon, I walked around outside after school to get some fresh air. A group of older elementary kids were standing near the ocher-painted building in the sunshine, just talking and chillin'. Boys and girls wore their fur parkas. They all had their fur ruffs up or wore stocking caps. The girls' parkas, covered with calico or other fabric, had skirts that fell to their knees. The boys' parkas were darker and covered their hips. They all wore mittens and boots. They smiled and posed themselves when I asked if I could take their picture, some goofy and all happy. I had gotten braver about asking to take their pictures. I thought it might be rude or against their culture, but it was neither of these. It was me being nervous and wanting to be respectful. Then, I went inside and prepared to catch my next flight on Wednesday morning.

Beringia awaited. Spellbound, I found the night passed quickly as trepidation fought with excitement in my head and heart. This adventure was just beginning. In the morning, composed and confident, I set foot into the bush plane and set off for Wainwright.

Kids will be kids. After school, April 1983. Photo: Kit Roberts

CHAPTER 22
Waiting for Break-up (Part 2)

Wainwright

There, in the small Barrow airport, waited about thirty local women and fifteen men. Warm in the well-lit room, sitting in several double rows of plastic chairs that attached back-to-back, the women glowed with happiness. Matrons and maidens alike relaxed in their calico kuspuks, with colorful trim, jeans, and warm boots. If they had a coat, it was a short, handmade parka that hung off their shoulders. Leaning this way and that, they spoke with affection to each other and passed on the news and tales of the day. The men were mostly quiet or just listening to the women. They all came for the jet from Anchorage—some to greet a passenger and some to catch it back.

Like the men, I, too, listened to the women, watching for my chartered plane to be displayed. While I didn't understand their words, I did understand their tone of voice. Filled with joy, happiness, and spunk, they gabbed, laughed, and interacted like any other delighted group of people I had ever seen. Why was I so impressed? Because they spoke their native language.

I had been led to believe that their language was dying. That was a shame and a sorrow for me. I knew that languages conveyed more than words. I wanted their meta-communication to remain with the people. That wouldn't happen if it faded into oblivion. Many native languages had already been lost or diminished. Now I felt the hope and heard the joy of people speaking their timeless, traditional words.

My chartered plane was ready. The pilot loaded my bags in the hold. As we pulled out of Barrow, I leaned back, took a deep breath, and relaxed into the matchless, divine openness of the North Slope tundra. Tranquil, I stared at it until my eagle eyes, bathed in white and blue light, closed with humility. A new village awaited. For now, rest.

Flying just eighty-six miles, we landed in Wainwright, located along the Chukchi Sea where it meets the Arctic Ocean. Its small population of 402 flourished on the western edge of the North Slope Borough, southwest of Barrow. I arrived mid-morning, wearing my full winter attire. A white man, who appeared to be in his late forties, waited for me in a white truck. It was the first pickup truck I had ever seen in a village. I looked forward to the warm cab. He yelled out the window, "You can put your things in the back seat."

"Thanks," I nodded, and he watched me load my bags.

"I'm Chuck," he said as I closed the door and we started to drive toward the village.

"Hi, I'm Kit Roberts, here to do some work at the school."

"Nice to meet you," he smiled. "I'm doing some construction here. The principal asked me to take you to the house. It's close to the school."

"The house?" I asked.

"Yep. Wainwright built a three-bedroom house for all of us travelers who come through town. You have your own room. Two of them are empty right now, so you have your pick."

"Oh, okay," I replied. Hmm, instead of sleeping in the school or with the teachers, I had a whole house. Fantastic. On the other hand, I didn't know this guy from Adam, so I was a bit guarded. He seemed nice enough.

Approaching the place, I noticed that a large swath of ground in front of it seemed to be an ice-skating rink. We drove up the slight grade to the front door.

"It's real slick here right now," he said. "With break-up coming, we've had some thawing during the day, then it freezes at night. It's glare ice all the way to the door, so be careful when you get out. I'm just gonna drop you off and get back over to my job. I'll be back later around dinner time. Do you need any help?"

"I think I can get it. Thanks."

My boots were great on crunchy snow, like at the airstrip, but on ice they turned glassy. As I opened the door and stepped onto the solid ice, I almost slipped. The soles of my boots were like smooth, hard plastic. Carefully, I opened the truck's back door and pulled out my luggage, the hard-sided, hot pink, high school graduation gift that I had lugged around ever since. Then my feet went right out from under me. My ribs crashed into the corner of the hard suitcase as I reflexively grabbed the door handle with my right hand and the back seat with my left. It did stop my fall, but I bruised a few ribs in the process.

"You okay?" my driver queried.

"I'm fine, I'm fine," I lied.

Tenderly and gingerly, I carried my luggage inside. It hurt to laugh or take a deep breath for several weeks. I didn't want to admit that I needed help. After all, I was as capable as a man. Subsequently, I bought a pair of crampons—metal spikes with adjustable straps that attached to the bottom of my boots, dug into the frozen ground, and made walking on ice much safer. Every time I went to a village, I learned I needed something new.

I arranged my gear, cautiously walked over to the school on some crunchy snow, and introduced myself to the principal. He was another middle-aged white man. I hoped to meet an Alaska native principal, but it hadn't happened yet. I explained that I would be here for the rest of the day and tomorrow. He showed me where to store my materials, and I began the usual screenings, including those for hearing. When I used the audiometer, I placed a pair of over-the-ear headphones on a child after I coached them to raise their hand when they heard a sound.

My directions went something like this. "You're going to hear some sounds now. Some sounds will be loud, and some will be soft. Some sounds will be *way up high*"—I said this in a high voice—"and some will be *way down low*"—in a low voice. "When you hear the sound, raise your hand like this"—I demonstrated. "Let's do a couple for practice. Remember to raise your hand when you hear it. Ready?"

Developed by audiologists, this ability to say "yes" or "no" by raising a hand or a finger in response to hearing a pure tone was a tried-and-true method for children and adults taking a hearing test. While still watching the audiometer, the tester saw the subject's hand lift in their periphery and changed the dial to the next sound level at the same time. I learned, however, that the native Alaskans had an even better way of saying "yes" and "no."

As I continued testing, I noticed that a child sometimes forgot to raise his or her hand when I knew they must have heard the sound. I gently reminded them again of how to show me they heard it by raising their hand. I started to observe what they were doing with their faces even before their hand came up. For "yes," a child raised his or her eyebrows, for "no," she lowered them. This was the standard way the Iñupiat indicated "yes" or "no" nonverbally.

Other people might nod or shake their heads for "yes" or "no." But this simple eyebrow movement was much more efficient. Of course, that meant that I, the tester, had to watch the child's face to determine if they had heard the sound. Only in Alaska.

When I evaluated a fourth grader named Evelyn, she did great on the speech screening. When I checked her hearing with the audiometer, it was fine. Then I examined her ears with the otoscope. I was stunned.

I had never seen this before. I had peered into hundreds of ears. Stopping myself from gasping, I calmly withdrew the otoscope, wiped it off, and looked again. Still astonished, I asked Evelyn if her ears ever hurt, especially *this* ear.

"No."

"Do you remember if you ever had any ear infections when you were younger?"

"Yes."

I asked her if she ever put anything sharp in her ear.

"No."

I couldn't diagnose the reason for her problem, but this girl needed to fly to Anchorage and have a consultation with an ENT, an ear, nose, and throat specialist, as soon as possible. She had a large hole in her eardrum—the tympanic membrane. The only remaining part was where the malleus attached to the back side of the membrane. I saw her entire middle ear, the three smallest bones in the body, and they had lots of "dust" on them. She needed a myringoplasty to repair her eardrum. During the middle of the day, I asked the principal to contact one of Evelyn's parents to have them come to talk with me.

Not much later, her father arrived at school. He wore a jacket, a plaid shirt, and jeans. We sat in the cafeteria. After introducing myself, he asked how the exam went.

"Well, Evelyn has good speech and good hearing. But when I looked in her ear with this light," I said, showing him my otoscope, "I saw that she has a hole deep inside her ear. That's not normal. Did she ever have ear infections when she was younger?"

"Yes, and the doctor gave her some medicine for it. She got over it okay."

"Did she have many ear infections or just one?" I asked.

"She had lots of them." he replied.

"Well, she probably got the hole from one of her ear infections, but it's not good to leave it like that. She might get more infections, and that would be bad for her hearing. We don't want her to get sick or be deaf in that ear."

"Can you fix it?" His brow tightened.

"No. Only an ear, nose, and throat doctor can do that. It takes a special kind of surgery, and she'll have to go to Anchorage. If I get it set up, can you take her there?" I asked.

"Sure. When?" He shifted from side to side.

"That I don't know yet. I'll talk to the principal about getting her a referral to Anchorage, and then you can work it out with him. I have to leave tomorrow."

I wondered how long Evelyn had endured this, undiagnosed and in possible jeopardy. At least she would get some help now. Bringing that otoscope along had turned out to be a good decision.

Girls on their Ski-Doo after school, April 1983. Photo: Kit Roberts

After school, I bundled up and traipsed around the village. I waved at a couple of girls, maybe ten years old, riding on their skidoo. The driver, wearing a pink stocking cap with red trim, sun glasses, a dark fur coat, and beige fur mittens, drove on the cold snow. The girl sitting in the back wore her fur parka with the brown ruff pulled snugly around her face. Her pink pants and red snow-boots were a bright flash of color against the black snowmobile. She flashed rabbit ears over the driver's head and laughed. Behind them, miles of flat, snowy tundra watched over them.

The village was only several acres, so I couldn't get lost. It was sunny, windy, and cold as I walked on the well-worn path. As I strolled around a corner, I saw a small dog on a short rope, chained to a stake. Dogs were common in villages, but this wasn't a big, furry dog like a Husky; he was a little dog like my mother-in-law in California might have. I stopped and looked at him. He sat on his haunches with his front legs hugged in tight. The wind came from the north, and he had positioned his back to it. He sat like a statue, stiff and still. His thin and scraggly hair trembled in the wind.

Flooded with concern, I stared at him. He weighed about nine pounds, not fifty-nine. He shouldn't have been out in the cold like that. I looked at him with sympathy. I thought about picking him up and tucking him inside my parka. But I didn't know this dog, and he didn't know me. He might be a Tasmanian Devil for all I knew and would rip me to shreds.

I contemplated stepping up to the house and knocking on the door to see if the owners were home. I would ask them why they chained the dog outside. I would plead his case, that it was too cold to leave him out there. Perhaps they chained him outside for a short time in the afternoon to get some sun and fresh air, which would be good for him, but he should wear a coat. But that was my cultural thinking, not theirs. He didn't make eye contact with me, just stared straight ahead, as if I didn't exist. The two of us were stuck in our cultures, me wanting to treat him like a California dog, him being an Alaskan village dog. I was the visitor; it was none of my business. He lived there and probably sat outside every day.

My heart filled with compassion for him having to be in the cold and for me having to leave him there. It was mind over matter for now. Just survive this moment. The polar wind blew steadily on both of us as we were left to our own devices. Compassion was the best I could offer that day. I didn't intervene.

As I continued around the village, I noticed some white fur skins hanging on a wooden drying rack. There were three of them, one large and two small, covered with snow. I found out later that three polar bears had stalked the village earlier in the winter. Once bears know where they can find food, that place becomes part of their daily path. They return again and again. Training these bears to stop coming was impossible. Having them anesthetized and moved away was out of the question. They had to be put down. Humans are prey to Nanook—polar bears.

A polar bear hide on a wooden drying rack, Wainwright, Alaska. April 1983. Photo: Kit Roberts

The stark reality of life in the Arctic moved through me like a cold wave from the Bering Sea. I rippled with the swirling choices that had to be made: kill or be killed, fight for your life or die. It was a choice that these peoples had made for thousands of years and still made. Sometimes we fight and only a part of us dies. But *ella* knows it all and remembers it and makes us whole in time. The harshness of Mother Nature had been hidden from me in the Lower 48, but it was on full display in Alaska. I never went long without seeing it. It took an emotional toll on me as I never wanted anyone or anything to suffer. The mother polar bear who saw her babies killed—or maybe it was the other way around, the babies who saw their mother killed—did they experience momentary fear or sadness?

I thought more and more about mothers and babies—that I was supposed to be a mother and have a baby. But I too had been skinned, and my ability to bear a child had been taken from me with a scalpel. For now, I accepted what I couldn't change, to "stay in my lane." I was the lone SLP on the entire North Slope at the moment, unaccompanied in unparalleled emptiness. I had the knowledge to help. That's what I did. In fact, caring for others filled me with tenderness and enthusiasm, two healthy feelings that counteracted my physical or emotional pain.

I walked back to the itinerant housing, and Chuck was there getting ready to cook his dinner. I now saw that he was about six feet tall and had gray hair. He was fit, and his face was tan. He sliced onions on the counter.

"Have you ever eaten walrus liver? How about muktuk?" he asked.

"No, I haven't," I said.

"Well, I'm making some walrus liver and onions. Do you want a piece?"

"Sure, I'll try a small piece, emphasis on 'small.' I used to eat beef liver and onions with ketchup when I was a kid. Since moving to Alaska I've even had buffalo liver, which tastes much better than beef liver to me."

He seemed like a regular guy at this point, no one to worry about. I relaxed into eating my unusual dinner.

He watched my face as I placed a bite of rubbery and sandy walrus liver in my mouth. It had to be chewed well. And each time I chomped down on it, I felt the grit of the sand in my teeth. I don't remember much about the taste, except that it had a fishy smell to it.

Now about the muktuk. This is frozen whale blubber cut in little cubes, and another traditional native food. My housemate took some from the freezer compartment of the white refrigerator in the kitchen. Muktuk had a yellowish-tan color, like most fat.

"Here, try this. Pop it in your mouth and swallow it down. Don't roll it around or let it begin to thaw and then chew it. Just chug it, so to speak."

"Okay."

Of course, I had to taste it, but I didn't hold onto it for long. It tasted like fishy fat. With the weather conditions in the Arctic in the winter, I imagined that I'd come to love a few pieces of muktuk to help me keep my weight up and keep me warm. Additionally, it was high in vitamins C and D.

Walrus liver and muktuk were two of the most

unique indigenous Alaskan subsistence foods I ever had the opportunity to eat. The ability to continue to hunt and consume subsistence animals is critical for people in the villages. Not only is other food scarce, especially in the winter, but as the saying goes, you are what you eat. The foods they ate made them who they were and kept their bodies healthy.

We finished dinner and talked about our impressions of this enduring Arctic village of Wainwright. The next day, after school, I was off once again to my next stop, the smallest village on the Slope.

CHAPTER 23
Waiting for Break-up (Part 3)

Point Lay

April 1983. Photo: Kit Roberts

I waited inside the warm truck for my plane to arrive. Silently, I thanked the weather gods that break-up hadn't ruined this runway yet. The pilot loaded my gear to Point Lay, the smallest village on the slope, with a recorded population of sixty-eight, sixty-three of whom were Iñupiat. Traditionally a fish camp and hunting spot, Point Lay officially organized into a village in 1972. Due to erosion, the village had to be moved to higher ground and rebuilt. Oil money paid for it all.

The people who populated Point Lay wanted to live a more traditional lifestyle. They got to do it with a new school, a large fire station, a community store with a post office inside, utility buildings, a public works building, and a village corporation–run camp. It also had North Slope Borough (NSB) housing.

NSB housing was a standard three-bedroom home with oil stove heating and running water. It reminded me of a house we had rented on Vashon Island, when I worked in Seattle. My whole neighborhood was filled with them. They were "kit" homes. They arrived with walls, floors, and roofs partially built, and a crew assembled the rest of it.

I hoped the contractors added in double-paned windows and better insulation for the houses of Point Lay. If they were like the single-paned windows and poorly insulated homes that we had on Vashon, they would have been extremely difficult to keep warm in the winter. Single-pane windows were close to worthless when the wind blew and the weather turned cold.

Once I arrived at the school, I met the pleasingly plump woman who taught the early grades. She was married to the principal, who taught the older students' classes. I got organized and began with a routine screening of the six-year-olds.

One boy caught my attention. He dressed in a buttoned, long-sleeved shirt, jeans, and sneakers. He was adorable, with his short haircut and gentle countenance. After giving him instructions to *say what I say*, I heard him struggle to speak sounds made in the front of his mouth.

"Say *rabbit*," I asked him with a smile.

"Wabbit," he replied, substituting a /w/ for an /r/ at the beginning of the word.

"Say *arrow*."

"Awow," he replied, substituting a /w/ for an /r/ in the middle of the word.

"Say *leaf*."

"Weaf," he replied, substituting a /w/ for a /l/ at the beginning of the word.

"Say *bathtub*."

"Batub," he replied, substituting a dentalized /t/ for a /th/ in the middle of the word.

"Say *teeth.*"

"Teet," he replied, again with his tongue tip down on the /th/, making a soft /t/ sound.

"Say *ball.*"

"Bah," he replied, omitting the /l/.

After checking twenty words, I stopped. The latest sound to develop in English is /r/. It can emerge at the age of eight and still be within normal limits. In fact, in Los Angeles, school SLPs weren't allowed to work with a child with an /r/ delay until the age of eight. But this child's pronunciation indicated something more problematic. To discover the issue, I gave him an oral exam.

"Open your mouth big and say *ah*, like this, *ahhhhhhh.*"

He took a big breath and said, "Ahhhhhhh."

While his mouth was open, I checked his palate, his teeth, and his bite. All normal.

"Now make the tip of your tongue touch the corner of your mouth like this." I demonstrated.

"Now touch the other corner, like this." As I watched each of his movements, I saw the blade of his tongue, not the tip. The tip was restricted behind and below his bottom lip.

Seeing that his tongue movement was severely impaired, I asked him for one last move. "Put your tongue way up high like me, all the way to your nose." I saw immediately that he had a tiny lingual frenulum on the underside of his tongue that attached all the way to his tongue tip.

The lingual frenulum is a short, white cord located under the tongue. It attaches at the base of the tongue and stretches about halfway up, to the sublingual gland. If it continues beyond that point, closer to the tip of the tongue, it restricts the articulation of the anterior lingual consonants such as /th/, /l/, /s/, /r/, /t/, /sh/, /d/, and /n/. By comparison, the posterior consonants—/k/, /g/, and vowels—are usually normal. This was true for him.

Tongue-tie is the common term for ankyloglossia. The lingual frenulum attaches too close to the tongue tip, which restricts tongue movement and impairs speech development. Unless the frenulum is clipped by an ENT doctor, the child's speech can't be corrected.

One more measurement was necessary to establish that the boy was, in fact, tongue-tied.

Using a Boley gauge, I quickly confirmed that the space between his lingual frenulum and his tongue-tip was fifty percent shorter than normal. He did have tongue-tie, and he would need to see an ENT doctor to correct it.

A six-year-old is mature enough to be aware of his own speech in comparison to others. If he starts to feel different or is teased about his speech, he might develop embarrassment or shame about speaking. Growing out of tongue-tie, a physical problem, is impossible. Speech therapy won't help until the frenulum is released.

I discussed the results with his teacher (the principal's wife) and his mother after school. They agreed that he should see an ENT in Anchorage. It could wait until summer, just several weeks away. After the frenotomy, which uses sterile scissors to snip the frenulum free, his speech would naturally correct. If he needed help shifting his articulation, then his parents and teacher would assist him to stimulate those changes. The SLP that came to school next year could check his progress and adjust his program as needed.

After lunch, I went to the upper grades where the principal worked. I looked through the window of his door and saw a room full of kids with their heads down. At first sight, I thought they were being punished. At second sight, I saw they were silent reading, their heads propped up by their hands. But I knew the statistics, and if half of these students were able to read at grade level, it would be a miracle. Statewide testing revealed that fewer than thirty percent, sometimes only fifteen percent, of students in the villages were proficient in language arts, which included reading scores.

There was no interaction happening in this drab room, which had only one map on the plain walls. Gone was the practice of reading to students after lunch, which stimulated their imagination, increased their vocabulary, and improved their attention span, at least in this room. I was hesitant to interrupt the stillness, but nonetheless, I had to screen the students.

Quietly, I knocked on the door and started the process of taking the children into the hall. I had never been in a classroom of such quiet children. The principal barely said two words to me. He never started a lecture or a different activity. Although I completed the screenings before school was out, the classroom remained silent.

On this spring day, I had time to roam around outside before I had dinner with the principal and his wife, and before my plane arrived. The snow crunched perfectly as I walked on it—no slip-and-slide. I took a deep breath of the clean and crisp, invigorating air. The sun shone brightly, and the sky displayed a color of azure blue I had only beheld in Alaska: so clear, so rich, and no haze to block it.

I decided to walk down by the ocean side and saw the Chukchi Sea in break-up. Putting my hand over my eyes for shade, I watched the ice floes saunter past and explored along the shoreline. Finally, the ocean was thawing, revealing the black water underneath.

What's that? Something was lying on the shore. Creeping closer, I saw a dead animal resembling a seal or a walrus with its head cut off. My eyes opened wide, and my stomach churned. What the?

I understood that native Alaskans killed walruses for subsistence, but when they did, they were expected to use most of it. Cutting off the head of a walrus, just to get its ivory tusks, was against the law, even for them.

When I went back to the school, I saw the janitor who was cleaning out some trash cans. I had met him earlier in the day.

"Hey, I noticed there is a headless walrus down there on the beach. What's that about?" I asked.

The janitor, a middle-aged local man, started to tell me.

"Well, Isaac is a walrus guide. He took a group of about ten men from Texas on a walrus hunt about a week ago."

From Texas? Why did men from Texas want a walrus? I hadn't heard of any walrus barbecues happening in Texas lately.

"What do you mean a walrus hunt?" I asked.

"Isaac is the one guy in the village who can take people on a walrus hunt. He earns money to do that because he's a guide," he said.

"What does he charge?" I asked him.

"Oh, about $1,000 each."

That's about $2,500 in today's money. Isaac would have made about $10,000 for the hunt. Since there are so few steady jobs in a village, that would be a great source of income.

"So what about that walrus. What happened?" I asked. "Why is its head cut off?"

"I don't know," was his answer. He turned and continued to pull the plastic bag out of the trash can, indicating the topic was closed.

Walrus remained a traditional native Alaskan subsistence food. Whites weren't allowed to own walrus ivory unless they found it lying on the beach. If they wanted to purchase ivory, it had to be carved or otherwise turned into a piece of art by a native Alaskan.

Hunting walrus takes care. Walrus were usually hunted on the ground, or if there were no islands or breeding grounds nearby, then the ice floes sufficed. The worst blunder was shooting a walrus on ice without the harpoon in it yet. The animal would sink like a rock and be lost. No one was happy with this waste. If it washed up on shore days later, then the meat would be spoiled.

What had happened to this headless walrus? It could have been a casualty of bad hunting, which sunk and washed up on shore later, too rotten to harvest. The only thing left to do would be to cut its head off for the ivory. Either that, or it was killed to get its ivory. I didn't know. Was the janitor's story about the Texans accurate or a tall tale?

Later, I found out that the Department of Fish and Game didn't allow this kind of guided hunt. Walrus and whale were official subsistence foods. They weren't hunted with licensed guides, as bears or moose were. Alternatively, ivory was a source of income for the locals. I tend to believe whatever I'm told unless I have a reason not to trust someone. I'm on the gullible side. I did learn that native Alaskans like to joke and tell farcical stories. Was I a rube that day? I can't imagine ten Texans out there, each trying to kill a walrus and ship it home.

This headless walrus made me think about what had happened to the People of the Snow a hundred years ago, first with the Russians and then with the Americans. They were conquered and had been cut off from their body of culture. The native Alaskans on the North Slope were thriving right now because of oil revenues. Every village I visited had a new, large school. They had *things*. But not long ago, they had been separated from their language, their dancing, and their singing. Every culture has language, dancing, and singing, unless they have been taken away. To decimate a culture, to see other humans as less than human, to make race something to divide rather than unite, is like cutting off its head. How had they coped, survived, and now, seemingly, thrived?

Before I left, I had dinner with the stern principal and his gentle teacher wife. After a full day of work, she cooked a lovely meal, like most working women did. They were an older couple, in their forties with no children. He had a slight European accent, and she spoke kindly in a midwestern voice. With my sensitivity to disrespectful male speech, he seemed a bit dismissive of her, interrupting her and telling her to be quiet. My gut tightened, and immediately I was afraid of him, concerned I might say something that would annoy him. Uneasy, I hurried through dinner, thanked them, and begged off to get ready to leave.

As I boarded my flight to Point Hope, I remembered how bleak the principal's classroom had been. I wondered if the kids were afraid to talk to him like I was. First impressions, like the silence in his classroom, might not be accurate. But my second impression at dinner added to my concerns.

Point Hope

It was seven o'clock in the evening, still light out and cool. After an early, although tense dinner with the principal and his wife in Point Lay, I resumed my journey across the North Slope of Alaska to Point Hope in a bush plane. It was Friday. School was out.

Escorted by the school janitor to a second-grade classroom—my home for the weekend—I set up my gear in a corner, away from the door window for privacy.

"There is going to be a dance in the gym pretty soon tonight if you want to come," he said as he left.

I had learned a long time ago that the janitor and the secretary were the two most important people to know at school. They knew everything and could help me with anything.

"Thanks," I smiled. "That sounds good. I'll get over there as soon as I get my stuff unpacked." Wherever the gym was, it wouldn't be hard to find. All I had to do was follow the people. Entertainment, whoopee! I was starved for it. What was going to happen?

A mix of spring slush and mud covered the ground as we all walked to the gym. The good weather was a gift, and like a spring bloom, the whole village burst into the gymnasium to be entertained by dancers.

Eager to see something different, I kicked the slush off my boots, walked in, and scanned the new, large gym. Young and old alike sat on the side of the room covered with bleachers. I took a seat about halfway up on an aisle. The audience was in a jovial mood. People smiled and talked to each other as they looked across the gym at their entertainers for the night. Nobody talked to me, but I smiled and made eye contact as much as I could. I, too, looked to the other side of the room.

There they mingled—the dancers, the musicians, and assorted families and children. They organized chairs, drums, and themselves. Some wore native dance costumes, some wore Western clothes, and all casually prepared to perform. No one was in a hurry. Hurry was an American invention.

Dancing had always been a social activity for the entire community. But historically, the first contracted churches with the BIA banned dancing. They were told to Christianize Alaskans. Dancing had to be stopped because it was considered heathen. Now, no longer illegal, a resurgence in dance and other Alaskan native cultural activities took place. Dancing wasn't done in isolation or secret anymore. Out in the open, in the gym, the dancers and musicians gave the "ready" sign. An announcer thanked everyone for coming and introduced the name of the troupe. The Point Hope dancers were preparing for a statewide festival.

Traditionally, dancing had also provided a way to give gifts to widows, orphans, and those who were alone. When people in need danced, the villagers presented a prize to them with items they needed—tools, kayaks, and goods. In that way, they were taken care of without embarrassing them. When the Americans came and took the dancing away, they ended this respectful and kind way of helping others.

As the drummers, seated in a long single row, started to beat their round, wooden frame drums and chant, my heart quickened, and I knew something was about to happen. The dancers lined up in front of the drummers and began their moves. Confidence showed in their choreography and in the performance. There were several men and women, old and young, drumming, singing, and dancing. Children wandered in and out and occasionally performed a few moves before leaving. They learned by watching and doing.

Each dance started easily and then built to a crescendo. The locals knew what the gestures meant and understood the story told by the dance. It frequently described how a man had captured an animal, very nonchalantly ignoring it at first, then engaging in a strong fight at the culmination to kill it and heroically, but modestly, bring the animal home to his people for food. As each song finished, the audience, including me, cheered and applauded for their talented neighbors.

I lucked out that night. I realized how telling stories through dance was more than passing down a tale. It was a delightful physical activity that could be relished during the winter. It brought the whole village together and gave them a chance to socialize while enhancing their well-being, cooperation, and friendliness—traditional qualities prized by native Alaskans. Dancing sustained and enriched their culture and history. What's not to like? It was perfect in all ways.

As I rarely got to interact with the local folks, I appreciated seeing them out and about. They were just like any other group of people, coming together to talk, see each other, and watch a show. In addition to Western clothes, many of the women wore handmade *kuspuks*. A *kuspuk* is a beautiful tunic-length blouse, usually made from a colorful calico cotton print. It had large pockets, a short skirt, and a hood. Decorative rickrack or trim outlined the pockets, the hood, and the hems. I had two of them and wore them when I went to the villages. Besides being fashionable, they were functional, with their hood and big pockets.

The spring temperatures meant that jackets were lightweight, and lots of people wore red tops on their feet. Red tops were simple pull-on, black rubber boots with a red line around the rim. I had an old pair that I bought when I lived on Vashon Island. Most Alaskans wore these in the spring and summer when the snow melted, the ground thawed, and mud puddles were on the rise.

After the dance was over and we were outside, a young woman walked toward me, holding hands with her two young boys.

"Are you from Anchorage?" she asked.

"Yes," I replied. A village is small, and even though I had flown in that evening, she already knew I was from Anchorage.

"When you go home, could you get me two pairs of red tops for my boys and send them back to me? We don't have any in the village, and it's so muddy now. They really need them," she said.

Even though this was a fairly large village, shopping was meager. Necessities had to be ordered from a catalog or flown in from a hub or a city like Anchorage or Fairbanks. Shipping by airplane was extremely expensive and out of reach for the average person.

I didn't know what size the boys wore, and neither did she. I didn't know where to get them or how to send them to her. It would be a week before I returned to Anchorage. With everything else I was juggling, I reluctantly told her I couldn't do it. I felt like a rat then and I still feel like one now.

The isolation of villages boggled my mind. When people in Anchorage or the politicians argued about how much money to disburse to the villages versus the cities for improvements, I knew one thing for sure—they had never been to a village. Had they seen how the First Peoples were living, how little they had and how much they needed, they would've thought like me. Give money to the villages. Help them upgrade to at least the basics that the rest of us took for granted.

The North Slope Borough was lucky. They had been able to upgrade their substandard living conditions. But other villages did not have the millions of oil dollars that the North Slope had. Their economies were concomitant with other developing nations, what used to be called Third World countries. And they were right here in Alaska. They had to rely on the state government for their money. Jobs were scarce, and any money earned did not go far. Everything was twice as expensive in a village than in Anchorage, and Anchorage was bad enough.

I had the whole weekend in Point Hope. I worked on reports and took some time to walk around. (I had learned that you don't hike in a village, you walk, and you don't walk fast because then you slip and fall.) I went down by the shore. Eventually, I saw a large carcass up on the beach, lying on mushy snow. As I got closer, I saw that it was a whale carcass. Picked mostly clean, it had some innards and baleen still on it. Soon, a rotten smell filled the air, and I saw the flies feasting on it. I stopped. I didn't need to go any farther. I knew it was a great boon and a tremendous effort for the people of the village to take a whale. It would be shared with everyone, the elderly first. It would be a reason to celebrate.

Yet they had to organize and petition the government to keep the right to "take a whale," something they had done for thousands of years, something life-giving they had to do to exist on the tundra. They weren't killing as many whales as possible, like the whaling companies. Each village needed one whale at the most, and would share it with others. *Ella* was both the whale and the people. She provided for them. Alaskan natives hadn't decimated the whale population; white man had done that, but Alaskan natives suffered the decisions of businesses that were made thousands of miles away, without their knowledge or input. Why? The villagers were considered inferior. Their opinions were not important. They didn't matter.

Native Alaskans kept trying to get a seat at the table, but so many customs had been taken away. So many communication barriers had been built as white people came in with their superior/inferior ideology, perhaps not always with malice but always with the presumption of superiority. It was men over women, conqueror over conquered, strong over weak, and organizations over individuals. When individuals dared to speak up, they were often ridiculed, ignored, or punished. Instead of listening to and learning from each other, communication was one way. Do as you're told, or else.

Add to this a communication disorder, which could make it difficult to communicate for a variety of reasons. Is the person ignored, pitied, humiliated, like Rose, or helped? What barriers have they faced, how difficult is it to find the proper help, and how supportive is the family and community? Was there a point to bringing me to a remote place to look for children with communication disorders? Absolutely! I had a voice that would have to be listened to. It was the law.

After screening the students on Monday and Tuesday, I

packed and prepared to leave first thing the next morning. My destination was the most southern and mountainous of all the villages on the North Slope. Not knowing what to expect, I didn't worry. I trusted that the pilot was capable and competent. The weather was good; the skies were blue. As wide open as the tundra, I received into my awareness whatever came before me and welcomed it, like the bright streams of sunlight, reflecting off the fresh spring snow, the grace of *ella*.

CHAPTER 24

Waiting for Break-up (Part 4)

Anaktuvuk Pass

I knew we were getting closer to the next village because we were climbing off the tundra into the mountains—the Brooks Range, to be exact, in northern Alaska.

"These are the Endicott Mountains," the pilot said. "Anaktuvuk Pass is coming up."

"Okay," I nodded.

As we drew closer, I sat in awe of the most dazzling, sweeping peaks and valleys of the Range. Then I saw it, Anaktuvuk Pass (Place of Caribou Droppings). Perched on one of the most scenic vistas imaginable, this village had a population of 203. I was privileged to work here. It was completely isolated. There were no roads in or out; the only transportation was by plane, landing on a gravel strip.

Fortunately, this morning the air temperature remained cold enough that our plane could land on the snow-covered gravel. I beheld the majesty of the region as we circled the village. Spring pushed forward, so under that snow, faint green appeared on the south-facing slopes of the mountains. Brown caribou with beige fur necks and C-shaped antlers that spread high above their heads were migrating, on their way to their summer feeding grounds on the tundra, north of the mountains. Surprisingly, I spotted them far and wide, lollygagging through the high valley, as the Creator intended.

The Nunamiut hunters knew well how to take the caribou. When the first of the herd came through (the scouts), the hunters watched closely, but they didn't kill any or get close enough to spook them. If they did, the caribou darted away and wouldn't return the next year. The creatures would find a new route.

If the hunters just waited a while, the rest of the herd, about ten thousand animals, would arrive shortly. Then, the hunters took as many animals as needed for food and hides. The caribou just kept coming and wouldn't run away at that point. This same herd had been migrating by their village for hundreds, if not thousands, of years. (White hunters, in their ignorance and entitlement, could have destroyed this pattern.)

"I'll be back about three," the pilot said as he dropped me off. "The snow is melting on the gravel, and it's getting soft. I wanna make sure I can get you out. It'll probably be too soft to get out in a couple of days." Soon he wouldn't be able to land for a few weeks, until the landing strip dried out.

The village buzzed with enthusiasm for the annual hunt. I watched men hop on their Ski-Doos to seek a caribou to kill. I noticed that many a doorway already had a caribou carcass hanging in it, with its hide stripped and its innards gutted. Everyone benefited. The hunt endured until the caribou left and as long as the weather stayed cool. Once it warmed up, however, the flies came and ruined the meat. For now, the abundant fresh caribou reminded everyone that the Creator was taking care of the people. There would be enough for the village to eat now and to store for the winter.

The small population of Anaktuvuk Pass required only a small school. Nonetheless, all the children needed to be screened for any speech or hearing problems. The classes were in session when I arrived, so I organized my things and sat in a child-sized chair in front of the kindergarten door. In a few minutes, recess started, which gave me time to introduce myself to the teacher and explain to her what I would be doing.

As soon as the bell rang, some children came out of the room. A sweet little girl noticed me right away and stood in front of me. Because I was sitting, we were almost the same height. Staring at me with curiosity, she studied my face and my hair, which was blond and came to my shoulders. Gently, she raised her hand to my hair and began to feel and stroke it. Then she looked at me and said, "You have *gussuk* hair."

I replied gently, "Yes, and you have Eskimo hair." Had she ever seen a blond person before? She had used the word *gussuk* as a generic term for a white person. She didn't insult me. She assigned me to a category in her brain, a normal thing to do at her age.

Unfortunately, I can't say the same about how people in the other villages felt about *gussuks*. A few villages in Alaska explicitly didn't care for white people; one had even banned whites. Who could blame them? Conditions and rules that outsiders had been making since the nineteenth century, and continued to make with state and federal policies, were often demeaning and hazardous. At the time, Anaktuvuk Pass disapproved of whites.

All the children were fine, and within a few hours, it came time for me to leave. As I walked down the short set of stairs with my bags and left the school, a local man was climbing up. He looked at me and hissed, "We don't want you here."

I felt the tightening of my stomach signaling violence, like the jaws of a wolf clamping down on a caribou calf. Racism breeds racism. In my thoughts, I replied, *I'm here to help your children if they need it. I'm only here for a couple of hours and then I'll be gone. I'm sorry for the bad experiences you have had that make you feel this way.* But I didn't dare speak those words. I just walked on as if I hadn't heard a thing.

I was an expert at hiding pain and negative feelings. As a woman traveling alone, I would never have confronted him about what he said to me. I suppose I could have followed him back into the school and asked him what he was thinking and feeling, except I knew what he was thinking—he didn't want me there. I didn't know how to address the terrible history his culture had experienced and the hatred he felt. Although I could never truly understand the experience of having my culture, language, and spiritual beliefs taken away from me by another race, I had empathy for native Alaskans and did what I could now to help, not hinder.

This was the first and only time I experienced blatant racism as a white woman while on the job in Alaska. In the Lower 48 I had worked with Americans of all different races—Hispanics, Asians, and Blacks. They were all kids to me, with hearts and minds, who deserved love and respect, along with a little speech therapy. Undoubtedly, all of them had experienced racism at some point, which made my heart sink.

In Alaska, I worked with many tribes—Yupik, Iñupiat, and Tlingit, to name a few. By being conquered, they had been subjected to racism. Now I had experienced it myself, and I didn't like the feeling. It made me feel unwanted, disliked, and despised. It made me want to retreat in shame.

Nuiqsut

"I want you all to know that anyone in this school or any school in our borough can attend any college in the United States, full tuition paid by us, as long as you meet the qualifications. I hope some of you will do your best and get one of these scholarships," Mayor George, from Barrow, announced to the student body.

On my last Friday afternoon, I listened to the mayor speak at the school assembly in the remote village of Nuiqsut, population 281. Surprised and impressed, I hoped that some of the children would take advantage of this generous offer in the future.

On a clear, thirty-degree April day, the sun sparkled. The flat tundra, covered with snow, extended to the horizon. The sky shaped a beautiful blue dome overhead. In the village, the crusted snow had packed down. It was good walking snow.

I walked past the P&J store, made of plywood and about the size of a two-car garage. Outside, a few big dogs, black and brown, walked around loose. Stores in the villages were meager at best. One wall held candy, another some refrigerated items like milk. Shelving in the middle stored canned and boxed food. A small freezer section, waist high, had basic frozen items. They were better than nothing.

I had journeyed on my itinerant speech therapy job for two weeks, making the rounds from village to village. This was the last one. I flew across the North Slope, testing children, writing reports, consulting with parents, teachers, and principals. But I had to admit, I was ready to return to Anchorage.

I wanted to sleep in my own waterbed, watch a rented video from Blockbuster, and eat my own popcorn drenched in butter and salt, while snuggled in with my husband, Bill; the cats, Arwen, Gandalf, and Mimosa; and the dogs, Sugar Bear and Cinnamon Bear. I wished to get in a car and drive somewhere on a paved road, call a friend and talk on the phone, and eat some fresh food. I missed dropping in on my neighbor and sharing a cup of tea with someone I had known for a few years. I was bushy, and I didn't like the hemmed-in, isolated, and anxious feeling.

My headaches had throbbed through the entire trip, as I dutifully took my hormones. The nausea always peaked after eating but improved after a couple of hours. That all would have happened in Anchorage. By going to the villages, I discovered new places and helped some children who otherwise may have had to suffer. I couldn't let them down. That helped me to ignore my pain. But I sure would have enjoyed it more if I didn't have this hot lava rock stuffed in my head, stabbing at my eyes.

The P&J Store in Nuiqsut. This was typical of the size of a store in many villages, basically a shed. April 1983. Photo: Kit Roberts

The small, chartered plane scheduled to carry me back to Barrow—and my flight to Anchorage—was due to pick me up at four in the afternoon. Because of the mayor's assembly, I couldn't accomplish anything further this afternoon, so I started packing.

Then I heard rumblings about the weather. A ceiling was coming in and dropping around three o'clock.

If there's one thing you pay attention to in Alaska, it's the weather. What appeared as a mild afternoon right now would soon be covered with low clouds. What did this mean?

It meant my chartered plane was canceled. If I couldn't catch that plane to Barrow, then I couldn't catch the jet to Anchorage. I had to get back that day or I'd be stuck until Monday. I was desperate. As the cloud cover began its descent, I too descended into an internal anxiety.

The mayor had flown to the village in a helicopter with ten seats. It handled eleven people, the pilot and ten passengers. As it turned out, the helicopter flew low, beneath the cloud cover. It didn't fly very fast, but if I could catch a ride in it with Mayor George, I could catch the jet home.

The scuttlebutt indicated that the mayor was leaving at three o'clock in the afternoon. His pilot wanted to be ahead of the ceiling as much as possible. I made a critical decision. *Get on that helicopter if it's the last thing you ever do.* Well, I hoped to get on it, anyway. Unfortunately, I heard several others were just as eager as I was to make that flight.

I felt a sudden urgency to my packing. I had to get everything finished up, buttoned up, and zipped up ASAP. Reaching the airstrip as fast as I could, I glanced toward the helicopter and saw a crowd of locals already standing around.

I counted. There were ten people, which was one too many. I was the only white person there, and I usually deferred to the locals. But this time, I had to assert myself. Like a group of ravens, jockeying for a position closer to the carrion, I inserted myself into that line and ended up as passenger number five. As

I got to the door, I handed my duffle bags to the person loading the helicopter. We were as crowded as kissin' cousins when that 'copter door shut. Whew.

The clouds were collapsing on our way back to Barrow, so the pilot flew particularly low. We weren't more than 300 to 400 feet off the ground. I saw the land so clearly. It appeared more rugged than it did from a higher altitude. The variability of the land surely indicated mounds of tundra vegetation: sedge meadows, lichen-heath mosses, wildflowers, grasses, and dwarf shrubs. It was April. Soon the snow would melt. Inevitably, the tundra plants would come to life again. The ground, saturated with water, made a breeding home for millions of mosquitos and migrating geese galore, coming to birth and rear their brood.

For two weeks I had traveled through Beringia. Parts of Beringia, the original land that crossed from Asia to North America, no longer existed. I had met with the ancestors of the people who crossed that land bridge and stayed. The rest of their ancestors went south and populated North and South America. They had become many peoples, tribes, and cultures. Like all members of an environment, they adapted to their new surroundings, new foods, and the gifts that came with each unique place.

It was getting dark as I boarded my flight to Anchorage. As I relaxed back into my seat, I marveled at the magnitude and diversity of land and life. I reflected on some of the traditional values in the villages and the sentience of the universe and its peoples, animals, seas, and lands. Respect was critical. Lacking respect equated to following one's own mind—a dangerous thing to do. With respect, one's life is beautiful.

Even so, the isolation was inconceivable to a person like me. I knew I couldn't adapt to full-time life in a village. After just two weeks, I was bushy. I decided to never go out on a job that long again. From then on, I limited my trips to the villages to one week at the most.

This Friday-night plane was filled with men coming off

the oil fields. I'd never been on such a noisy and jocular flight. These guys were yelling over the isles, getting up and walking around to talk to different people, and, of course, drinking. They laughed and told stories the whole way to Anchorage. I love Alaska Airlines.

CHAPTER 25

Movin' On Up

When we strive to become better than we are, everything around us becomes better too.
—Paulo Coelho

"We're going for a ride," said Janice and Kathleen.

Puzzled, having just returned from a weeklong trip to the villages in 1987, I let them take me by the hand. We had been renting office space together for two years, ever since the IRS debacle. I had cancelled my SLP contracts with them, and they became independent providers. We stayed in the same space and shared office expenses, which was great. We had sublet the largest room in our suite to a doctor, so it felt cramped.

Janice was a few years younger than I and had moved to Alaska with her husband in the early 1980s. Kathleen and her husband had lived in Anchorage for many years, and they had an adult daughter. Kathleen knew everyone and had experience with state-level programs for children with special needs. The two of them chatted happily as they drove and refused to tell me where we were going or why.

"Okay, what is this all about?" I asked.

"You'll just have to wait and see," said Janice.

Alaska is a state of contradictions. We had days of darkness and nights of light, volcanic eruptions and ancient glaciers, and big cities and tiny villages. Even in Anchorage, the largest city in Alaska, we didn't have all the advantages that people in big cities in the Lower 48 had. Frankly, we liked it that way. We didn't have satellite TV or lots of stores. We also didn't have drive-by shootings, crazy amounts of traffic, or unemployment. The rich and the poor sat together in the same bars and churches as they did at the Performing Arts Center. I couldn't tell them apart.

The entire time I lived in Anchorage, the town was on an upward trajectory. The jobs for the pipeline attracted more people, which created more business, which attracted more people. Both blue- and white-collar jobs remained available. Like the winds blowing off the Prince William Sound, a wind behind my back sent me on a higher and wider trajectory. As the town grew, so did my knowledge and skills and the numbers of people I could help. I wasn't making anything happen. *Ella* did it. She gave me my drive, enthusiasm, and strength.

After five minutes, Kathleen turned into the Dimond Mall, the only mall in Anchorage and Alaska at the time. Comparable to shopping malls in the Lower 48, it had two levels of shops, a basement level with an ice-skating rink, and a six-story professional building.

"Come with us," said Kathleen after parking near the professional building entrance.

"What are we doing here? I asked.

Janice and Kathleen led me to the third floor of the professional building.

"While you were gone, we did some looking around. Our office is too small. So is the waiting area. We found the perfect place to move," said Kathleen.

Move? Who said anything about moving? Was I in on that conversation? I wasn't so sure about that. I was certain that an office space in the mall would be very expensive. And I sure didn't want to go through the hassle of moving and changing addresses with all the doctors, hospitals, school districts, clients, phone book, business cards, stationery, IRS, State of Alaska corporation registration, Borough Business License, state SLP association, and national SLP association. Then moving the furniture, my materials, and library would fall to just Bill, me, and our pickup. Setting up computers and printers, which we had upgraded since 1984, would definitely require Bill's help. I was exhausted just thinking about it. Then we went inside.

"It's right here," said Janice, opening the office door. "You're going to love it."

Love it? I'll see about that. Hmm. The waiting area was bright and roomy. Then came the waist-high, built-in cabinets, countertop, and a swinging half-door that blocked off the waiting room from the professional offices, which I could see on the other side. The offices all had windows that faced east toward the Chugach Mountains. The view was tremendous.

As we toured the suite, I learned that in addition to our offices, we each had our own treatment room with a large window. We would have to pay to change the plain glass to one-way mirrored glass in those windows. A parent could look through the window and watch their child receiving therapy, just like the first SLP I ever saw through a mirrored window, working at the Crippled Children's Services clinic. As a general rule, I didn't allow parents in the treatment room, but I did want them to know what their child was capable of doing. The mirrored window provided the perfect solution.

Despite my misgivings about moving, after exploring the openness, the extra space, and the view, I was sold. I did love it. All the anxiety of being "taken for a ride" dissolved.

The three of us leased this suite and moved. I approved of the professional look. I felt the joy of experiencing something new again. The mall had security guards, and I felt protected and safe in this new place.

We each settled into our own niche. I worked with adults with a variety of disorders or children who stuttered. Janice worked primarily with people who were moderately to severely disabled. Kathleen treated children ages five and under with delayed speech and language development. We split the cost of a part-time office manager who did the billing, took messages, and checked-in clients. It worked nicely, and we felt more professional.

Partnering with this group of women was particularly gratifying. We were all busy and working independently, sharing expenses. I still traveled to the villages and worked at the hospitals. Janice had her own contracts with different facilities. We learned from each other.

I loved watching Kathleen work with her little ones. She made the therapy so much fun. Each year on the children's birthdays, she took them to the toy store in the mall and bought them a birthday present. Of course, the children took part in this. After comparing toys—using speech and language—and selecting the right present, they went to the check-out counter, and Kathleen gave the child some money. The child handed the money to the clerk, received the change, and said, "Thank you." Every step was a teaching moment.

Janice impressed me with her ability to work with people with some of the most challenging problems: moderate-to-severe developmental disabilities, including autism. She created augmentative and alternative communication systems (AAC), from simple to intricate, such as picture exchange systems or touch-screen devices for her totally nonverbal clients. She was vigilant and on the leading edge for computer-assisted communication.

One day, late in the afternoon, I remained in my office doing paperwork. I didn't have more clients that day. A large, lumpy man entered the waiting room with two children. The older one went with Janice, while the man and his daughter (I assumed), who was about eighteen-months to two years old, stayed in the waiting area. He was a young man, maybe twenty-five years old. He still had pimples and was casually dressed in jeans and a big tee shirt. He spread across the couch while his little girl toddled around. We had plenty of toys and books in the corner to interest children while they waited with their parents for their family member.

Gradually, I became aware of a loud, male voice. I peeked around the corner just in time to see this man trip his little girl on purpose.

"Ha, ha, ha," he laughed. "You can't even walk. You're so stupid."

He picked her up roughly and started her on her way again with another gruff put-down.

"Go away. Get away from me," he said. "What a loser."

She picked up a toy and brought it back to show him. He forcefully grabbed it out of her hand.

"This is dumb. You can't even find a good toy. Don't bother me."

He threw the toy back over in the corner where she found it. Again, he pushed her away firmly, this time with the bottom of his shoe. She lurched but didn't fall down.

His body remained sprawled on the couch like a beached beluga. He bullied her with his whole body, through the reach of his long legs, long arms, vile words, and monstrous tone of voice. My stomach turned. In my opinion, I was witnessing child abuse—and this out in public. Who knew how much worse it could be at home?

What should I do? He was Janice's client, not mine. If I said something to him, he might make it worse for the little girl. He might come after me. He might pull his child out of therapy and not come back. I didn't know anything about him or how he might react. And there was no way I could win a physical altercation with him.

What if I yelled, "Hey, what do you think you're doing? Stop that right now or I'm going to call the police. You leave that little girl alone. Stop calling her names. Stop tripping her. That is physical and emotional abuse! If I hear or see anything like that again, I'll call security."

Instead of saying any of that, I stayed mum. But later I asked Janice for his information to report him to Child Protective Services (CPS). That much I had to do.

I called the number, my heart racing. I had never before reported anyone to CPS or any authority for that matter, but I knew I had to say something. After a few rings, a woman with a tired voice answered the phone.

"Hello," I said, mustering my courage. "My name is Kit Roberts and I'm a speech-language pathologist. I want to report a man for possible child abuse."

"What's his name and address?" she asked, not even asking what he'd done.

I told her. Then I described what I had witnessed.

"Can you make a site visit to his home and evaluate the

situation?" I implored.

"He has to have three complaints against him. You're the first one."

"So you're not going to do anything?" I asked, incredulous. Was a child supposed to be neglected, abused, or beaten three times before someone intervened?

"We have to wait for three complaints. I'll put your complaint in the record."

"Okay. Thank you."

Really?

We know so much more now about bullies and being bullied. I could have swept into the waiting room and interacted directly with the child.

"Who is this sweet little girl?"

"My, aren't you smart with that toy?"

"Let's look at the book together. Where's the dog? Right. Show me the bear. Yes. You know so many things. What a smart girl you are!"

"Do you want to play with the baby doll? You can hold her. Show me how to rock her. We have to be very gentle and smile at her. We want her to be happy and feel safe. Let's put her to bed now. Slow and careful so she doesn't get hurt. Now her blanket. There we go. You are so gentle."

I could have modeled for him how to play with his child. Of course, it wouldn't have changed his behavior, and I still would have reported him. The law states that SLPs must report suspected child abuse. We are mandatory reporters in the United States.

I don't know if there was any resolution to this problem. Our paths never crossed again. His evilness froze in my memory, like the hard winter snow. I was disappointed in the system, once again. So many people needed so much help. There was only so much of me to go around.

CHAPTER 26

Flight Attendant Loses Her Wings

What is speech therapy? For me it meant that the therapist would help me find my way back to a degree of normalcy in every single endeavor that required using my mind as it struggled for new strategies in getting thoughts through a damaged brain to the world outside.

—Helen Harlan Wulf, Aphasia, My World Alone

"What is the chief complaint about your voice right now?" I asked.

"My voice is hoarse, and it hurts to talk sometimes. I'm the lead flight attendant, and I make the overhead announcements. Sometimes, it's hard to hear them."

"So it's affecting your job. That must be difficult."

"Yes, it is. I've worked fifteen years and have a senior position. I don't want to lose it."

Linda looked classy, dressed in her French-navy flight attendant uniform for Alaska Airlines. Her flight schedule began after our appointment, which meant she would be flying to Seattle, back to Anchorage, over to Russia for the night, and back to Anchorage. Then she would wait a few days and do it again.

After meeting in the waiting room, I had invited her into my treatment room and began her formal evaluation, although I had already heard the hoarseness in her voice.

As I had become an established SLP in the growing town of Anchorage, the ENT doctors began referring their patients with vocal disorders to me. Lacking a standardized evaluation routine and a sequenced plan of treatment, I knew it was time to get professional training in this area. I liked certainty, not uncertainty. My experience told me that if I learned the most up-to-date information about vocal disorders, my insecurities would melt away like a May snowfall. The doctors trusted me to be competent. I expected to be excellent. It wouldn't help my headaches, but it might mitigate them by giving my brain something new to think about that would benefit someone else.

At this point, my trips to the Lower 48 for training had become common. Flying five-and-a-half hours to Minneapolis, crossing concourses to find my next gate, then embarking on the next flight to Cincinnati turned into a hobby, like orienteering. But where was my pink, hard-sided luggage that had trekked through the villages and saved me from a broken rib? It had slowly been gouged to death, like a tree trunk gashed by a logger's hatchet. It came back after each flight with another chunk of it missing. Eventually, it went to the dump, and I purchased new soft-sided luggage.

Having attended three different voice symposiums and inviting a PhD SLP voice specialist to my office to train me and other SLPs in the diagnosis and treatment of vocal disorders, I felt secure. Confident that I knew the *best practices*—a new term that had started to pervade the clinical arena—I prepared for my new clients. Like the rain in August, a steady stream of referrals came from the ENTs. But before I started evaluating anyone, I needed some equipment.

To work with people with voice disorders, I purchased a five-octave electronic keyboard to assess vocal range, a sound-level meter to assess volume, and a nasometer to assess abnormal nasal air omission. I bought a professional tape recorder, which cost $450. I almost gagged on that one, but the sound quality was amazing. Since I recorded every session and sent it home with the client, it had to be high quality. I had tried the basic Radio Shack tape recorder, and the amount of static made it difficult to hear voices sharply. This would not do, because the final purpose of recording the sessions was to hear the improvement of the client's voice over time.

Having my own business, I had to buy everything myself from what I earned. Somehow, buying equipment and materials was never a problem for me. If I needed it, even for one patient, then I bought it. If I didn't have the right equipment, then I wasn't doing my best. If I wasn't doing my best, then the patient wouldn't improve. That was not an option for me. I had to eliminate their problem to the greatest degree possible. I could not fake it. I had to be real.

By the time Linda made an appointment with me, I was confident in my diagnosis and treatment of people with dysphonia. Her ENT had diagnosed her with a vocal cord nodule and referred her to me. Dysphonia is a medical problem of the voice. A nodule is like a blister on the vocal cord that doesn't go away unless the underlying pattern of vocalization is altered. I now had the knowledge to help her make that change.

"When did you first notice the problem?" I continued.

"It was about four months ago."

"Did you notice the problem suddenly, or did it occur over time?"

"Well, a little bit of both. My voice would get tired and it would be hard to get volume, so I would just push it to make it louder. Then one day, I just felt like I couldn't get a voice out at all," she said in her raspy, harsh voice, a voice that wouldn't project well.

"Do you think the problem is any different now—worse, better, or the same?"

"It's worse, because it's not going away. It used to go in and out; now, it's always scratchy."

"In your opinion, what do you think caused it? Were there any accidents, illnesses, or emotional events surrounding the onset?" I asked.

"Well, now that I think about it, I caught a cold. I was coughing a lot. When I was making the overhead announcements, it was hard to get my voice out, and I would cough. It never really got better after that."

One common cause of a vocal nodule is coughing during an illness. There are small mucous glands underneath the vocal folds (vocal cords). These glands are there to hydrate the vocal cords, so your voice doesn't dry out. But when the mucous increases due to an illness, people will feel it in their throat and try to cough it away. At the same time, they are ramming their vocal cords together, hard, over and over, which causes the formation of a fluid filled sac, like a blister. If we catch it within two years of onset, we can get rid of it without surgery.

"Did you ever completely lose your voice?"

"Maybe for a couple of days when my cold was the worst. Otherwise, no."

"Is there a history of vocal problems in your family?"

"No."

"How do your friends and family react to your voice?"

"They just kept telling me I should have it looked at because it wasn't going away. That's when I finally went to the ENT. Everyone was worried I might have throat cancer, even though I'm not a smoker. But I work in a smoking environment."

Smoking wasn't banned on Alaska Airlines until 1990.

"Do you have any pain or tension in your throat?"

"Yes, it feels like a sore throat the more I talk, and it starts to give out on me if I have to talk more than a couple minutes."

At this point I got up and asked her if I could feel her throat. She agreed. I located the tip of her Adam's apple. From there I slid my thumb and index finger back to the laryngeal horns and gently massaged them. She signaled the right side was sore, indicating excessive tension on that side, the same side as her nodule.

I asked her several more questions, then did an analysis of her voice. I measured her volume for speaking and for making overhead announcements, her pitch range, her habitual pitch, her optimal pitch, her s/z ratio (how long she can sustain an /s/ sound versus a /z/ sound), the amount of time she could sustain the vowel /o/, her breath supply and control, her singing, her hard glottal attack, her vocal focus, and her laryngeal rise.

During her evaluation, I determined that Linda's pitch was too low. In the 1980s, voice coaches taught women to lower their vocal pitch. Theoretically, it gave them more authority because they sounded more masculine. But when she lowered her pitch, she lowered her vocal focus into her throat at the same time instead of keeping the focus in the facial mask. The facial mask is the area between the chin and the eyebrows. It's where your voice should be focused.

Focusing the voice in the throat is dangerous territory; it can cause vocal strain, nodules, and polyps. She changed the way she spoke without the critical knowledge that if she increased her volume, she would damage her vocal cords. Naturally, she had to speak louder at work because she competed with the sound of jet engines. After having a cold, this was her final downfall and prevented the nodule from healing.

Linda complained of chronic hoarseness, an inability to talk at will and at length, and a tone change from a clear voice to a breathy or rough voice. She cleared her throat frequently, but it was non-productive. The more she talked, the more her voice tired, and she soon felt tension and tightness in her throat. Knowing she had a nodule explained all of her sensory symptoms.

Additionally, Linda spoke with hard glottal attack —a staccato-like sound on vowel sounds. This indicates hypercontraction of the vocal muscles involved with the vocal cords. Because of this, she had lost vocal range and the ability to sustain a tone. The resulting nodule was interfering with several of the vocal parameters I measured.

Linda didn't use diaphragmatic breathing, meaning instead of breathing from the navel area, she was breathing with her upper chest and raising her shoulders on inhalation. This is incorrect breathing for speech and would have to be addressed.

As the lead member of her team, she had to make announcements, but her voice had become so hoarse that it didn't project over the speaker anymore. It impaired her job performance, and she was at risk of losing her "wings." If she learned how to use her voice correctly, her nodule would fade away, and the overhead announcements would be a breeze again. I needed to help her. Her livelihood was at stake.

There were only four essential things I needed to teach a person with an ailing voice: how to reduce laryngeal tension, how to breathe correctly, where to focus her voice, and how to speak at her optimum pitch. I loved working with people who had voice issues. Their problems usually resolved quickly, and they became independent in their ability to maintain a healthy voice.

When I finished her evaluation, I reviewed all of my findings with her. Then, I told Linda, "To summarize, I need to teach you how to reduce laryngeal tension, raise your habitual pitch slightly, breathe from the diaphragm, and focus your voice in the facial mask. Since you haven't had your vocal nodule for more than two years, the research tells us that it should dissolve within a couple of months—if you do what I say."

"That sounds good to me," she said.

"If you want to start treatment, it will take six sessions for me to teach you everything I know about correcting your voice. We'll meet once a week, and I'll give you handouts and a recording of each session to practice with at home. By the end of the six weeks, you should be able to speak correctly for a ten-minute conversation. At that point, your voice will be stable, and you'll continue on your own. We can always add in a session or two later for a refresher, or if you run into problems."

"Okay, I can come next week about this time."

"Sounds good; I'll see you then. In the meantime, speak as little as possible. Put yourself on voice rest unless you have to talk. Have a safe flight," I replied.

A week later, she returned, and we got started.

<u>First Exercise</u>

"Hi Linda, come on back," I said, directing her to the treatment room. "Today I'm going to show you how the vocal cords work, teach you how to reduce the tension in your voice, and show you how to get your voice out of the basement (your throat), and into the facial mask."

With the tips of my two index fingers together making an upside-down V shape, I demonstrated how the vocal cords are together in the front and apart in the back, how they don't vibrate unless we pass air through them, and how to keep them from hypercontracting, which causes a myriad of problems, including nodules.

Then I gave her an exercise to reduce laryngeal tension. "For your first exercise, I want you to pretend that you're eating a big piece of crusty bread on your back teeth. Chew slowly and calmly, and keep your mouth closed."

I watched her as she pretended to slowly chew.

"Now add a hum. Do that for several chews and take a breath through your nose when you need it." I demonstrated and she responded.

"Hmmummumm. Hummummum. Hummummumm," she hummed and chewed.

"Very good. Now I want you to do something your mother probably told you never to do: chew with your mouth open. Imagine you are chewing that bread again, but this time when you hum, open your mouth. Take a breath through your mouth, keep chewing and keep the sound going. It will be mushy and sloppy, that's what I want, like you have been to the dentist and are numb with novocaine. Don't let the sound come out of your nose; keep it coming out of your mouth." Again, I demonstrated and she responded.

"Yawyawyawyawyawyaw," she chewed and hummed with her mouth open.

"Now do the same thing, but do it at this pitch." I played her optimum pitch on the keyboard, which raised her pitch slightly, and modeled for her how that sounded.

"Yawyawyawyawyawyaw."

She did very well, and after a few rounds I asked her some questions. "Compared to how you usually talk, how does your throat feel now? Is it more open or more closed?"

"More open," she said.

"How about the amount of air coming through your throat; is there more air or less air?"

"More air," she replied.

"And what about your voice; is it more smooth or more

scratchy?"

"Definitely more smooth," she said. "It feels good."

"That's right," I acknowledged. "Everything I'm going to teach you is to make your throat more open, so more air can get through, and your voice will get smooth again. It will take the pressure off the nodule."

I demonstrated the last few steps of the exercise and put a copy of it in her folder to take home and practice.

Second Exercise

"Now I'm going to show you how to get your voice in the facial mask. Right now, your voice is in the lower throat and we want it up here in the mid to upper throat." I pointed to a line drawing of a head in profile that showed the throat, lips, nose, and eyes. "That's where the voice should be aimed," I said, pointing to the nose/eye area, "up here between your chin and your eyebrows. Now, I want you to say the word hum and hold it until you can feel the sound vibrating on your nose and lips."

"Hummmmmm."

"Put your mind in the mask," I said. Her pitch had naturally normalized, as it often does.

"Hummmmmm."

"Did you feel it vibrating?"

"Yes, I did. It was buzzing on my lips and nose."

"That's perfect. That's where I want you to aim your voice every time we practice. Now I'm going to add some syllables. But first, I want to show you the magic voice button." She looked at me with curiosity. "I'm going to be pressing right here, a couple of inches above your navel. Is that all right with you?"

"Sure," she said.

We practiced a few more hums while I jiggled the magic voice button. This supports the diaphragm and moves air up and out, right into the facial mask. After she was able to get her voice in the facial mask saying *hum*, I added syllables, words, and sentences. She jiggled her voice button by herself. Catching on quickly, she became independent by the end of the session.

I added more homework to her folder to practice speaking in the facial mask, gave her the recording of the session, and encouraged her to practice with it every day.

Our first session completed, I had relaxed her vocal cords during phonation and changed the focus of her voice. These are the two most important parameters to correct first. If she hadn't learned to relax her vocal cords with the chewing approach, I would have used other techniques before moving on. The root of her problem was laryngeal tension.

At each appointment I added another parameter—how to breathe, speak at the correct pitch for her, and speak loudly without injuring her vocal cords. She understood and quickly implemented each step, which promptly changed her voice. Before I discharged her, she was able to use the overhead microphone system without any problems.

By the end of the sixth session, she was ready for discharge. Her nodule had disappeared. A few months later, I received a nice card from her, thanking me for helping her with her voice. She didn't have further problems and was able to accomplish her job. She followed her calling; she kept her wings.

Sometimes, after discharging a successful client, I realized that what could have been a deterrent to following my calling hadn't held me back. My parents moving away when I was in college, my husband moving us to Alaska, my problem with the IRS, my hormone headaches—none of these incidents had stopped me. Was my calling going to put me to work no matter what? Did it have a plan for me to follow, no matter the setting? I was given the courage, the skills, and the desire to help people with communication disorders. Did humans come with a predetermined destiny, or was it all random?

As I grew in my field, I began to believe that my work was a calling, that it was meant to be, and that it had revealed itself to me in the fourth grade. By following my calling, others, like Linda, continued to follow theirs. I was changing, too. My initial insecurities, doubts, and submissiveness to others had decreased. More confident, I wasn't higher than anyone else. If anything, I was still lower. But I was slowly becoming even with others—except for doctors. They were always higher.

CHAPTER 27
Transgender

And I would find myself again. Not the same version of me that I was looking for, but a stronger version. A wiser version . . . A woman who had been tried in the fire but instead of being burned by it, came out gold. A woman who finally after doubting and questioning and striving and hustling for her worth for years . . . came to the realization that she was and is and has always been . . . Enough.
—Mandy Hale

While Alaska is a macho place, it has its share of gay men. That's not to say that homosexuals aren't macho. Heck, contending with Alaska, I would consider myself macho compared to most women in the Lower 48. At the time I was there, the new statistics indicated that at least one out of ten people were homosexual. That included lesbians as well. Other sexual and gender minorities were not acknowledged at the time.

In Anchorage, the gay/lesbian community organized in 1977, then went through a series of changes over the years to include all sexual minorities. They had their own nightclub downtown and a community center.

Every so often, the LGBTQ+ community hosted a national convention at the Anchorage Convention Center. I attended one year. It was a lot of fun. Everyone dressed to the nines. As I rode the escalator going up, crowded with noisy patrons, a man on the equally packed and loud escalator going down, looked at me, pointed to me, and exclaimed, "I love your outfit."

"Thank you," I yelled back. And let's face it, a clothing compliment from a gay man is a good compliment.

It didn't seem like anyone in Anchorage had a problem with the gay/lesbian community. I never heard any reports about attacks on gays or lesbians, although it's probable that there were. It would be naïve of me to think otherwise. It was somewhat different for the transgender community.

One day, I got a call from a transgender woman who wanted to work on her voice. After that, several transgender women came to me for help with their voices. All of my transgender clients (we used the term transsexual at that time) were male-to-female. Interestingly, most of them worked in super-macho fields: a bear guide, a Fish and Game ranger, a police officer, and a pharmacist. The bear guide had the thickest beard and deepest voice of all. She told me, "I came to Alaska to prove to myself and my family that I was a man." But eventually, she had to surrender to the fact that she was a woman on the inside and wanted to be one on the outside, too.

These women had been in jeopardy many times. They endured physical violence, job discrimination, and harassment. They faced internal and external obstacles to experiencing their truth. Victory was a moving target.

The police officer made the smoothest transition. Her special surgery in Thailand to minimize her brow and jawbones had made a big difference. She also had delicate features, which made her appear more feminine. She shopped at Nordstrom, an upscale department store, and had great taste in clothing. Her nicely styled brown hair fell to her shoulders. Her makeup was appropriate. She achieved a lovely transformation in the style of an American woman.

All of these women wanted to sound more feminine, which is what I helped them to do. Most men have an average habitual pitch of C below middle C on a piano, while women have an average habitual pitch of G below middle C. So first, I raised their pitch to the most comfortable level for them, as close to G as possible, usually E or F below middle C. While I recorded them, they practiced speaking at their new pitch repeatedly. Then I played it back to them, so their brains started hearing and accepting their new voice. That is called "ear training." I sent the recordings home with them to practice.

Voice placement was particularly important. Most men have what we called a "chest voice." I wanted these clients to place their voices in their heads instead of their chests. The "head voice" simply meant that you directed your voice upward and forward into the facial mask, between the eyebrows and the lips. Additionally, in their cases, I wanted them to adopt the Julia Child voice, speaking as an English lady (sans accent). This caused them to phonate on the thinner edge of the vocal folds instead of the thicker edge, which is how they currently spoke. I addressed other parameters of speech, such as prosody (melody of voice), intonation, rate of speech, and nonverbal communication (for example, don't sit with your legs open).

These women were remarkably vigilant. After our six sessions together to transform their voices, treatment ended. I hoped for all of them that their journey into womanhood was a pleasing one.

Working with this group also helped me realize, once again, how women are conditioned in our culture to look a certain way, act a certain way, and be a certain way to be deemed acceptable. I embraced and encouraged my clients wherever they were on their becoming. I did what I could to give them the dignity to be themselves. That is what I wanted for myself and why I pursued my career, even though I lacked confidence at the beginning. The more I learned and the more I did, the more confident I became. But sometimes, confidence is not enough.

CHAPTER 28
A Seizure Killed the Deal

I will seize fate by the throat; it shall certainly never wholly overcome me.
—Ludwig van Beethoven

"Hello, my name is Phillip Hanson, here for my appointment."

Phillip showed up at my office door unable to speak. He wrote what he wanted to say on a pad of paper and had prewritten his introduction.

I invited him into my office and asked him to take a seat. In 1987, he was in his early sixties, had a slight build, and nicely cut graying hair. About my height, he dressed in casual slacks and a long-sleeved, button-down shirt. He clearly took pride in his appearance. Then I saw the hole in his neck. It all started with cigarettes.

During his evaluation, Phillip answered my questions on his notepad or by nodding. He had smoked a pack or two of cigarettes a day for years. He developed a hoarse voice and made an appointment with an ENT. When the doctor finally diagnosed him with cancer of the larynx, he had a dire decision to make: have a laryngectomy and live, or ignore it and die. He chose laryngectomy.

Laryngectomy, which is the surgical removal of the larynx —usually for cancer—causes a total loss of the voice because the larynx houses the vocal cords. As a substitute, a small hole is made in the patient's neck, and their trachea is directly attached to it; it's called a stoma. Through the stoma the person breathes, coughs, and laughs. They chew and swallow as before the surgery, but they can't sniff their food. Since they can't smell, their taste is usually diminished.

After surgery, special techniques and equipment may restore a laryngectomee's voice to a certain degree. The client learns a kind of burping technique to make a speech-like sound, called esophageal speech.

There are electrical devices, such as the artificial larynx, used to provide a voice. About the size of an electric shaver, the laryngectomee holds it in his hand, places it against his throat, and presses the "on" button. A buzzing tone is emitted and remains until the user releases the button. It is adjustable for pitch and volume. With the correct neck placement, the client finds a "sweet spot" that propels the sound up into his mouth where it is articulated into words. It can sound robotic because the pitch, once it is set, does not change. In therapy, the client practices words, sentences, and conversations with the artificial larynx. These were the standards of treatment explained at a five-day Laryngectomee Rehabilitation Seminar I attended at the Mayo Clinic in 1984.

Recently recovered from having his laryngectomy, Phillip came to me for speech therapy, in the hope of communicating with oral speech again. He was tired of writing everything he wanted to say.

"Can you teach me esophageal speech?" he had pre-written.

"Yes, I can teach you esophageal speech, but let's get you an artificial larynx for now. It will make your life much easier while you are learning it." I picked up my loaner Electrolarynx and demonstrated how to use it.

In the back of my mind, however, I was thinking of something else. My laryngectomy rehabilitation skills had taken a giant leap forward recently. I had trained in the use of the tracheoesophageal puncture technique, which restored the laryngectomee's voice immediately after a simple, ten-minute surgery. Developed by Eric Blom, PhD-SLP, and Mark Singer, MD, the technique added a puncture into the patient's throat and a plastic tube (initially stainless steel) that fit into that puncture, providing a new source of vocal sound.

We were a group of five SLPs from around the world participating in a five-day training at the Head and Neck Cancer Institute in Indianapolis. Each of us was given a fellowship for the visiting clinician training.

On our first day there, we observed a laryngectomee (a person who has already had a laryngectomy) as he went through the brief tracheoesophageal puncture surgery with a local anesthetic. Twenty minutes later we spoke with that patient, who indicated by nodding that he did not feel any pain. Within a couple of days, we encountered that same man in the office for the placement of his voice prosthesis, which would restore a voice to him.

The prosthesis was simple to fit. I inserted it. "Take an easy breath and say ah," I said.

"Ahhhh," said the client. We both looked at each other with glee. It worked for him, and it worked for me. Compared to all the other laryngectomee patients I had worked with, this was marvelous. He had a big smile on his face and I looked like a parent who had just watched their child open a Christmas present.

"Now, I'm going to have you answer a few questions. What's your first name?"

"Paul," he said.

"Good. How did that feel? Was it simple or hard?"

"It was fine," he answered, with his new voice. We both laughed.

"Tell me the days of the week. Take a breath when you need one."

He continued to practice, speaking with sentences, reading a paragraph, and then having a short conversation with me. He talked the way he always had. Because he was vocalizing through a prosthesis—and not his true vocal cords—he didn't sound exactly the same as he used to, but he spoke with ease. No burping or holding a device to his neck and sounding robotic. After a full week with Dr. Blom and his patients, the five of us were ready to go home and apply what we had learned.

I was so appreciative of what the Blom-Singer device had done for people with laryngectomy. What a difficult decision they had to make in the first place, having their voice removed or dying of cancer. And what a major trauma to the body having that surgery. These people had been through so much. I wanted to offer this advanced treatment to them in Alaska.

I couldn't wait to get back to Anchorage to use it. The one issue stopping me was the need for an ENT to perform the surgery. Without that, we wouldn't have this brand-new option available in Alaska. Although some laryngectomees couldn't tolerate the Blom-Singer method because of poor tissue condition or other medical, visual, or dexterity problems, I'd give it my best shot.

I prepared to inform the handful of ENTs in town that I had this current knowledge and was excited to use it. Since I had worked with all their patients at one time or another, I decided to meet with them individually to let them know.

Dr. Mathison had a beautiful office. I had arranged to see him at the end of the day so that he wouldn't be distracted by his next patient. When I entered his empty waiting room, I gawked at the large, spectacular panels of sandblasted glass depicting Alaskan wildlife. One wall had a huge, beautifully lit aquarium. I felt hopeful he was a man who would appreciate innovation. I brought a voice prosthesis with me to show him how it worked if he didn't already know, and I had my efficiently honed spiel ready; I didn't want to waste his time. Since everyone, including his staff, was gone, I went to the hall and said hello in a raised voice.

Dr. Mathison came out of his office and waved me down the hall. We introduced ourselves and he told me to take a seat on the other side of his desk. It was scattered with paper and files, much like my own. I started to tell him about my recent training. "If you have any laryngectomy patients, I can offer the latest treatment for them."

He raised his hand up as if to say "Stop." Then he said, "I'm not going to be working with laryngectomy patients anymore. They have to be in the hospital for too many days, and I have to make rounds. They require too much time. I send them to Seattle for their surgery now, because we just don't have that many up here. Anyway, I'm going to be doing something different now."

As I sat on the other side of his desk, I noticed that he had been passing something back and forth between his hands, like a bean bag.

"I'm going to be doing these now," he said, throwing the mystery item across the desk to me. Reflexively, I caught it. It was no beanbag; it was a breast implant!

This doctor had just thrown me, a woman, a silicone breast implant like it was a ball. I couldn't believe it. But he wasn't through.

He went on, telling me, "I'm a plastic surgeon now; this is where the money is. I'll be performing breast implants from now on." He motioned to a framed certificate on his office wall that showed he had 300 hours of training, establishing him as a plastic surgeon.

Basically, he was boasting that it only took eight weeks for an ear, nose, and throat specialist to become a plastic surgeon. That scared me. I thought the American Medical Association had more common sense than that.

I sat there in a state between freeze and flight. I couldn't budge, but I wanted to get out of there as fast as possible. After an awkward moment, I thanked him for his time and left. I couldn't believe what had just happened. It was offensive, ludicrous, and sickening. But his story wasn't over.

In August of 1999, the first allegations of incompetence would be filed against Dr. Mathison with the Alaska State Medical Board. After further allegations surfaced of professional incompetence, repeated negligent conduct, and violation of malpractice reporting laws, it was determined that his continued practice posed a clear and immediate danger to the public. In April of 2002, he surrendered his medical license while in an administrative hearing, thankfully ending his practice and career in Alaska.

Meanwhile, I met with three ENTs who worked together in a different clinic. The first one was doing double duty between Seattle and Anchorage, so I knew better than to ask him. The second one told me he wasn't taking any additional patients because he would be retiring soon. That left only one doctor. I asked the last man standing. "Dr. Roman, I wanted to let you know that I have the training to fit a Blom-Singer voice prosthesis. If you ever have a laryngectomy patient that you would like to try it with, I'm available. Can you do the surgery?"

"Yes, I can. In fact, the laryngectomee I sent you, Phillip, would be a good candidate."

"Oh, that's great," I said. "That would be wonderful for him."

Phillip's simple surgery went well. I went to Dr. Roman's office with all of my paraphernalia to insert the prosthesis. Dr. Blom insisted that the insertion of the prosthesis be done in a physician's office, in case anything went wrong. I got there ahead of time to organize all the implements I needed to insert the prosthesis.

"Are you ready for this?" I asked Phillip when he arrived.

Phillip, smiling, answered with his electrolarynx, "Oh yes. I want to get rid of this thing."

I started by inserting a long, hollow red rubber tube through his insertion site, the tracheal-esophageal puncture the doctor had performed. Then I blew into it and listened for the sound of the air coming back up from his esophagus. When I heard it, I knew that physically, he was ready for the prosthesis placement. The red rubber tube wouldn't be needed again; I threw it away.

Then, I handed Phillip a large hand-mirror, asked him to watch what I was doing, and explained everything as I placed the voice prosthesis. All went well. I had Phillip say "ah." Eureka! He was speaking right away, just like the patients at Dr. Blom's office.

We were a couple of minutes into a simple conversation, with everything going beautifully, when he had a seizure. I was stunned, devastated, and momentarily terrified that his seizure would be serious. But thankfully, it was mercifully short and mild, only five or six seconds of fluttering eyelids. When it was over, he just leaned back in his chair and closed his eyes. Luckily, the chair had a high back and a headrest. I didn't have one of those chairs in my office. I learned with this experience why Dr. Blom had made the rule that prosthetic placement needed to be done in a doctor's office. He was right.

After the seizure, I had Phillip rest for a few minutes without talking. Then I went and found the doctor. He checked Phillip's vitals, which were normal. We weighed the options and concluded that I should remove the prosthesis, let the puncture site close on its own, and proceed with esophageal speech and the artificial larynx. I hid my disappointment but understood the decision. Phillip's seizure could have been random, but on the other hand, he might be more prone to a seizure when speaking. He had never mentioned the fact that he had seizures on my intake evaluation, so it wasn't taken into consideration.

This demonstrates the importance of getting a thorough history. Sometimes people leave out information because they think it might be a deal-breaker. Sadly, this was indeed a deal-breaker for Phillip. For the few minutes that he used the voice prosthesis, he talked as easily as you and I. His seizure killed the deal.

CHAPTER 29

Hypernasality

Let people catch something from your heart that will cause no discomfort, but help them to sing.
—Rumi

One of the other problems people endure related to the voice is hypernasality. Hypernasality is usually caused by a cleft palate or by a short soft palate, which does not contact the back wall of the throat. Speech, therefore, sounds as if it is coming through the speaker's nose. We call that sound hypernasal. Stanley, my fourth-grade friend, had this.

In Alaska, all children born with cleft palate and lip were assisted by a team of specialists contracted with the state. This system worked well. No matter where in Alaska a baby was born with a cleft palate or lip, this team convened and took care of her or him. The parents were trained in feeding techniques. Surgery schedules were arranged. After surgery, speech therapy started. For this reason, I never worked with a child with a cleft palate in my private practice. I did, however, work with a grown man who had hypernasality. Something was wrong.

Mike was in his thirties when he met me. He was single but didn't want to be, and he thought his speech had something to do with it. He had a lifelong problem. His speech had too much sound coming through his nose. I did an oral exam and discovered that his soft palate was too short to contact the back of his throat. Therefore, air escaped through his nose that should have gone through his mouth. He was born this way; it was a birth defect. This kind of physiological problem can only be corrected by surgery. He needed to consult an ENT.

I sent Mike to Dr. Williams. I had worked with many of Dr. Williams's patients who had vocal nodules, hoarseness, and polyps. He'd performed many cleft palate surgeries, and I knew he'd be able to take care of Mike. After surgery, Mike would return to me for any follow-up speech therapy.

Not long after I referred him, I received a phone call from Dr. Williams's office. "Would you like to come to the outpatient surgery center to watch Mike's operation?" his assistant asked me.

I calmly answered, "Yes, I'd appreciate that," but inside, I ballooned with excitement. I had the opportunity to watch a master at work on one of my own patients. What could be more interesting than that?

On the day of surgery, Dr. Williams asked me to stand at the top and to the left of the narrow operating table. It was in a small room; the walls were lined with equipment and covered by those gray, metal cabinets, and the shelves were loaded with boxes of medical supplies. The operating room I imagined from the movies didn't look like this. It looked like a storage closet with surgery taking place in the middle of it. Then Dr. Williams began.

Obviously, Mike was under anesthesia. His head was tilted back, and his mouth was open. Dr. Williams stood behind Mike's head and looked down into his mouth. He placed a bite block between Mike's back teeth so his mouth stayed open. Then he took a medical instrument, like a tiny hoe, and forcefully scraped the skin off of the roof of Mike's mouth, back and away from his hard palate.

The difference in the roof of the mouth can be felt by the tongue. Beginning from front to back, a hard surface is felt in the front, which changes to soft skin about halfway back. This back part, known as the soft palate or the velum, had to be pushed back. To do that, the tissue had to be scraped loose from the hard palate in the front. It was stunning to witness; this appeared radical to me. It also looked painful.

Next, Dr. Williams turned his attention to the back wall of Mike's throat, the pharynx. On the pharynx, he made a little flap from the skin by slicing under a small piece of tissue on three sides, leaving the top of the flap attached. Then, he brought this flap forward and sewed it to Mike's soft palate, which was now farther back. This was called a pharyngeal flap. It helped close the opening between Mike's soft palate and the back of his nose, causing his voice to exit through his mouth instead of his nasal passages. If all went according to plan, this procedure would significantly reduce his hypernasality.

A couple of weeks later, Mike came to me for his first post-op appointment. The outcome thrilled me. His hypernasality was virtually gone. I only had a few things to teach him. We went through some exercises, and I discharged him. Before he left, I had to ask that one question.

"Did it hurt?"

"No, not at all," he answered, to my surprise.

I relaxed with relief.

A few months later, Mike dropped by my clinic around closing time.

"Mike, what are you doing here?" I asked him with a smile.

"Hi, Mrs. Roberts," he said. "I wanted to come by and thank you." He was so happy. "Do you have a minute?"

"Sure," I answered, "come and sit down. How's everything going?"

"Well, my life has completely changed since I saw you last. I left my old job and got a better one. I make more money and have more responsibility. I think my speech is the reason for that."

"That's wonderful," I nodded. He had confided in me the difficulties of having a speech disorder, including how he had been judged as less intelligent and felt less lovable as a result.

"Also, I got a new girlfriend. We've been going out for a couple of months now. Everything is going so great. I'm not as shy as I used to be, and I just talk with her and I'm not embarrassed or afraid. Everything is going so well, and I just wanted you to know how much you helped me."

I was so proud and appreciative of him for taking the time to visit me. I rarely had the opportunity to see the outcome of my work because after discharge, patients typically left and got on with their lives.

Since the surgery, his speech and his life had completely changed. Mike had a new self-confidence. He wasn't embarrassed to speak, and when he did, he wasn't being ridiculed for it. I felt humbled and honored to have been a member of the team that made it possible for him to have the life he'd always wanted. He reminded me of why I did what I did.

As I sat in my office chair after he left, a warm feeling of gratitude and love came over me. My calling not only helped people with communication disorders; it helped me. There is a great satisfaction in seeing others improve their lives with my assistance. Seeing the changes in their communication encouraged me to be more confident in mine.

CHAPTER 30
He Spelled Out "Gun"

Don't tell someone to get over it. Help them to get through it.
—Sue Fitzmaurice

It took four and a half hours to drive south from Anchorage to the town of Kenai. Holly, no longer a floor nurse but working for an insurance agency to direct patient rehabilitation, hired me to work with a middle-aged man who had recently returned to his home. He had been in hospital and rehabilitation after having a construction accident that resulted in locked-in syndrome. Many of the healthy middle-aged men I worked with in hospitals were there for that same reason —construction injuries. Luckily, Alaska had a great worker's compensation program. They paid for services as billed. This man was no exception.

When I first met Ken, he lay in a hospital bed, his head raised, in his bedroom in Kenai. With locked-in syndrome, he was worse off than a total quadriplegic. He had no movement below his neck or above his neck, except for his eyebrows. He had a percutaneous endoscopic gastrostomy (PEG) tube for feeding and was on a respirator. Mentally, he was fine. He lacked a way to communicate. I couldn't leave him like this.

SLPs create augmentative and alternative communication systems (AAC), which are designed to support, enhance, or supplement the communication of people who cannot talk, either temporarily or permanently. A simple AAC is an alphabet board on which the individual points to letters and spells out words to his communication partner. Picture systems are made for those who can't spell. But what if they couldn't point? Is an eyebrow enough to control an AAC? Absolutely, yes!

I had designed simple AAC systems when I was in college. We didn't have computers then. As time went on, computers were designed with programs that spoke for an individual. The notable physicist, Stephen Hawking, used a computer for his AAC. He selected words and commands using a hand clicker. But Ken couldn't tap even one finger. Luckily, he could move one eyebrow.

For Ken, I ordered a computerized AAC system with an eyebrow switch. Once everything was in place, I asked Mary, a local, private practice SLP, to step in for regular visits to train him. I flew to Kenai once a month on a twenty-minute flight to troubleshoot, see how things were progressing, and update his treatment plan. I scheduled therapy more often if needed, and Mary and I consulted on the phone as well. Quickly, we all decided on a simple program. His computer screen displayed the alphabet in a particular configuration, with the vowels together on one side. Ken spelled out words and sentences with his eyebrow switch. This worked well for him, and he communicated this way as long as he wanted.

One day, Mary called me with a disturbing situation. Ken had spelled *gun* and *closet*, for days and days. His health aide worried that he wanted to kill himself. Eventually, the family decided to get his gun out of the closet, a rifle. He spelled *stock*. This part of the gun presses to the shoulder and is the butt of the rifle. Then he spelled *open*. They opened the stock of the gun and were surprised to find three thousand dollars hidden inside. Ken didn't want to shoot himself. He wanted to provide for his family.

Many people hid cash in their homes for emergencies. This was a clever hiding place; I had to give him that. His relieved family now knew that his message was the opposite of what we all were thinking. Here was yet another example of how important it is to be able to communicate. Even if you can indicate just one letter at a time, it is enough. SLPs can help; it is our calling.

On one of my trips to visit Ken in Kenai, I flew on a daily flight out of Anchorage. The plane had twenty seats. The Cook Inlet lies between Anchorage and Kenai and is notorious for rough winds. The mornin flight was steady and relaxed, but on the way back, the rolling, gusty, tossing, buffeting winds were endless. There was no respite from one bump to the next. We jostled. Our heads bounced. Then we shook left to right, each wing of the plane plunging side-to-side. Every passenger tightly belted themselves and hung onto their armrests, their feet holding down carry-ons. Then, the big one hit.

As the plane plunged, a sharp jolt propelled all of our heads toward the low ceiling of the plane at the same time, even with our seatbelts fastened. It looked funny until two rows ahead of me, the chairs bolted to the floor broke loose. The people pitched forward and caught themselves on the back of the seats in front of them. As quickly as possible, they scrambled to unoccupied seats that were still attached to the plane. This harrowing ride took twenty minutes.

Thank the Lord it was such a short flight. That was the worst turbulence I ever experienced in all of my flying days in Alaska. When we touched down, everyone applauded, cheered, and laughed. That pilot was masterful. From that day on, I gauged the turbulence of future flights by this trip from Kenai.

Since I lived through that voyage, I knew I didn't have to worry about turbulence again, unless it became worse. There could never be a more turbulent flight than that one. It was like being on a roller coaster at the carnival, exciting and terrible, both at the same time. The adventures in Alaska just kept on coming, each one leading me to the next.

My bumpy ride at home had taken a turn with computers as well. Bill now spent hours in the back of the living room during the evening playing computer games. He killed people with machine-gun bullet sounds and "blood" splattering all over the screen. He dropped bombs on ships at sea with great explosions. In his computer-generated car, he ran over computer-generated people walking on the side of the road, causing them to cry out. Need I say more?

I had to find some peace. I took up meditation, hoping to get some relief from my migraines. Instead, I discovered a fountain of love inside myself. Even through my headaches, I experienced an incredible feeling of happiness. My life force returned to me, the force of love that I had used to freeze myself in time so that I wouldn't have to suffer the loss of my father.

Knowing how tense Bill was, looking at him with the great love I felt, I invited him to join me. Instead, reducing me to tears, he ridiculed meditation, me, and my teacher. He became so opposed to it that he told me to never speak to him about meditation again. I felt like he threw a part of me, a lovely part, into that volcano I could see from our living room window, a mountain whose aboriginal Athabaskan name literally meant "burning inside." I had hoped, like boating on the Prince William Sound, that this could be another "us" activity, not another rugged individual pastime. Once the topic of meditation blazed out of our reality as a couple, a practice that I had found so affirming, gentle, and amazing, I felt fear and sadness grow hotter in my gut.

Like a private in Bill's private army, I had to take his harsh orders. He made a decision, and I had to follow it to make him happy. What about my happiness? He seemed incapable of acknowledging it or recognizing it. Intentionally stuffed down by my own husband, the one I loved the most, I started to find this disrespectful situation unbearable. Now when I meditated, I meditated on loving myself. He might be able to control my outside, but he couldn't control my inside. I would merge into love without him.

Thankfully, my work allowed me to stay sane. My patients were helping me, although I never mixed my personal life with my professional life. In some cases, I could see that my plight was worse than theirs. I could fix that vocal nodule in six weeks. Voilà! But my problem at home was a day-to-day grind, four seasons of slush and trudge, summer never bringing relief. Too hot for the northern lights, too cold for fresh leaves on the trees. I felt left in a constant cloud cover of drizzle, stuck in the glacial mud that clung to my boots, and my headaches were getting the best of me. I started to take Wednesdays off to rest and reduce stress.

It made me wonder about my patients' families. How much support did they get? With the exception of truly evil people, like Genie and Robert's parents, I think with the children, the support was great. Parents had to bring them to therapy, pick them up, and practice at home. But these were the children I saw. What about the families that didn't even know about speech therapy or didn't want to admit their child had a problem?

That's what is so great about the public schools screening for children with speech disorders. The SLP will find them, and the child can be treated at school. But in the villages, I might find that child, but who was going to treat them?

I eventually stopped traveling to the bush in the late 1990s because I felt like a token therapist. The school followed the law by having me screen, but I was never invited back to treat. I had to do something to get more services into the village schools. I had to work at a systems level. I had to use my voice. I turned to the educational system.

First, I spoke with several principals and encouraged them to employ a year-round SLP, one who could continually make the rounds from village to village. The North Slope Borough and the Nome school district followed through on that suggestion. Encouraged, I moved on to my next idea.

I started an Associate of Arts (AA) program with the only junior college in Alaska. We developed a distance learning program for speech therapy assistants, based on successful programs in the Lower 48. We sent each student a box of materials at the beginning of the semester containing all the books, materials, and exams. Classes were held over the phone. Low tech was important because computer access was still limited throughout Alaska except for the larger cities. Graduates would be qualified to work as a Speech-Language Pathology Assistant in a school or private practice.

The program was a great success. The only problem was that no one in the villages took the classes. The students were primarily from Anchorage, Fairbanks, and Juneau. After the first year, I had to drop out of administration of the program due to health. The college sent course offerings to all the schools in Alaska, but recruiting in the bush wasn't itemized. I don't think the high school kids in the villages knew about the program. If they did know, they didn't understand what it meant. None of us could afford to go on a recruiting trip. It was extremely expensive to fly to the villages.

The AA program continued to be highly successful and recently became part of the UAA distance learning program for speech-language pathology. Hopefully, they have done a better job advertising in the villages. Unfortunately, the units per class are much more expensive than at the junior college.

CHAPTER 31
Dyslexia

Tell me and I forget. Teach me and I remember. Involve me and I learn.
—Benjamin Franklin

I entered the small conference room at a downtown hotel and took a seat. There were about fifteen chairs set up in a U shape around some tables. It was June 1994, warm, and the sun streamed in through the windows. I usually went into a course open-minded but a little skeptical at the same time. Methods needed to be proven to me or I wasn't interested. If it didn't get results quickly, then it wasn't the best practice. I wanted to use superior programs with my clients. I did not want to waste their time or mine. Thus, I tended to think, this had better be as good as I had heard it was.

This workshop had been on my radar for a long time. Expensive? Yes, because it took five days to complete. But I did not have to fly to the Lower 48 and rent a hotel room, so it was a deal.

Turning on the overhead projector, the trainer gave us the grim statistics on dyslexia and the even grimmer statistics on the state of school reading scores across the country. Dyslexia is a learning disability. It is the largest learning disability identified in public education: eighty to ninety percent of students in special education are there because they cannot read. These children drop out of high school at twice the rate of their non-disabled peers. Most do not get identified until the age of eleven, and that is too late, especially when only twenty-one percent of teachers feel adequately prepared to accommodate students with learning disabilities in their classrooms.

One of the most important skills our students learn by the end of twelfth grade is oral and written language comprehension and expression. Unfortunately, between kindergarten and third grade, about thirty percent of children begin to fail in one of the three sensory-cognitive skills necessary for reading, spelling, and comprehension—phonemic awareness, symbol imagery, and concept imagery. Even though their lower skill levels can be identified, stimulated, and improved, without that help they tend to peak at a fourth-grade level and are labeled dyslexic. Children who cannot read or comprehend will not be successful in school. They may not be able to learn independently or reach their potential.

As the week continued, I learned how to stimulate and improve the sensory-cognitive skills to overcome dyslexia. And in fact, the program's research using fMRI showed changes in the brains of the dyslexic subjects who went through their curriculum, demonstrating the principals of neuroplasticity inherent in the program. These programs not only changed their client's reading, spelling, and comprehension, but they also changed their brains.

The programs were research-validated (a better designation than scientifically based), and they applied directly to a group of clients I worked with: those who had difficulty with phonemic awareness and symbol imagery (speaking, reading, spelling) and concept imagery (comprehending oral and written speech). In other words, children with delayed speech and language development. By the end of the five days, I wanted to start using the programs right away.

If a child's reading skills are six months behind at the end of first grade, the research shows that their abilities will likely level off no higher than a fourth-grade level. That is when teachers stop teaching reading. Without intervention, they are doomed to low self-esteem, failure in school, behavior problems, and a higher probability of dropping out of school.

At the end of the week, the facilitator announced they planned to hold an intensive summer clinic for children in Eagle River during the month of August. Eagle River was a town about twenty minute out of Anchorage. A clinic there would be close enough for me to see the program in action. In fact, I wanted to work in that summer clinic.

I garnered my courage and wrote to the facilitator's offices, proposing that I work at the Eagle River intensive as one of their clinicians. I loved total immersion. I learned best by doing, and if I could work with experienced clinicians, I knew I'd get the most out of my training.

I still had my own office to run in the Dimond Mall, so I couldn't work full-time, but I could work half-time. Would they be willing to hire me for half a day? They said yes.

Well, let's just say that it was the best thing I ever did. They paid me the wages of a beginning clinician, seven dollars and change per hour. I charged $120 an hour for services at my clinic, so I took a substantial pay cut. But it was worth it. When I involved myself in the program, I learned it.

I learned how the whole program melded together over time. I witnessed how easily one thing led to another and how, for the children, the pacing made learning effortless. I experienced the brilliance of intensive treatment—four hours a day, five days a week, for six weeks. I read the pre- and post-testing scores and was amazed at the progress the children made. Depending on their age, they improved a shocking four years or more in their reading scores. Finally, I experienced the importance of intensive treatment related to neuroplasticity. This program was on the cutting edge, the gold standard.

At the end of the month-long clinic, a fourth-grade boy needed more treatment. He came to my clinic for follow-up therapy. I booked him for one hour, on Tuesday and Thursday after school. Yes, he continued to make progress, but after working intensively, I was disappointed with the lack of momentum. In the back of my mind, I knew that if I decided to offer this program at my clinic, I would have to do it intensively.

Contemplating the necessary details to start a clinic large enough to incorporate the program into my services, I thought about the employees I would have to hire. My aversion to having employees was still strong. The whole thing was too daunting.

But I had that nagging feeling—an intuition that if I didn't do it, who would? People needed this program everywhere. Anchorage was no exception. Anxiety defeated me. I decided not to do it.

Then Bill came home one night and told me, "Dan is starting his own engineering business with a couple other guys, and they're moving into your building." Bill worked with Dan at the power company.

"Really?" I said. "Where's their office going to be?"

"On the fourth floor in the corner, looking north at Denali and east at the Chugach Range," he said. We described everything in relation to our landscape.

"Wow, that's going to be expensive. Do you know what they are paying?" I asked.

The answer wasn't good. They were paying less than we were, by two dollars a square foot.

After six years, it was time for Kathleen, Janice, and me to renew our three-year lease. The economy had slumped in Anchorage, and I didn't want to pay an increase in rent. Plus, thoughts of opening an intensive clinic for people with dyslexia meant I would have to move to a bigger space.

I thought about how we could renegotiate our current lease. I knew Dan had just opened an office one floor above us in the corner. Higher floors had higher rents. Corner suites were more expensive than inside suites, like ours. Naturally, I thought they would pay more than we did.

We had been there for six years; we were proven renters, on a lower floor, and no corner. The new guys, who were on the higher floor and in a corner suite, were paying less. When we renegotiated our lease, I wanted a decrease. I did not want to pay more than the engineers paid. That seemed fair to me.

The three of us went to the sixth floor, the highest floor, for our rent negotiation. I informed Janice and Kathleen that I'd leave if we didn't get a decrease in our rental contract. They were okay with that. Janice knew an SLP who would rent my office space if I left.

It was the principle of it. Since the first landlord who took advantage of me, I had learned my lesson. I also didn't like the smell of gender discrimination. These men were given a better deal than the women.

We entered the corner suite of the man who ran the Dimond Mall. It had windows on two sides, with an incredible view of Denali. He wore a suit; so did I. He sat on the other side of a large, imposing desk. That didn't scare me. Yes, he thought he was important, and he was. I didn't think I was important, but I thought I was right. Let the negotiations begin.

Before we were through, he was actually screaming at us—well, mostly me. I couldn't believe his unprofessional behavior. He refused to reduce our rent in any way, shape, or form, no matter how much logical information I presented to him. Men are so emotional. How did it conclude? Kathleen and Janice stayed with an increase in rent. I left.

CHAPTER 32

Now or Never

Learning is not attained by chance, it must be sought for with ardor and attended to with diligence.
—Abigail Adams

As I deepened my intention to help all people with communication disorders, I struggled. Reading and writing are more abstract, higher-level forms of communication, which I now knew how to stimulate and improve. In our time, illiteracy is a huge barrier to participating fully in life. To eliminate my fear of proceeding, I had to get over my aversion to the IRS, hiring employees, having a large clinic, making payroll, and being a boss. These thoughts that held me back also had the domino effect of holding back all the potential people who needed help.

I kept seeing the faces of those people. If I just let go of the limitations I created in my mind, the people would blossom, like the fuchsia fireweed that blankets the land in August. Even with my constant migraine and nausea, I had to mature. I had to assume a role greater than any I had ever anticipated. Fulfilling the idea could make a profound difference in peoples' futures. A fresh passion filled me at the thought of opening a clinic with intensive instruction. Overcoming my fearful soul, I followed that passion into a unique way of working, not just for myself but for all Alaskans.

When I chose not to renew my office space at the Dimond Mall, I knew I had an important decision to make. I constantly thought about adding the dyslexia program to my already long list of efforts. There was something about meditating that had increased my life force, opened my heart, and increased my courage even more. Within a few months, I took the plunge. Hopefully, that plunge wouldn't end up like the Cook Inlet, drowning in quicksand. I found a larger office space at the Emerald Building, across the street from the Dimond Mall.

I rented a couple thousand square feet. Large windows lined the two outside walls facing south and west, the best directions. Plenty of sun poured into each treatment room. I added one-way mirror windows in between each one. A small kitchen area tripled as a place to prepare our lunches, keep snacks, and store the client's working folders. A proper check-in area, enclosed with glass, complete with a sliding window, accommodated my clinical assistant. Bill ordered and customized new computers and printers for the whole office.

I hired a professional decorator to make the office inviting and beautiful. She used rich teal accents on an entry wall, tabletops, and the fabric on the hardwood chairs, just like the mauve ones at the hospital. This office was my pride and joy.

Emerald Speech and Learning Clinic, Inc., opened in 1996. It was the largest speech-language pathology clinic in the history of Alaska at the time. I was nervous. I had just rented a tremendous amount of space. The decorating cost alone was five thousand dollars. But it was beautiful. I walked into my clinic every morning filled with delight.

Now that I had this inviting and large clinic, how could I inform people about our services? What was the most effective way to advertise? Not surprisingly, it turned out to be television. The production people advised me that it would cost six thousand dollars (ouch) to have a commercial made to run five times a week for six weeks, including once a week during the extremely popular *Oprah Winfrey Show*. If they had dead time, the television station would air it during the wee hours of the night for free. Once again, I decided to bite the bullet, spend the money, and see what happened.

In the commercial, I promoted our speech therapy services and the new reading program. At the end of the commercial, my two small, white Maltese dogs were filmed individually walking down the hallway. As they walked, the camera zoomed in on one dog, Honey Bear, and a voiceover said,

"I learned how to talk at Emerald Speech and Learning Clinic." Then, filming the other dog, Yogi Bear said, "And I learned how to read, too." Okay, cheesy, I know, to use my doggies, but they were so cute. And let's face it, dogs get our attention.

What happened? People quickly signed up. We were full in no time. After that, we never advertised again; it was all word of mouth. Someone told a friend how well their child or loved one learned at our clinic, and the friend signed up. The physicians saw what a great difference we made in their young patients, and they referred to us. We were usually booked out one or two sessions for reading. Each session lasted six weeks. Summer booked up by March. We had waiting lists.

I never felt like the clinic was *mine*; I felt like it was *ours*, all eleven of us. By "ours," I mean all of the nine therapists and the office manager who worked there with me. Without them, nothing would have happened. The nagging feeling I'd had was correct. I did need to open this clinic; I did need to serve this population; I did need to mature and grow and overcome my outdated fears of employees and the IRS.

Children and adults from all over the state enrolled in the six-week intensive programs. It was extremely rewarding to see the tremendous amounts of progress made by each person in such a short time. It was gratifying to see the pride on each client's face as they left the clinic, now able to read, compared with how they had entered it.

I remember a little boy and girl specifically. The boy, who had just started second grade, came to the clinic in the afternoons. He walked in the door like a tough guy, ready to knock somebody's block off.

This was one of the three ways children's behavior changed if they didn't learn how to read like the other children in their classroom. They acted out against others, they acted inward on themselves, or they withdrew, even to the point of falling asleep in school. And, by the way, nobody had to tell him that he couldn't read. He knew it.

On Friday of the first week, we sent a simple book home

with him to read to his parents. On Monday, he walked in the front door and said, with joy, "You taught me more about reading in one week than I learned in a whole year at school."

Obviously, he had heard an adult say this and repeated it. A seven-year-old cannot make that connection. But he was proud. He could learn. By the time he finished his six weeks with us, he was reading beyond his grade level.

The little girl, starting third grade in the fall, came for the summer program. She lived in another town with her father during the school year, and over the summer she lived with her mother in Anchorage. She walked through the door with her head down, eyes watching the floor, and her shoulders rounded forward. She appeared defeated.

This was the second way children who could not read reacted. She was ashamed of herself and insecure. She started to have headaches and did not want to go to school.

Because her testing was so low (below first grade), I wanted to work with this girl first. She had a severe phonemic awareness disorder. Her history revealed that she had multiple ear infections when she was younger. This medical problem can cause poor phonemic awareness, which thirty percent of the population exhibits. In fact, there is a fifty-two percent higher incidence of otitis media (ear infections) in the state of Alaska compared to the rest of the country.

Otitis media is a persistent middle ear effusion. It's like hearing under water. Studies indicate that recurrent otitis media episodes before the age of three years correlate significantly to several types of deficits, some of which have persisted to at least the age of eighteen. They include language deficits; speech sound sensitivity; articulation errors; poor ability to discriminate speech sounds in a quiet environment; depressed verbal intelligence scores; pervasive auditory processing deficits; significantly poorer reading ability; hyperactive and inattentive behavior problems; adverse effect on reading comprehension; lower performance in mathematical skills; poor classroom concentration; lower scores on tests of cognitive ability, verbal ability, auditory decoding, and spelling skills; poor auditory-visual integration; and auditory perception disorders.

Poor phonemic awareness causes failure to read because it interferes with a person's ability to perceive sounds. I explained to this eight-year-old what we were going to be doing: learning a new way to think about sounds. After I had her discover how the brain—the thinker—works for reading, with the eyes looking, the ears hearing, and the mouth moving, I added feeling. This is the missing piece for many children and the key to unlocking the door to phonemic awareness. The first sound I asked her to say was /p/.

"Match me. Say /p/." I modeled it for her and had her copy me.

"/p/"

"What did you feel moving—your lips or your tongue?" I asked. Most children quickly said, "My lips."

She answered, "Tongue," because it was the last word she heard me say. She did not feel what her lips and tongue were doing; she did not perceive it. If she did not have the sensory perception that her lips moved, she had no self-awareness of what she was doing. Without self-awareness, she could not self-correct and become independent. She would always need someone by her side to correct her. My goal with her was independence. She needed to become self-aware.

"Let's check and see. Match me, say /p/." This time I over articulated the sound.

"/p/," she said.

"What did you feel, your lips or your tongue?"

"My tongue."

"If it was your tongue, it would look like this /t/, or this, / l/. Is that what you felt?"

She nodded her head "yes."

"Let's look in the mirror." I gave her a small hand mirror. "Look at your mouth. Touch your lips. Show me your tongue. Lift your tongue up, like this. Put your tongue down, like this.

Very good."

"Now look in the mirror and say /p/. What do you see moving, your lips or your tongue?"

"My tongue."

"Look at me when I say /p/. What did you see moving, my lips or my tongue?'

"Your lips."

"Good thinking," I said with a smile. "Did they pop open or stay shut?"

"Pop . . . open?" she asked.

"Good checking."

"Now you try it. Say /p/ and tell me what you feel moving, your lips or your tongue?"

It took her about seven minutes of stimulation before she told me that she felt her lips. She had a severe phonemic awareness disorder.

By the time she left our clinic, she read at a solid third grade level and was ready for school that year. She left the clinic with her head up, her eyes forward, and her shoulders relaxed. I said goodbye with a big smile, gratified by her wonderful progress.

Sometimes, as in the case of this young lady, we didn't get paid. We billed her insurance, which covered speech therapy. Unfortunately, the services were declined because her speech coverage ended on her eighth birthday. She had already turned eight. Therefore, we had to bill her mother.

Her mother said, "I don't have the money to pay for that, send the bill to her father."

Let it begin; the battle of the divorced "adults."

We billed her father, and he also refused to pay. I decided to call Daddy on the phone, because I knew he made more money than Mommy, and he could make some payments.

"Hello, this is Kit Roberts from Emerald Speech and Learning Clinic in Anchorage."

Silence.

"Is this Mr. Doe?"

"Yes."

"Well, you know that your insurance declined any payment for Jane because she already had her eighth birthday. I was wondering if you could make any payments?"

"No. I already told you this whole thing was her mother's idea, and she can pay for it."

"She's a hairdresser and barely makes enough money to support herself."

"I'm not paying anything," he said.

"Your daughter couldn't read at all when she came to us, she had very serious problems. We worked with her intensively for six weeks. Couldn't you pay something? We taught Jane how to read. She's at a third-grade level now. She's a completely different girl."

"Let her mother pay for it." Click.

He hung up on me. He was angry. When I reminded him that we taught his little girl how to read, he didn't even say, "Thank you." *You're welcome*, I thought to myself after I hung up.

Jane had just completed 120 hours of treatment, for which I had to pay my clinicians. And I wasn't paying seven dollars an hour; I was paying twenty to forty an hour. So I lost a minimum of $2,400 of cold, hard cash. I had just paid for his child to receive treatment through our clinic. I sent both parents bills for a few months and then gave up. I did my part. That was their karma. As a parent, I would have been mortified to stiff someone who had helped my child so much. But they weren't even the worst.

I lost about ten thousand dollars a year from people who never paid, even with a collection agency. Considering the number of people who attended our clinic, I decided to let go of the frustration of it. I was "paying it forward." I considered it a donation to the children who needed it. The parents weren't my problem. I took care of my problem: the children who needed my help.

Then, after I opened my clinic, a great boon arrived—Denali Kid Care. It came from the Children's Health Insurance Program (CHIP), which provided speech therapy benefits to children who qualified for the program beginning in 1997. It derived from a bill at the federal level, where a group of our representatives did something at the highest level of government to help these children who "fell through the cracks" because their parents couldn't afford health insurance.

Suddenly, children whose families would not have been able to afford speech therapy could attend my clinic. I could bill the federally funded Denali Kid Care program for their services. What a return on investment. Preventing reading disorders and improving literacy would decrease the numbers of children in special education and increase the earning power of every child who came to my clinic. Those children would grow up, get a job, and pay taxes—taxes that would be turned around and used to maintain the CHIP. Once again, I love it when everybody wins.

At the same time, a group of parents whose children had autism lobbied to get their children's private rehabilitation services paid for through Denali Kid Care. Insurance companies had squirmed out of paying for autism treatment by saying that it wasn't a medical problem; it was developmental. These children needed speech, occupational, and physical therapy year-round, not just when they were in school. They also needed it as early as possible, before they entered school. I'm very proud of those parents who finally got treatment for autism covered by the Alaskan CHIP program. Speaking up is important. Sometimes it's easier to do for the love of others than for ourselves. But speak up we must.

At home, Bill spoke up. "I want a divorce."

"Can't we please go see a psychologist, at least once—talk to a trained professional to help us with our problems? I'll find a male psychologist," I said, thinking that would make him more comfortable.

"Okay, just one time," said Bill.

As we entered the office downtown, we sat across from the psychologist. He was about our age, in his forties, and wore a dark suit.

"So, why are you here today?" he asked.

Bill spoke first. "I don't like her meditating, I'm tired of it and I want a divorce."

"What is your background with similar things, like church? Do you go to church?" he asked Bill.

"No. I was raised Catholic, and I stopped going when I was seven years old."

"Did anything bad happen to you?" the psychologist asked.

"No. My mom made me go. I was an altar boy. But my dad stayed home and watched football on Sundays. I didn't like it and I didn't want to go, so I stopped."

"What about you?" he turned and looked at me.

"I was raised Lutheran, but since marrying Bill, I haven't attended any church. I started meditating when I was thirty-eight to help with migraine headaches. That was the first time I learned how to feel my inner love, what people might call spiritual love. I asked Bill to come one time, because he is under a lot of stress and is always gritting his teeth. I thought it would be good if he could relax and feel that love too. He refused to try it, and he doesn't like me doing it. Sometimes our meditation group meets at our house. Then he has to hang out in the bedroom and watch TV downstairs. He doesn't like that either."

"So, Bill, is this a deal breaker for you?"

"Yes. I want a divorce."

"What about you, Kit?"

"I'm not going to stop developing my inner self. I've given him everything else. I do everything he wants to do. When he wanted me to be a certified scuba diver, I did that. When he wanted me to ride motorcycles, I did that. I learned how to down-hill ski, drive a boat, camp, hike, fish, and explore. I enjoyed them all. I've asked him to come to meditation one time and see for himself if it is anything he might like. I haven't said he has to do it forever. If he thinks that one little thing is going to kill him, I haven't been able to change his mind. That's why we are here today," I said.

I had met Bill during the hippie generation, when "love will steer the stars." I had an unconscious contract with him when we married. We would share love, not just sex. When I found that deeper love, I expected to share it with him. I realized that was my hope, my aspiration—not his. I hadn't tried to change him before, but oh, how I wanted him to join me now.

"Well, Bill," the psychologist asked, "are you willing to go just once?"

"No."

"Well, then, there's your final answer. Thank you for coming today."

The psychologist walked to his heavy office door and opened it, like a boulder opening into a dark cave. Bill went through first. Then as I walked through, the psychologist paused, looked into my eyes and said, "Well, I guess that didn't go the way you wanted it to, did it?"

Shocked by his snide comment, in my mind I replied, "What an unprofessional thing to say. I'll be reporting you to the licensing board for that." But my throat was locked tight, trying to hold back the tears now that I was going to be getting a divorce. I felt like I would burst, but I didn't want Bill to know. I had to keep myself together, to continue the big lie that I was tough, like him, and nothing would make my frozen tears fall where he could see them. I could cry later when he wasn't around.

Bill found an arbitrator to help with the divorce. She was less expensive than using an attorney, and Bill always thought about the money. I just went along with it like everything else Bill did. After about a month of gathering accounts, deeds, and vehicle titles, we were getting to the point of finishing.

I had spent the month overwhelmed with my busy office and employees. I thought about where I was going to live. Prices had gone up in Anchorage over the years. In a private practice, income is variable. All my business contacts were here, I had signed an expensive lease, and I never thought about moving out of the state. That meant being on my own. I had never been on my own. I had been with Bill since graduating from high school. I lived in a low-lying fog, which I couldn't dispel. If I did, that meant I had penetrated it, fathomed it, and emerged from it in peace.

Before I had a chance to clear that fog, Bill came home from work one day and said, "I don't want to get a divorce anymore."

"What? What is going to change, what is going to be different? You still aren't going to be happy about me meditating," I said matter-of-factly and irritated.

"Well, we can agree to disagree."

I was surprised. But I was relieved. I didn't want to break up everything we had built. It wasn't all bad. As a "feminist," I should be able to let him live his life while I have my life. We weren't joined at the hip. Plus, I had made a vow, for better or for worse. I had hoped he might join me in meditation, enjoy the love, and share it with me. But I was a big girl. If he could let go of his anger over it, I could let go of wanting to share it with him. We would have sex, not love.

In a way, it reminded me of my initial break from my father. Once again, wanting to share love with another was taken from me. What was life trying to teach me as I turned inside once again, not out of fear this time, but out of love? Life had another contract with me, one that I would understand in time. Sadness, longing, and desire melted slowly, like a glacier, but with time, reaching the sea would be worth it.

In the end, the real reason he changed his mind was, "It's cheaper to keep her."

CHAPTER 33

Barbara Lefler: The Woman Who Made the School District Pay

Frederick Douglass taught that literacy is the path from slavery to freedom. There are many kinds of slavery and many kinds of freedom, but reading is still the path.
—Carl Sagan

Concerned parents packed the room, some standing along the back wall. A group of them succeeded in getting reading disorders on the agenda. The school board had a tight grip on the school system. Pitifully, only thirty percent of students in Anchorage scored at the proficient level for reading.

A nervous wreck, filled with statistics, I prepared to ask the Anchorage School Board to add the dyslexia program to its schools for the sake of the children. But I didn't speak first; Neal did.

The moderator called our names, and we walked up to a small table with two chairs in the front of the room. As I sat straight and watched Neal read from the speech he had prepared, I almost started to cry. I was so proud of him. There was no way he could have done that without our help. He was so confident. I thought to myself, *Look at this young man, who just learned how to read a couple of months ago. He is up here in front of all these people, cool as a cucumber. What is wrong with you, Kit? Relax. If he can do it, you can do it.*

Can you imagine? *He* gave me confidence. I had to laugh at myself, silently, as I physically relaxed back in my chair. I doubt I would have ever addressed the Seattle School Board. Only in Alaska.

People in Anchorage expected the public schools to teach their children how to read and write, just like any other town in the nation. Unfortunately, that didn't always happen. I taught hundreds of students from the Anchorage School District to read. One of them, Neal Lefler, stands out in my mind for two reasons: his tremendous progress and his mother, Barbara. She was the first parent to make the Anchorage School District pay for her son's program at our clinic.

Neal, a tall, slim young man with sandy brown hair, had just started the eleventh grade when he came to Emerald Speech and Learning Clinic. His reading test scores averaged around the fourth grade. Some of his scores, such as phonemic awareness, were as low as the first grade. He had one year left in high school, and his mother was determined to make the best of it. He would learn how to read, come hell or high water (but she probably wouldn't have said "hell").

After his evaluation, which clearly demonstrated the connection between his poor phonemic awareness skills and his low reading and spelling scores, she arranged for the district to pay for Neal's treatment. After all, they'd had him for eleven years and failed. By law, schools had to provide treatment for children with learning disabilities, such as dyslexia. If they did not, they had to pay for those services elsewhere. She was the first and only parent who ever took advantage of this technicality in PL94-142 (now the Individuals with Disabilities Education Act, IDEA). By doing so, she changed his life.

Before beginning treatment, I called Neal's school principal, whom I knew on a personal level. He cautioned me about any expectations of improvement I might have, given Neal's age. He basically dismissed the process before it even started. And he did not like the fact that Neal would miss six weeks of school after lunch. I urged him to keep an open mind because this dyslexia program was different. It was intense, and our prognosis for Neal's improvement was good, based on his evaluation. It turned out I was right.

At the end of treatment, his phonemic awareness had improved from a six-year age level to completely mature. He performed all types of phonemic awareness, including phoneme segmentation (breaking a word into its separate sounds), phoneme deletion (recognizing the word that remains when a phoneme is removed from the word), phoneme addition (making a new word by adding a phoneme to an existing word), phoneme substitution (substituting one phoneme for another to make a new word), and phoneme repetition (repeating the same phoneme in a word). Once he laid that foundation, he thrived. This could have been done in the first grade, but because it hadn't, he had floundered, because poor phonemic awareness is the number-one cause of dyslexia.

As a result of achieving this foundation, his average reading and written comprehension scores improved by four to seven years. Where reading was concerned, he finally left elementary school and got into high school. Neal decoded words and sentences and comprehended written information from a seventh-grade to an eleventh-grade level. He could read his textbooks and understand what he read. As he returned to a full-time student, he left us with a new confidence.

A couple of months later, I sat next to Neal at a small table, as we addressed the school board. We made our pitch to them, which fell on deaf ears. He told them how he had learned to read at our clinic, after eleven years of illiteracy in the Anchorage School District.

When it was my turn, I urged them to train personnel and administer the program to the students who showed a six-month delay in reading at the end of second grade. This was my prescription for the seventy percent of children in Anchorage who were falling behind. The president of the board explained that they could not mandate a specific program to be used in their classrooms. I wondered why they used the program currently in use. Who mandated that? Santa Claus? Clearly, it was not working.

Our pleas fell on deaf ears. The private sector urging the public sector to make a change for the good of others was ignored. Our attempt to communicate at the system-wide level failed. I had addressed the board directly. There was nothing else I could do. My voice was considerate and confident, but ultimately disregarded. To follow my voice, I had to do it myself, with my own business.

In 2017, I checked the updated reading scores in Alaska, and only a paltry fourteen percent of students were proficient. I thought a score of thirty percent proficient was poor. Why school districts resisted research-validated programs to teach their students mystified me. As someone who always strived to offer the best treatment to my clients, I couldn't understand the limiting approach the board took. What could have been so bad about a trial program, just to see what would happen?

To join the military, an applicant must pass a written test. Many young men and women in Alaska wanted to join, but they did not qualify because they couldn't read the test. A few years later, after his family moved to the Lower 48, Neal passed the test to join the Air Force. As an airman, he moved back to Alaska with his wife and started a family. This was the kind of difference reading made in one person's life. I wish I could have made that difference in everyone's life in Alaska.

Thanks to his determined mother, Barbara Lefler, and the school district that paid, this story had a happy ending for Neal.

CHAPTER 34
Fraud

The only thing worth writing about is the human heart in conflict with itself.

—William Faulkner

"You got this in the mail today," said my office manager, Patti, handing me an envelope.

Patti was one of the most kind and gentle people I ever employed. Yes, when I interviewed her, she had the required billing, bookkeeping, and payroll skills necessary to open my clinic, but so did the several others I interviewed. Her manner emerged as the defining quality for hiring. When a potential client called my clinic for the first time, they heard her voice —kind, soothing, and gentle. I wanted them to feel that, not encounter a sergeant running a battalion. She set the tone for the whole office.

I took the envelope and sat down. Removing the newspaper clipping inside, I noticed it had a note attached to it from the sender, an SLP in Homer, Alaska. She had written FYI and signed her name. I read the clipping. A man in Homer had advertised himself in the local paper as a speech therapist. He had a bachelor's degree in psychology, but that did not make him an SLP.

My blood boiled.

Like the January winds that buffeted our house at 110 miles per hour, causing the spider plant that hung from the ceiling to sway like a pendulum chandelier, I reeled from the news and immediately called the SLP who'd sent the clipping and talked to her about it. She was as stunned as I was when she read it. We commiserated about the fact that a potential and unsuspecting client would not only receive fake services but also waste their hard-earned money. The worst part, however, was that there was nothing we could do about it.

Except for five states, SLPs had to be licensed to work in a school, private practice, hospital, or clinic. Alaska was one of the exceptions. We had no licensing, meaning that anyone could say she or he was an SLP, put their name on the door, and scam the public.

People attracted to Alaska didn't like laws. They didn't like people telling them what to do. In 1976, a person could drive with an open liquor bottle in his car. The devastation of drunk driving was predictable. Thankfully, Mothers Against Drunk Drivers lobbied our state legislature to pass laws to prevent drunk driving, and the incidents declined significantly. I needed the legislature of the State of Alaska to write and pass a bill to license SLPs. This was 1999, and it was almost the new millennium. A new law was coming to town.

Now, it was our turn. Working with members of the Alaska Speech and Hearing Association (AKSHA), I took on the project. I contacted the American Speech and Hearing Association (ASHA) for help. They had been through this fight before and had great resources for us.

ASHA is the national organization that licenses SLPs and audiologists for clinical work, similar to the American Medical Association for physicians. ASHA granted the Certificate of Clinical Competence (CCC). This involved being supervised by another SLP who already had their CCC. To be eligible, a master's degree in communication disorders/speech-language pathology was required. After a year of supervised work with a variety of clients, a comprehensive test was administered. If an applicant passed the test, she was awarded the CCC and could now work in any setting and bill insurance. The Certificate of Clinical Competence guaranteed a proficient level of knowledge and experience in the field, enough to work independently. Being able to add SLP-CCC when I signed my name was empowering.

That faker in Homer had neither a degree in SLP nor the CCC. Time for action. I contacted the state representative for my district, Con Bunde, about this matter. As it turned out, he had a bachelor's degree in speech therapy. He had worked as a speech therapist and taught at the university in Anchorage many years ago. Then it became necessary to have a master of arts or master of science degree to work as an entry-level SLP. There were no master's-level programs in Alaska at that time, so he was out of a job. At some point, he ran for office and served as my representative in Juneau, the capital of Alaska. He was willing to take on the licensing issue for us and present a bill for consideration. I think *ella* was behind all of this. What are the odds that my congressman would have been an SLP?

I wanted to make it easy for Con. I contacted the State Licensing Board and found out what they needed from us. From ASHA, I researched samples of other SLP licensing bills. A flurry of phone calls and faxes ensued. I wrote up a bill and had it sent out to members of AKSHA for input. The final version was sent to Juneau to be written in the correct format. In the meantime, we garnered letters of support from parents and professionals.

Eventually, it came time to testify to the committee that was hearing the bill in Juneau. Because Juneau was so far away, they used a teleconference system to receive testimony from citizens who could not be there in person. Along with SLPs and other interested parties, I attended the hearing from the state building in downtown Anchorage. I went to listen and give my testimony.

An impressive wooden conference table, enormous and unreasonably thick, took up most of the room. Chairs were placed around the table with barely enough room to squeeze into them; they were so close to the wall. A small microphone, connected by a wire to a speaker box in the middle of the table, sat by each chair. When it came time for the meeting, we heard the committee members in Juneau through the speaker box, and they heard us through our microphones. People from other towns were also on that call, and we listened to them through the speaker as well. It was quite a state-of-the-art system at the time.

Con was not the leader of this committee; he was the representative who introduced the bill to the committee and was there for this testimony. By the tone of voice of the man who was running the meeting, he was irritated, gruff, and couldn't be bothered. He made it clear to Con that he didn't want this meeting to take a long time, and that Con had better have his ducks in a row. Internally, I shook my head in disbelief at the pecking-order attitude. Externally, I was intimidated. Was this a battle? If so, why? Why did there have to be such stress in communication?

Thanks to Con, House Bill 105, Licensing Speech Pathologists and Audiologists, passed on May 11, 2000. Occupational therapists and physical therapists had been licensed for years. We finally took our place among the licensed professionals in the State of Alaska.

Why did *ella* make that clipping come to me? Why did she think I would take on this monumental project with my headaches, nausea, and frozen voice? How did my state representative come to be in the right place at the right time? Who did I think I was, getting state licensing for speech-language pathologists? I never would have done that in California or Washington—only in Alaska, with the help of so many others on the national and local level. Why? Because it was my calling.

After it passed and I had some quiet time, I thought back to Rose's face, blood red with fear and terror, and how Stanly withdrew into the background like wallpaper, friendless and isolated. They had been with me on this whole quest. Now, all people in Alaska would receive real services from qualified people. Although my career continued, this seemed like the most impactful thing I would ever do. I had gone from working alone with one child at a time to working with many at the systems level. Both levels are necessary, the difference being the advancement of one person or an entire field. I used my frozen voice to create a law that officially protected people with communication disorders. Perhaps it had finally thawed, in this frozen land, without my notice. Even tundra thawed in the summer.

CHAPTER 35

See You

Be soft. Do not let the world make you hard. Do not let the pain make you hate. Do not let the bitterness steal your sweetness. Take pride in the fact that even though the rest of the world may disagree, you still believe it to be a beautiful place.
—Iain Thomas

"What are you doing home?" I asked Bill. I usually got home before him.

"I injured my back at work today. They sent me for an X-ray, and I have a slipped disc. Tomorrow I go to get a steroid shot for the pain. After that, I'm supposed to rest for a few days, then start physical therapy," Bill said from the couch.

"Oh my god. How are you feeling?"

"It's okay if I don't move. I have ice on it right now. Then I'm supposed to put some heat on it and alternate that a few times. I need to be as still as possible and not lift anything heavy."

"Of course not. I'll get the heating pad. Are you hungry or thirsty? Do you need anything before I start dinner?"

"You can bring me some more water. I have to take another muscle relaxer."

I took him a glass of water and made some dinner. He decided to sleep on the fold-out couch and not go down the stairs to our bedroom. The next day I helped him into the truck to get his steroid shot. That would help reduce the pain. At least that was the plan.

When the doctor gave Bill the injection, he punctured Bill's spinal cord. If he knew it, he didn't say anything. It would take a year and a half to diagnose the pounding headaches Bill got after standing up and going to work. But after lying down for an hour or so, the headaches went away. He had a spinal puncture headache that came and went two to three times a day.

Because it was always leaking, Bill's spinal fluid could

never replace itself, especially when he stood up. Gravity drained it from his head. Having lived with a constant migraine headache since the age of thirty-two, I had an understanding of what he was going through. I thought of the irony that he now had what I had had, but for a different reason.

Bill could no longer enjoy what Alaska had to offer. No more snowmobile treks, no more fishing, and no more skiing. He was stuck inside both the house and his head, and that wasn't healthy. He used alcohol to numb his pain and became increasingly belligerent. I walked on hot coals around him and kept myself as busy as possible to avoid his hostility and combativeness.

Since I had my own share of health issues, we both decided it was time to leave this faraway place of unfathomable beauty. We had lived here for thirty-one years, in the prime of our lives, and experienced so much together and apart.

As we drove south on the Alcan highway, along perilous, opaque glacial rivers, our memories rushed out of sight. Like a frosty wind, we couldn't quite catch the right words to say. Our feelings were deep, from the heart, but silent, like the Prince William Sound.

We eventually divorced after forty-one years of marriage. Both of us remarried. For myself, I knew my worth and wasn't going to settle for a handsome face with a hot car this time. I met a kind man who could be honest in his communication and listened when I raised my concerns. He was conscious of the importance of communication and helped me to stop acting like a tough guy on a hair trigger when it came to dealing with men. I calmed down considerably and felt tenderness, connection, and honesty with my partner. I could relax again. I felt my anxiety thawing. On our first date, he took me to meditation. Together we are pure joy, love, and happiness.

I was guarded the last day I saw Bill, standing in the garage. After picking up a few items, he said, "This is all you get. Don't come back again, and I'm changing the locks." He still berated and bullied me, and I was still afraid of him.

He didn't know it yet, but I had removed all the guns from his gun case in the garage and put them in storage. He had been extremely nasty to me for years, but his drinking and behavior had taken a downturn. He was depressed, but he refused counseling. I didn't want him to do something stupid to himself or to me. I would never be able to turn into what he wanted, and I was relieved when he asked me for the divorce. A few months later, when he figured out the guns were gone, he called me, and I returned them.

In the garage, he seemed to soften momentarily and mentioned something about his pension. I walked over to him, and with tears in my eyes, I hugged him and said, "Thank you for taking me to Alaska." Then I left. I had learned in Alaska that there are many forms of communication.

Being in Alaska, communing with all it had to offer, had helped me to realize that communication is a gift, filled with beauty and grace. Denali communicated strength, austerity, and boldness. I heard the silence of the Great One as it whispered its qualities into me. There was no finality to its supreme dignity, no insult it could not bear. Of all the natural wonders in Alaska, I loved Denali the most.

The Alaskan moon, given to guide the way during polar night, is better than all the rest. The January moon, a full moon, in the still dark-blue morning light, resting over the mountain peaks, communicated the gentle wonder of the Greatland. With its soft glow on the ridge, I stared at it so long through my living room window that I felt the rotation of the planet as it rolled away from that heavenly body. Where else but in Alaska could I feel the planet move?

I fulfilled my calling in Alaska. I had my feet in two worlds —the modern world of science and service and the ancient world of land and love. I married the two together and somehow accomplished more than I ever could have dreamt through one adventure after the next. I achieved levels of career growth in my life that I never would have thought possible, all because I wanted to care for people with communication disorders.

Just as important, in Alaska I found my voice. Little by little, I learned that I had self-agency, that I could think for myself and know what was right for me. That did not mean everything was effortless or always went my way. It did not mean that I always had the courage to use my voice. There are times to be silent.

I was raised to follow orders, do it all, know it all, and make things right for others. But for myself, my advocacy was minimal. I gave up too easily when it came to protecting me.

Instead of listening to my body and stopping the hormones, I took them for twenty years—finally quitting them against doctor's orders in 2002, when I had such a severe illness that I had to close my clinic after six years of achievements. The important results of what became known as the Nurses' Health Study had finally been released, too late for me. After two years of taking Premarin, the research was stopped because so many women were having heart attacks and strokes and developing cancer. And the number-one complaint—migraine. My body knew it couldn't tolerate those hormones, but I was conditioned to do what the doctor said, without question. Since then, I have become a bad patient. I now agree to try a treatment with the caveat that if my body doesn't like it, I will stop it. And I do.

Instead of taking quiet time, which I so loved in the bush, I kept busy with outward activities to ignore my bodily pain. Our last year in Alaska, a couple of years after I closed my clinic, I took a position at the University of Alaska, Anchorage, coordinating the three-year old speech-language-pathology program, teaching as an adjunct professor, and supervising the summer clinic, where students worked with patients. It was one of the first distance programs in the country to offer the bachelor's degree in SLP and to receive a master's degree through a partnership with East Carolina University. We wanted to "grow our own" as SLP positions in Alaska still went unfilled. I took the theoretically "part time" job for one year when the developer of the program was asked to substitute as an assistant dean in the College of Education. I loved every minute of it.

Looking back, it's hard to believe I did it, I was in so much pain after my illness. Luckily, I could work from home in my bathrobe while prepping classes and grading term papers and tests. I went to the university, physically, to teach classes online using Blackboard Internet, coordinate with other adjunct professors and clients, and attend meetings. The summer clinic was full-time work, which almost broke me. But I was able to pass along what I had learned to new students during the seven-week, hands-on clinic in the summer. It seemed I had come full-circle, from the time I had worked with Genie in my CSUN summer clinic.

I drank the American Kool-Aid to go-go-go and never stop. That's what my father liked—a woman who got a lot done. And that's what Bill liked. I felt compelled to do it their way; the masculine way. Living in Alaska, however, made everything worth it. Alaska was a giant present to me. It didn't matter where I went or what I did, I enjoyed it all.

While I was there, First Peoples brought back the teaching of their native languages in school. The kids could hear, speak, read, and write their ancient language, without fear of breaking the law. They hired native Alaskan teachers.

Native dancing returned, right in their own gymnasiums, which until the 1960s was considered heathen. The children learned by watching the elders with pride, just as they had always done.

All of these changes were like a renaissance for First Peoples. Their true natures were being supported again. They brought back what had not been lost from their culture, gained self-respect, and spoke up.

Now, the first generations of students have grown up who never had to leave home to go to high school. Those were the children I worked with. They escaped the trauma that some pupils experienced in boarding schools. They were not taught that they were lowly and stupid or punished for speaking their native language. Many are working in engineering, in marine biology, and as doctors, dentists, and administrators. We even have our first female congressperson representing Alaskans in Washington, DC. Nonetheless, generational trauma remains and requires attention and resolution.

With the research on our emotional IQ that started to appear in the late 1990s and now the work on trauma that is available online, in books, and through classes, I understand that most of us have been traumatized. Not by what happened to us, but by how we made ourselves smaller, afraid, and alone as a result. Almost everyone has some version of impaired communication. Individuals, families, groups, organizations, and political regimes need to understand this. The days of the rugged individual, so popularized by white men in Alaska, are over. Indigenous Alaskans learned that lesson thousands of years ago. Cooperation kept them alive. Gentle, humorous cooperation is the key.

Humans are the same species—the only species given the gift of articulate speech and language. At our core, we are love and compassion. Our communication skills are on a continuum, from weak to strong. We have all been silenced in our own ways, either by others or by ourselves, not understanding how we have been affected. From our cultural conditioning, to our educational and work experiences, to our childhood traumas, we all suffer. Unless a person has worked rigorously to understand their communication problems and to change, they still have work to do. That includes me.

Don't take speech for granted. Give me a person with a communication disorder, and I will show you someone who suffers. I will show you someone who wants help. They themselves, however, are perfect. We all need help with our communication, to learn to use our voice, and we are all perfect as we learn and grow. We are here to help one another. And we are all here to care for one another. There is help for all of us. We need to take a chance and ask for that help. We don't have to do it alone.

Because of my clients, I grew in love, compassion, and humility. I learned to express those qualities to myself as well as to others. These are inherent qualities we all need to develop and express, from individuals to institutions. My love for people who cannot communicate is real. I understand the fear and the frustration. It is my sincerest wish that all who need help, will find it.

I discovered that a life in the service of others is a life well lived. I had empathy for people with communication disorders. That empathy led me to my path. By helping them to live a full life, I lived a full life. My path found me, and I walked it, even when I got sick. Even though no one could help me completely eradicate my problem, like my headaches, I walked my path.

Doing one thing led to another; just like volunteering at Crippled Children's Services led me to becoming a speech-language pathologist. My life unfolded. I did not have to know everything ahead of time. I have learned to let the *mystery* come to me, in its own time. It is always the right time.

The Power of Speech

When words are on the tip of your tongue, but you can't get them out—

When thoughts are in the back of your mind, but you can't bring them forward—

When ideas are at the tips of your fingers, but you can't write them down—

When kindness is in the depth of your being, but you can't express it—

your life is restricted.

Words can free you. Words can build the life you want, whether they are oral, written, or sign. The power to improve these skills is within you.

Never give up hope. Seek help. There is someone who cares about you and knows what to do. It is their calling.

ACKNOWLEDGEMENT

My gratitude to Melinda Bessett, Heather Double, Jim Brock, Toby Parsonage, Anne Ver Hoef, Posie Boggs, Sue Sparling Micks, and Cheryl Campbell for being my Beta readers. After their comments, I sent my manuscript to a professional editor, Janice Harper, who told me, "You have three books in here and none of them are memoir." She offered to help me write a memoir, which I discovered is not the same as writing a report. Julie Artz guided me to shorten my timeline and cut, cut, cut. And thanks to Annie Mydia, who fostered my ability to share feelings, not just facts.

I want to express my appreciation to my husband, Eric Johnson, who encouraged me to keep going, even though it took four years of writing and revising to finish this book. He also took my press photo and composed the cover of the book.

Finally, to Alaska and her people. You can take the girl out of Alaska, but you can't take Alaska out of the girl. Bravo to the intrepid humans who have found this amazing place and call it home.